HAS GOD
MANY NAMES?

To Maggie

HAS GOD MANY NAMES?

An Introduction to RELIGIOUS STUDIES

Dewi Arwel HUGHES

APOLLOS (an imprint of Inter-Varsity Press),
38 De Montfort Street, Leicester LE1 7GP, England

First published 1996

British Library Cataloguing in Publication Data
A catalogue record for this book is available from the British Library.

ISBN 0-85111-448-2

Set in Garamond no. 3

Typeset in Great Britain by Parker Typesetting Service, Leicester

Printed in England by Clays Ltd, St Ives plc

CONTENTS

PREFACE

I have very vivid memories of attending my first conference run by the British Association for the History of Religions. We were not long into the programme before I was made to feel like an intellectual leper because speaker after speaker took pleasure in mocking the type of traditional Christian position that I represented. I am sure that, if they had known that there was an evangelical in their midst, they would not have been so unkind. But they must have assumed that the type of study of religions done by their association would exclude Christians like myself. On my way home, I realized that we evangelicals very often behave just as badly in our own 'ghetto gatherings', and I hate to think what a 'liberal' would feel like if one happened to slip in unawares. I vowed that I would make every effort from that point to be as gracious as I can when speaking or writing about those from whom I differ. Resorting to mockery is irrational and evidence of losing an argument. Being a very fallible human being I sometimes transgress my best intentions, so I am very grateful for the friends that have helped me to get rid of any weeds of this sort from this volume.

As I returned from that conference, I also felt very strongly that an evangelical has as much right to be heard as anyone else in the academic world of Religious Studies. This volume is the result of a lot of reflection on the discipline that I had the pleasure of teaching at the Polytechnic of Wales (now the University of Glamorgan) from 1975 to 1986. That reflection began with my doctoral thesis on 'The History and Principles of Comparative Religion in Britain from 1850–1950', which was examined and commended by Professor Geoffrey Parrinder. I have seen no reason to compromise my evangelical faith throughout my study of the world's great religious traditions and of the methodology of Religious Studies. In fact, since someone of my convictions is rare in Religious Studies, I have the advantage of an outsider who can often see things more clearly than an

PREFACE

insider. What I have written is not an evangelical tract but a reasoned introduction to a subject which I love. There has been much discussion and disagreement about methodology in Religious Studies, and in many ways the discipline is still searching for an adequate method. I would be more than happy if this volume could be viewed as a contribution to that discussion.

Producing even a modest volume like this is never just an individual effort. The work on this started long ago, during my days as a teacher at the Polytechnic of Wales. I am grateful for the stimulation of discussion with students and with my colleagues Alan Hill and Hefin Elias during that time. Interestingly, it was after joining Tear Fund's staff that I had the opportunity to experience one of the great Eastern religions at first hand. I have now visited India four times, which has been a great help in my understanding of the Hindu tradition. My time teaching Hinduism at the South Asia Institute for Advanced Christian Studies at Bangalore was particularly valuable, and I am very grateful to Graham Fairbairn, Tear Fund's Home Director, for making it possible.

The book was finished as a result of a grant from the Universities and Colleges Christian Fellowship Research Committee, which made possible my release from Tear Fund work for the first three months of 1995. I am grateful to UCCF and to Stephen Rand, the Communications Director of Tear Fund, for this. In bringing the work to completion, I have received a lot of support and encouragement from David Kingdon, then theological books editor of Inter-Varsity Press, for which I am very grateful. A number of people also made helpful comments on the manuscript. Professor Stephen Williams of Union Theological College, Belfast, sent in a long list of comments and suggestions. I have taken note of most of them, and I am sure the volume will be much better than it would have been as a result. 'Perfume and incense bring joy to the heart, and the pleasantness of one's friend springs from his earnest counsel' (Pr. 27:9, NIV).

Finally, my greatest debt of thanks goes to my wife, Maggie. She persuaded me that it would be a shame to waste all the work that I had put in to research for this volume while still teaching. Since I put my hand to the plough in January 1995, she has continued to support me in many different ways. I hope that the publication of the book will be some compensation for those hours spent in the study which could have been spent on holiday, decorating the house, *etc.*! I am not sure of the origin or significance of the practice of dedicating books, but if dedication is an expression of love and esteem then I gladly dedicate this volume to my wife.

February 1996

Dewi Hughes
Pontypridd

INTRODUCTION

This book has been written in the impersonal way that is expected of an academic discourse, but I would like to begin on a note of personal reminiscence. Some years ago, I taught Religious Studies in a polytechnic. Since then the polytechnics have grown up into universities, and with the change in name they have perhaps lost something of the strong association with science and technology which they once had. As a part of polite conversation with strangers I used to be asked quite often what I taught at the polytechnic. My answer of 'Religious Studies' did not seem to enlighten folk very much, and tended to be something of a conversation-stopper. If the enquirer could break through the barrier of the science and engineering image of polytechnics and persisted in wanting to find out more, then I used to say something similar to what follows.

Whatever one says about the status of religion in our own society at the moment, it is impossible to deny that there was a time not so very long ago when it had a very important role. The many religious buildings dotted about everywhere witness to that. In many other countries in the world, religion is still a dominant force in people's lives, the Islamic countries such as Iran or Pakistan being particularly good examples. Religious Studies attempts to introduce students to some aspects of this important world of religion. Since Christianity has contributed so much to our history and culture in Western countries, it is important, first of all, to introduce students to something of its history and central ideas – and particularly the history and ideas that had most impact on the part of the world where the polytechnic was located. Secondly, it is important to appreciate the way in which the Bible, as the authoritative book of the Christians, has been viewed and understood. Thirdly, since we are increasingly living in a global village, it is important that we get to know something of the religious ideas and practices of our neighbours – Jews, Muslims, Hindus and

Buddhists in particular. These are topics to which we try to introduce students who opt for Religious Studies courses as a substantial component in their overall Humanities degree course. The type of degree course with which I was involved was not untypical then and is even more common now. Religious Studies is firmly established on the academic map. The newest element in these courses is the study of religions other than Christianity. This is the one element that makes the new schemes '*Religious* Studies' rather than 'Biblical Studies' or 'Theology'.[1]

Thirty years ago, if one wanted to study religion of any sort at higher-education level, it was almost inevitable that one read Theology or Biblical Studies. At that time both these subjects had a somewhat vocational orientation. Theology was generally read by those preparing for the Christian ministry, while Biblical Studies was read by those who were equipping themselves to be school-teachers. This division reflected the agreement that had been made towards the end of the nineteenth century on the question of Religious Education between Anglicans on the one hand and Non-conformists on the other. The Non-conformists had insisted that denominational teaching should be excluded from schools that were coming increasingly under state control. Teaching about Christianity was to be the responsibility of the churches. But pupils could be taught the Bible in school as long as its content was presented in a somewhat objective manner. Non-conformists thought that this accommodation would hinder the established Church with its greater resources from taking an unfair advantage in using the schools to make converts to Anglicanism. So in teacher training colleges and in universities for much of the twentieth century, most of what could be described as 'religious teaching' was Biblical Studies. Theology also had strong links with the university in many cases, even though it was very much a denominational activity and was seen as preparation for service in the church. Since men were being prepared to communicate the Christian message to the world, it was in Theology, on the whole, that the opportunity was found to learn about religions other than Christianity.

IMPERIAL EXPANSION *and* LITERATE RELIGIONS

At the risk of being charged with being simplistic, it can be argued that Religious Studies first appeared in the academic firmament as a result of imperial expansion, coupled with technological and intellectual developments in the

---

[0] For a recent book on Religious Studies as a discipline, see Ursula King (ed.), *Turning Points in Religious Studies: Essays in Honour of Geoffrey Parrinder* (Edinburgh: T. & T. Clark, 1990).

INTRODUCTION

West since the beginning of the nineteenth century. To claim that Religious Studies has found a place in the academic world in the last thirty years because of such factors that have their root almost two hundred years ago demands some explanation.

The first factor is the growth in the availability of information about the world's religious traditions. This is the direct result of imperial expansion and the development of Western technology. In the nineteenth century, Europeans, the British in particular, subdued much of the East militarily and commercially, and in the process discovered ancient religious traditions with profound and sophisticated literatures. The growth of British power in India is an excellent example of this development. English imperial policy was strongly in favour of not disturbing the traditions of the people that were being colonized. This meant that administrators needed some understanding of the religion and law of the subject people. So colleges were eventually established to teach Indian languages and traditions – which included religious traditions. To teach adequately, relevant Indian literature was needed. By the beginning of the nineteenth century East India House in London, the headquarters of the East India Company, had a fine collection of Indian literature. It was to this library that Max Müller, who is regarded as the father of 'Religious Studies', came to edit the ancient Indian religious text, the Rig Veda, in the 1830s.

In the eighteenth century religions were classified into four categories: Christian, Jewish, Muslim and pagan. All religions other than the three Semitic traditions were included under the one heading of 'pagan'. By 1900 a significant proportion of the literatures of the Eastern religions had been translated into various European languages and it had become very obvious that a more adequate classification than 'paganism' was required. It was as a result of the study of these literatures that the '-isms' were born that are such commonplaces of Religious Studies still, though questions are now being asked about the reality behind these terms: Hinduism, Buddhism, Jainism, Sikhism, Confucianism, Taoism and Shintoism.

Discovery of 'primitive' peoples

The delineation of these -isms did not exhaust the meaning of what had once been called 'paganism'. In Africa south of the Sahara, Australasia and numerous islands dotted about the Pacific, the all-conquering Europeans discovered peoples without literatures, living at a much more basic level technologically than themselves. A few Europeans believed for a short time, in the second half of the nineteenth century, that some of these peoples were devoid of any religious beliefs. They were soon proved wrong, as accounts of such people's beliefs and rituals came flooding in from all directions. When this material was added to accounts of the traditional beliefs and practices of native Americans of North and South America, there was an enormous body of literature calling for scholarly understanding and interpretation. The felt need to interpret the information flooding in about societies living at a simple level of technology in turn led to the gathering of yet more information and to the development of sophisticated methods for gathering it.

Christian missions

Another important factor in the opening up of world religion to the West was the tremendous expansion of Christianity in the nineteenth century. It has been called 'The Great Century' in the history of Christianity. The attitude of missionaries towards the religious traditions of those to whom they brought the message of Christ was generally very negative. After all, they had left the comforts of home and gone, often at great personal cost to themselves, to make converts to Christ. It is not surprising that the religion of the 'natives' was often portrayed in very dark colours to the supporters of the mission at home. But there were many missionaries who also realized that understanding the religious traditions of those they were trying to reach was important if their mission was to succeed. In the Protestant missionary movement the translation of the Bible into vernacular languages was a central plank of missionary policy. To do this demanded an understanding of the religious language of the people in order to facilitate the translation of biblical concepts into a new cultural form. Doing this adequately called for an understanding of a people's religious tradition. So the work of missionaries made an important contribution to the stock of knowledge about religions other than Christianity.

Yet another important factor is that commercial, imperial and 'scientific' interest often followed the missionaries to what were remote and inhospitable parts of the world. The opening up of Papua New Guinea towards the end of the nineteenth century is a good example of this type of development.[2]

IMMIGRATION *and the* COMMUNICATIONS REVOLUTION

By the end of the nineteenth century, there was some recognition that the study of religions should be recognized in higher education. But provision for such study was very scant until quite recently. Among the many factors that have contributed to this change, immigration and the communications revolution

[2] See R. Lovett, *James Chalmers* (Oxford: Religious Tract Society, 1902).

must be primary. The demise of imperial power in the mid-twentieth century led to the movement of significant numbers of people, from countries that were formerly under imperial control, to the country that once controlled them. For example, a significant number of Asians have moved to Britain since the demise of empire particularly in India, Pakistan and Bangladesh. These immigrants brought their religions with them, so that in some parts of Britain in cities like Bradford and Leicester, Islam or Hinduism are no longer a distant reality but the religion of very close neighbours. This was bound to have an effect on thinking about education, particularly in areas where there is a concentration of immigrants. It is not surprising, therefore, that pressure for recognizing the reality of the plurality of religions came from the colleges responsible for training teachers.

The impact of the communications revolution is more difficult to define, but there is no doubt that television and the increasing ease of travel has made information which has been available since the nineteenth century much more accessible to the masses. In consequence, an ethos has arisen which creates a presumption that the study of religion must mean the study of a plurality of religions. In the world in which we live, to confine ourselves to the study of the Christian tradition or to Biblical Studies will not do. Plurality is our reality, and an academic study of religion must recognize that fact. The fact that many Biblical Studies departments in universities have changed their name to Religious Studies, and expanded their curriculum to include the study of religions other than Christianity in the last few years, witnesses to this reality.

A Fundamental Assumption

Running parallel with these historical developments, there is a story of attempts to understand, interpret and explain the reality of religious plurality. This is the story on which this volume is focused. If it has a central theme at all, it is that the foundations of contemporary theories of religion were laid at the beginning of the nineteenth century and that those foundations are inadequate. They are inadequate because one of their fundamental presuppositions is that God cannot communicate with human beings in such a way as to enable them to say that certain statements about God are true. The traditional Christian claim that God has spoken, in the Bible and through his Son, in such a way that those who know the Bible and Jesus can say that they know what God is really like, is ruled out of court from the beginning. Obviously, if traditional Christian doctrine is true knowledge of God, then Buddhist or Islamic doctrine that contradicts it cannot be true as well. This is why traditional Christian teaching has been described as exclusivist. Modern and post-modern theories of religion assume that exlusivism is untenable.

This fundamental assumption makes life rather difficult for a Christian who is committed to a traditional view of Christian doctrine but who is also very interested in other religious traditions. It certainly complicates the whole business of dialogue with the contemporary world of Religious Studies. The difficulty of talking with those who assume that the traditional views of revelation and the inspiration of the Bible cannot be true is obvious. What happens is that both parties make a series of unconnected statements which are a denial of each other's positions. This book tries to bridge that gap, and to enter into dialogue with the contemporary world of Religious Studies. This is why very little of the familiar language of traditional Christian doctrine will be found in it. But this does not mean that that doctrine is in any way forsaken or sacrificed.

In view in this book are both students who are coming into contact with Religious Studies for the first time as committed Christians, and those who are without any real religious commitment. What is attempted is an explanation of the prevailing theory of Religious Studies, which will raise questions about its adequacy from within its own conceptual framework. To realize that some of its principles may not be satisfactory, even according to its own criteria, should help a student either to survive in an antagonistic atmosphere or to begin asking about a better way. The author is profoundly convinced that Jesus alone is that better Way.

IDEALIST *and* POSITIVIST TRADITIONS

The framework of this book is determined by the conviction that there are two main intellectual traditions, both with roots in the Enlightenment, that have given birth to a whole series of theories of religion. They are called the 'idealist' and 'positivist' approaches in this volume.

The idealist approach has its roots in Germany and particularly in the thought of Immanuel Kant, Friedrich Schleiermacher and G. W. F. Hegel. Unlike the rationalists of the eighteenth century who believed in a natural religion and condemned the institutions of Christianity as oppressive priestcraft, they saw historical religions as the necessary outward shell of the inward essence of religion. The history of religions was for them the history of the increasing realization of the essence of religion in and through its forms. The task of Religious Studies, a term which is used anachronistically here, was the discovery of the essence of religion. The ultimate reality in the universe for the idealists is

INTRODUCTION

spiritual, and on the whole they identified 'spiritual' with some form of Christianity. Their focus was mainly on those religions that have a literary tradition. Their theories were the result of studying various scriptures.

The roots of the positivist approach are to be found in the empiricist tradition of the Enlightenment, with its very heavy emphasis on the natural sciences. Positivists saw religion as something to be explained away. For them it was now a hindrance to human development, though it may have been a help at a more primitive stage of human history. For them the ultimate reality was not spiritual but natural. If there was any reality in religion, it had to be something other than what it claimed to be. Their theories are reductionist in that they reduce religious reality to some natural reality such as bad reasoning, society and so on. Not surprisingly, particularly when the theory of evolution became dominant, the positivists were particularly attracted by the religions of contemporary peoples living at a very basic level of technological culture. It was to their advantage that religion should be seen as a primitive phenomenon, hence they freely used the term 'primitive' religion.

Although the idealist tradition has gained the upper hand in Religious Studies in the twentieth century, the positivist tradition has left a legacy which is still very much alive in certain areas of the discipline.

A VARIETY of NAMES for a DISCIPLINE

Before giving an outline of the contents of this book, it may be helpful to say a little about the terms that have been used in the past to describe what is now called Religious Studies. Idealist scholars under German influence first called it 'The Science of Religion' (*Religionswissenschaft*). This reflects the wider meaning of 'science' in continental Europe. In Britain this term has not found favour, because of the identification of 'science' with natural science. The term favoured by the beginning of the twentieth century in Britain was 'Comparative Religion'. Attempts were made without any great success to establish Comparative Religion as a subject in the curricula of universities. Even today some still call a study of various religious traditions 'Comparative Religion'. Another term which became popular in the second half of the twentieth century was 'the History of Religions'. This again is more popular on the continent and reflects the desire to get away from the evolutionist implications of 'Comparative Religion' and to focus on the individual histories of the various religions. It is only recently that 'Religious Studies' has become generally accepted. Since this is the term that is now used to describe academic courses which include the study of Christianity and other religions, it is the term that is used throughout this volume.

OUTLINE OF CONTENTS

PART ONE

This book is divided into three parts. The first part looks at those who laid the intellectual foundations of Religious Studies. The general heading for this part is 'The classics'. A classic is a work of acknowledged excellence in any discipline. The authors considered in this part belong to the nineteenth and early twentieth centuries. If the reader is only interested in what may be of immediate contemporary relevance, then he or she may go straight to the Conclusion of Part One, which is designed to serve as a shorter introduction to the rest of the volume.

The classics are divided into three types: idealist, positivist and ambivalent. Chapter 1 looks at the philosophical and theological foundations laid by Immanuel Kant (1724–1804), Friedrich Schleiermacher (1768–1834) and G. W. F. Hegel (1770–1831), before going on to consider the work of Max Müller (1823–1900) and Rudolph Otto (1869–1937). The author would not claim to have a keen philosophical mind but he can understand enough to appreciate how crucial Kant is to the development of modern thought. In the theological realm Schleiermacher's contribution has been as significant as Kant's in philosophy. They laid the foundations which were built on by Müller and Otto, who produced classics, in the strict sense of the term, in Religious Studies.

Chapter 2 follows the same pattern in that the contribution of Auguste Comte (1798–1857) and Charles Darwin (1809–82), who together laid the foundations of the positivist approach to religion, are examined first. Since positivism identified strongly with natural science, it is not surprising that theories of religion were formulated by some of the classic authors in a number of new disciplines, making claims to being natural sciences, that appeared in the nineteenth century. The three that are considered in this chapter are James G. Frazer (1854–1941), who represents anthropology, Sigmund Freud (1856–1939), representing psychology, and Emile Durkheim (1858–1917), sociology. Finally, the work of some of the British school of functionalist social anthropology is considered as an example of combining themes from anthropology and sociology. The work of all the authors in this section are clearly reductionist.

Chapter 3 looks at the work of a psychologist, an anthropologist and a sociologist who, though they speak the language of one of the intellectual traditions examined in the first two chapters, were obviously attracted to the other tradition. Both William James (1842–1910), the psychologist, and R. R. Marett (1866–1943), the anthropologist, use the language of positivism, but they are much nearer the idealist position in the last analysis. Max Weber (1864–1920), the sociologist, was bred in the idealist tradition, but he clearly leans in the direction of positivism at times. He is probably the only one of the three that is really ambivalent.

The Conclusion to Part One forms chapter 4, and it can, as already indicated, serve as an introduction to the rest of the volume, if so required.

PART TWO

In this part, various approaches to religion that are still current, and which have been built on the foundations of the classics, are considered.

Chapter 5 examines the 'History of Religion' approach. This chapter is not a study of the tremendous work that has been done since the nineteenth century to tell the stories of individual religions. Rather, it is concerned with the idea that there is a unified essence of religion which is manifested in and through the historical religions. This is the belief that there is a story of religion in the singular that is being told in and through the stories of the plurality of religions. The meaning and significance of the History of Religions is a crucial issue for this approach. The two authors considered in the chapter represent two approaches. E. O. James (1888–1972), who belongs intellectually to the first half of the twentieth century, was an idealist evolutionist who saw the essence of religion being gradually realized through its historical forms. Wilfred Cantwell Smith (1916–), who was still writing in the 1990s, is more difficult to characterize. He is clearly not an evolutionist in the same way as E. O. James. His position may be described as hoping for the historical convergence of religions in the faith of liberal Protestantism.

Chapter 6 deals with the phenomenology of religion. Like many modern and post-modern movements, phenomenology is very difficult to pin down. Fundamental to it is the desire for objectivity. In one sense it is a reaction against reductionism of every kind. Focusing on the classical work of this genre produced by Gerardus van der Leeuw (1890–1950) and the contemporary contributions of Peter McKenzie and Ninian Smart (1927–), this chapter questions the possibility of being completely objective in describing anything.

Chapter 7 looks at various approaches to religion as a social phenomenon. Two disciplines, social anthropology and sociology, have focused particularly on the social dimension of religion. Both disciplines with their positivist roots have been, and continue to be to a great extent, reductionist in their approach. The claim to scientific objectivity has been a dogma for both disciplines, though there is some evidence that some anthropologists and sociologists are becoming uneasy with it. This chapter does not focus so much on particular authors, although it does contain a substantial section on the structuralist theory of Claude Levi-Strauss (1908–).

The penultimate section of chapter 7, which contains a summary of D. A. Fraser and Tony Campolo's sociological analysis of the attitude of social science to religion, is particularly significant in helping to understand the thrust of the whole book.

Chapter 8 examines psychological theories. This begins by looking at psychology in very broad terms and argues that many of the theories of religion considered in other chapters are in fact psychological. It is argued that in the tradition of Schleiermacher much theology has in fact been reduced to psychology, so that liberal theological theories of religion are actually psychological theories. Ninian Smart is cited as an example of this. The whole discussion of psychology is put in the context of the idea that we are witnessing the psychologization of Western human beings. The prophets of this movement are the likes of Carl Gustav Jung (1885–1961), Carl Rogers (1902–87) and Abraham Maslow (1908–70). They have founded the cult of self-actualization, which fits in very neatly with the New Age movement that is gathering momentum in the West.

Chapter 9 is devoted to an analysis of the work of Mircea Eliade (1907–86). Because he combines so many contemporary approaches to religion in his work, this chapter in fact serves as a conclusion to Part Two as well. Eliade fits the model of an authentic contemporary classic of Religious Studies. He is much admired and criticized. He epitomizes the dilemma of Religious Studies. He is profoundly convinced of the crucial importance of religion for human beings, yet trapped within a modern scientific mentality which freezes religious reality to death. It is interesting that some of his admirers have cut the Gordian knot of science and plunged into experimentation with practices such as shamanism, in search of renewed access to the life-giving religious dimension to life.

PART THREE

This part of the volume focuses on a number of basic issues, in order to illustrate some of the difficulties connected with the essentialist view that has dominated Religious Studies.

Chapter 10 considers the issue of authority in religion. One of the main points of this chapter is to show how thinking about the nature of religious authority in the West has influenced the way authority is viewed in religion in general. It is a significant fact that the study of authority in religion has been almost completely neglected, despite the fact that it has more power to determine the direction of people's lives than anything else.

INTRODUCTION

Chapter 11 goes on to look at mysticism. Mysticism has been a favourite focus of Religious Studies because it is in this somewhat rare and often esoteric form of various religions that experience seems to be in the ascendancy. Beginning with what T. H. Huxley (1825–95) believed to be an experience of the *philosophia perennis* under the influence of mescalin, the whole issue of the relationship between the experience and the way it is expressed is examined. This chapter also includes a short section on John Hick's (1922–) idea of the Real as the one focus of all religious experience.

Chapter 12, the final chapter, considers the claim that the same divine is the object of different religions by focusing particularly on the doctrine of God in the Christian tradition, and Brahman in the Indian tradition. The framework for the discussion is the inclusivist and pluralist claim that the same Ultimate is, or can be, found through the many religions. The conclusion is that the transcendent beings in the two traditions – Christian and Indian – are not the same, if the reports of those who experience them are to be taken seriously. The chapter ends back with Schleiermacher and Kant, where the whole story began.

I

THE CLASSICS

– 1 –

the IDEALIST CLASSICS

INTRODUCTION

Any brief account of some of the major movements of thought in the nineteenth century is bound to appear simplistic, but the attempt must be made if we are to understand some of the fundamental issues which still occupy students of religion today.

Although at the threshold of a period of great expansion at the beginning of the nineteenth century, Christianity had already suffered a century of severe intellectual challenge. Those who rejected Christianity as it was traditionally understood spoke in the name of reason and science, and displayed a loss of confidence in the efficacy of Christian faith, which is characteristic of our modern age. What this meant practically was the questioning of the veracity of the Bible and of Christian doctrine.

In the eighteenth century, an increasing number of intellectuals found it difficult to accept doctrines such as the infallibility of the Bible, the deity of Christ, original sin, the eternal punishment of unrepentant sinners, and the atonement. Particularly offensive to these rationalist critics were the miracles recorded in both Old and New Testaments. However, they did not reject the whole structure of traditional Christian thought in the name of atheism but rather in the name of a rational, or what was often called 'natural', religion. They made a sharp distinction between what might be called 'historical religion' and 'natural religion'. Positive religion is religion as found in human history with its doctrines, rites and institutional structures. For most of the eighteenth-century rationalists, this would mean Christianity, but they were also very conscious of the existence of other religions. For them, religion in this historical sense was the cause of untold misery and trouble for humankind. It had been used by crafty rulers to oppress the people – what they called 'priestcraft' – and had been the cause of endless conflict, persecution and repression. As a historical phenomenon, therefore, religion was to be rejected. But, despite the disastrous history of religion, there was still some truth in it, and this truth could be discovered by the use of reason. Simply by sitting down and thinking a little, the rationalists believed that it was possible to discover the basic tenets of true or natural religion, and thus to by-pass completely all the irrational teachings and paraphernalia of the historical religions. As early as 1624, Lord Herbert of Cherbury (1583–1648) had listed the tenets of natural religion.[1] The last, and probably the greatest, advocate of natural religion was Immanuel Kant (1724–1804), who set the scene for many developments in modern thought.

IMMANUEL KANT

Those who had freed themselves from what they perceived to be the bondage of Christian dogma and ecclesiastical authority in the eighteenth century had done so in the name of reason. They sought by reason to prove both the folly of traditional belief and the truth of their own belief in God, the guardian and rewarder of virtue. But a few scholars – the Scottish philosopher David Hume (1711–76) being the best example – subjected this belief in reason to analysis. Hume came to the conclusion that there was no certainty even here. He argued that it is impossible to assume that human nature is the same everywhere and that, therefore, the highest human faculty, reason, may not lead one to indubitable truth. Immanuel Kant, one of the few who took Hume's challenge seriously, states, in one of his rare autobiographical comments, that he was 'awoken from his dogmatic slumber' by him. Kant set out to examine reason and to discover what certainties, if any, are available by following its path.

In his *Critique of Pure Reason*, Kant came to the conclusion that, though we can know for certain that things external to us exist, we can never know their precise nature, because all our knowledge of them is determined by the 'categories of our understanding'. When I look at a tree, the fact that I recognize it as a tree is not determined by its nature as an object but by what my mind brings to the process of observation. My mind is pre-programmed in such a way that, when a tree appears before it, I am able to recognize it as a tree. Kant's term for this 'appearance' before the mind is 'phenomenon' and, according to him, we have

---

[1] The five doctrines of Cherbury's natural religion are: (1) God exists; (2) it is a duty to worship him (3) the practice of virtue is the true mode of honouring him; (4) man is under an obligation to repent of his sin; and (5) there will be rewards and punishment after death.

THE IDEALIST CLASSICS

knowledge only of phenomena. The external object lying behind the phenomenon, which he calls 'the thing-in-itself' or 'noumenon', cannot be known. That phenomenological knowledge presupposes the categories of the understanding was, in Kant's mind, a refutation of Hume's scepticism, and enabled Kant to reaffirm that reason could lead to certainty.

This certainty was only possible in the realm of the phenomenal since the categories of the understanding were bound to perception. Knowledge comes only by means of perception. The observation of phenomena had led scientists to the conclusion that there was a 'law' of cause and effect at work in the world. This 'law' for Kant is, of course, a construct of the mind, but it could never have become such a construct apart from the perception of phenomena, that is, what appears to the mind of the mysterious and unknowable noumena. There is no knowledge *without* noumena, although there can be no knowledge *of* noumena.

All this talk of phenomena and noumena might seem abstruse and irrelevant to us, but the implications of Kant's *Critique* for ideas about religion were very significant. Most significant, maybe, were the implications of his theory for the traditional proofs for the existence of God. We can take the argument from the first cause as an example. Put simply, the argument goes thus: 'Every effect must have an adequate cause. The world is an effect. Therefore the world must have had a cause outside of itself and adequate to account for its existence.' Kant's theory means that we can never know whether or not the world has a cause outside of itself since we cannot know anything apart from the world. The noumena are unknowable. Other traditional proofs for the existence of God founder in the same way so that, according to Kant, it was impossible to prove God's existence by pure reason. In this way he demolished the foundation of what had come to be understood as natural religion.

The cause of natural religion was not completely lost, however, because Kant went on to discuss another type of reason, which he called 'practical reason'. He believed that, through this second type of reason, he could establish religion on a sound foundation. Human beings can discover in themselves not only those categories of the understanding which make the external world intelligible, but also categorical imperatives which direct their moral life in the world. These categorical imperatives are universal rules of duty that demand obedience, not for the sake of human happiness, but simply for the sake of virtue. Kant emphasized the fact that to do what is right is very often contrary to doing that which will bring one happiness in this world.

Unlike many rationalists, Kant also believed that humans are radically evil, so obedience to the demands of the categorical imperatives called for a tremendous effort of will on their behalf. He believed that this effort could not possibly be consummated in a single lifetime, so he argued that human beings must be immortal in order to have the time that they need to perfect virtue. Having argued that in this world happiness and virtue are mutually exclusive, Kant could not believe that virtue and happiness are eternally divorced. In the end, the virtuous person must also be the happy person.[2] God is Kant's answer to this contradiction in human moral experience.

This conclusion, one of the most obscure in Kant's difficult philosophy, has caused much debate among his interpreters as to precisely what he means by his belief in God, with some emphasizing God's role as the guardian of the moral law and others emphasizing the very peripheral role which the concept of God plays in the system. It is sufficient for us to understand that for Kant religion means morality, and that his idea of morality in some sense demands the idea of God and immortality. There is no question of knowing God, but simply of doing what the categorical imperatives demand in the hope that the contradictions implied by obedience will at some point be transcended. This, according to Kant, is the one true religion which is to be distinguished from the many 'faiths':

> . . . there is only *one* [true] *religion* but there can be *faiths* of several kinds. We can say further that even in the various churches, severed from one another by reason of the diversity of their modes of belief, one and the same religion can yet be found.[3]

Since Kant goes on to include Judaism and Islam among the 'faiths', he obviously believed that his rational religion was in fact the essence of all religions. This idea belongs very much to the eighteenth-century tradition of natural religion with its belief that the true religion of nature is discoverable in all the religions of the world, though often obscured by unnecessary dogmas, rituals and institutional structures. The major difference is that Kant's religion is not arrived at by the study of nature but is located in immediate experience. The rationalists of previous generations had drawn up their dogmas on the basis of a rational analysis of the natural world. Kant shut the door for many on such a procedure, and opened it for those who would locate the source of religion in inner experience. For Kant that inward experience was moral, but those who

---

[2] N. Smart, J. Clayton, P. Sherry and S. T. Katz (eds.), *Nineteenth Century Religious Thought in the West*, vol. 1 (Cambridge: CUP, 1985), p. 28; A. W. Wood, 'Rational theology, moral faith and religion', in *The Cambridge Companion to Kant*, ed. P. Guyer (Cambridge: CUP, 1992), pp. 401ff.

[3] Immanuel Kant, *Religion within the Limits of Reason Alone*, trans. T. M. Greene and H. H. Hudson (New York: Harper, 1960), p. 98.

came after him found its source in some other aspect of human inward experience.

FRIEDRICH SCHLEIERMACHER

Friedrich Schleiermacher (1768–1834), who has been described as 'arguably the greatest theologian of the nineteenth century, if not of the entire modern age',[4] was definitely post-Kantian in his view of religion, but whereas Kant emphasized people's moral nature Schleiermacher emphasized their emotional nature. Like Kant, he came from a pious Christian background, but lost his early faith when he came into contact with the rationalist challenge to orthodoxy. For some time he became a follower of Kant, and as a young preacher was a zealous advocate of moralism. By this stage he was resident in Berlin where he became involved in an *avant-garde* group of Romantic aesthetes. He found them contemptuous of religion, but at the same time they reminded him of some of the characteristics of his early pietist[5] upbringing. Under their influence, he came to believe that he had rediscovered the essence of his early faith while being freed from its dogmatism. He also believed that he had found the essence of religion free from the dogmatism of the rationalists and the moralism of Kant.

In 1799 he published anonymously *On Religion: Speeches to its Cultured Despisers*, in which he called upon his Romantic friends to reconsider the claim of religion. This volume, which contains Schleiermacher's description of religion in general, lays down the foundations for his work as a theologian. In 1821, as a professor in the University of Berlin, he completed the edifice with his *The Christian Faith*, which describes the specifically Christian type of his general description of religion.

Schleiermacher, in identifying himself with the Romantics of Berlin, was

---

[4] Smart *et al.*, *op. cit.*, p. 9. For other helpful studies of Schleiermacher, see K. Clements, *Friedrich Schleiermacher: Pioneer of Modern Theology* (London: Collins, 1987); B. M. G. Reardon, *Religion in the Age of Romanticism* (Cambridge: CUP, 1985), pp. 29ff.; C. Welch, *Protestant Thought in the Nineteenth Century*, vol. 1 (Yale: Yale University Press, 1972), pp. 59ff.

[5] Pietism was a movement in the Lutheran Church in Germany which began with the work of Philipp Jakob Spener (1633–1705) in the last quarter of the seventeenth century. In its emphasis on devotion, intense study of the Bible and experience, it bears many similarities to the Methodist movement in Britain. For a brief introduction, see article 'Pietism', in *New Dictionary of Theology*, ed. S. B. Ferguson and D. F. Wright (Leicester: IVP, 1988).

caught up in a movement that emphasized the importance of the emotional as opposed to the rational response to the world. In many ways it was inevitable that there should be a reaction in favour of feelings, since for the previous century the emphasis had been so much on rationality, clarity, logic and mathematics that to call someone 'an enthusiast' was considered an insult. The universe having been reduced to the laws of mechanics, it was to be expected that at some point someone would again be struck by the sheer wonder of it all. The rediscovery of feelings in European culture is known as 'Romanticism'. A couplet from a poem by the historian J. G. Herder (1744–1803) captures the mood perfectly:

> I am not here to think! – To be! To feel!
> To live! And to rejoice![6]

The same hectic and exclamatory spirit pervades Schleiermacher's *Speeches*, as he emphasizes that religion is not a matter of accepting a body of doctrine or a question of following certain moral imperatives, but is essentially a question of feelings. But then what does he mean by 'feeling'? It is the most fundamental way in which humans relate to the world around them, according to Schleiermacher. A person can relate to the world *theoretically* by making the world subservient through the exercise of reason. This is what the scientist does when looking at the world. On the other hand, people can relate to the world *practically*, and here they seek to influence the world by their moral and cultural activity. But people can also relate to the world *religiously*. Here they neither analyse the world nor seek to change it but are passive with regard to it. Here it is the world that has an effect upon the person.[7] In this context the experience is one of unity rather than diversity, dependence rather than dominance.

The formula which Schleiermacher coined to express this response was 'the feeling of absolute dependence'.[8] As an irreducible part of the spectrum of human experience, there is this kind of feeling or immediate self-consciousness which is at the root of all piety or religion. This feeling or immediate self-consciousness belongs to a human being as a human being, or is a part of a

---

[6] Quoted from K. Barth, *Protestant Theology in the Nineteenth Century* (London: SCM, 1972), p. 319.

[7] F. Schleiermacher, *On Religion: Speeches to its Cultured Despisers* (New York: Harper, 1958), p. 31: 'Piety cannot be an instinct craving for a mess of metaphysical or ethical crumbs.'

[8] F. Schleiermacher, *The Christian Faith*, ed. and trans. H. R. Mackintosh and J. S. Stewart (Edinburgh: T. & T. Clark, 1928), p. 12; *cf. On Religion*, p. 36.

person's psychological make-up and is constantly pushing upwards into conscious life. What Schleiermacher was saying was that the root of what we know as historical religion is beyond verbalization or moral principle, but its upsurge into consciousness inevitably involves these elements. It is possible to have beliefs and moral principles without genuine religion or piety – which was a charge levelled by Schleiermacher against the rationalism and orthodoxy of his day – but it is not possible to have genuine religion or piety without beliefs and a moral code.

This position has far-reaching consequences for the way in which Schleiermacher and his followers think about Christianity and religion in general. Christianity becomes one historical expression of a primordial feeling. This can be seen clearly, for example, from the way in which *The Christian Faith* is structured. Schleiermacher begins his volume by discussing religion in general before going on to consider Christianity as a specific type of religion. The title of the first part is 'The development of that religious self-consciousness which is always both presupposed by and contained in every Christian religious affection'.[9] A number of conclusions follow from this basic premise.

1. Christians cannot claim that their religion as a historical phenomenon is true while other historical religions are false: all historical religions have the immediate self-consciousness of the Universe as their basic impulse.

2. Christians can claim only that their religion is different from other religions in external manifestation, the internal religious impulse being the same in every case. Schleiermacher does argue, however, on the basis of a somewhat superficial comparison that Christianity is the superior form or manifestation of religion. But it is important to emphasize that Christianity is not superior in the sense of truth being superior to error, but in the sense that Christianity gives better expression to the primal truth shared by all truly religious persons. One person can be a better poet than another person while both possess the true spirit of poetry.[10]

Schleiermacher's discussion of revelation illustrates this crucial point very clearly. He admits that the term 'revelation' presupposes a divine communication and declaration, and that it points to that which lies at the root of religion. 'But', he states, 'I am unwilling to accept the further definition that it operates upon man as a cognitive being. For that would make the revelation to be originally and essentially doctrine.'[11] What he is saying is that revelation by definition is essentially non-verbal, an idea which was very radical in 1821 but which has

[9] *The Christian Faith*, p. ix; *cf.* p. 33, and Smart *et al.*, *op. cit.*, p. 131.
[10] *The Christian Faith*, pp. 37ff.
[11] *Ibid.*, 49; *cf.* pp. 16, 17, and Smart *et al.*, *op. cit.*, p. 186.

become one of the unexamined assumptions of modern Western theology, and of much modern thinking about religion in general.

3. While maintaining that Christianity or any other religion must resign its claims to truth in any verbal or dogmatic sense, Schleiermacher is concerned to emphasize that this does not lead to a despising of historical religion, as was the case with older rationalists. On the contrary, historical — or what Schleiermacher himself calls positive — religion is the only access we have to the life-giving source of the feeling of absolute dependence, to the experience of 'God'. The original emotional intuition, because of the unity of the human personality, must inevitably be captured in history. This occurs, first of all, in a communion with others who come to share the original intuition, and then in a communal attempt to give verbal and moral expression to it. The verbal or doctrinal and moral expression, however, can never be identified with the original intuition or feeling and can in time become divorced from it.

The way in which Schleiermacher viewed the origin of Christianity will clearly illustrate this approach. Jesus was seen as the bearer of an intense intuition of 'God'. He attracted to himself a number of followers who shared this original feeling. In due course they tried to express it in terms of lifestyle and doctrine. The moral and doctrinal expression, however, can never be identified with the original feeling or intuition, and can even in time become divorced from the foundational experience. In fact, according to Schleiermacher, the situation can become so serious that doctrines and a certain view of morality may need to be rejected, in favour of a return to the original intuition, whereby the whole process of verbalization and moralization begins again. Schleiermacher believed himself to be engaged in this process of returning to the original intuition of Christianity. In doing so, he fashioned a definition of the essence of religion, which he left as a legacy that is still very much alive in Religious Studies.

G. W. F. HEGEL

Schleiermacher's views did not receive universal acclaim in his own day. In fact he was very much overshadowed by G. W. F. Hegel (1770–1831), who was a fellow professor at the University of Berlin. Hegel, who was immensely famous in his own day, was one of the main opponents of Schleiermacher's idea that religion has its source in the feelings. Hegel's contempt for Schleiermacher's view is clearly seen in his statement that, if the feeling of absolute dependence is the root of religion, then the dog is the most religious creature on earth![12] He placed

---

[12] See H. R. Mackintosh, *Types of Modern Theology* (London: Nisbet, 1937), p. 102.

feeling in a lowly position in the scale of human attributes, below imagination, understanding and reason.

Hegel believed, like Schleiermacher, that religion has to do with the very essence of what it means to be human, but he maintained that it has to do with the higher human attributes. Because there is no higher attribute than reason, religion must be rational in the last analysis. To prove this, Hegel set out to explain reality in its entirety, to construct an immense rational system that would bring everything into a final synthesis. The method which he used to grasp the meaning of reality throughout the system is constant, being the eternal play between individual subject or spirit, the particular quality of the object or nature and the universal principle or logical idea. This sounds terribly abstract and abstruse – and in fact it is! – but this is what is meant by the famous dialectic of thesis–antithesis–synthesis which is the favourite way of expressing the method which underlies Hegel's gigantic system, though Hegel himself hardly ever uses these terms.[13]

Hegel's system is notoriously difficult to grasp as a whole, or in its details, but it is apparent throughout that he is concerned with thought or the development of the mind. His idea of the Trinity may be used to illustrate the method at work. The thesis is God the Father who as Absolute Spirit is the sum of all individual spirits. Hegel believed that every individual human mind or spirit is a moment of the divine mind or spirit. The totality of these moments is God the Father. The antithesis is the Absolute Spirit divesting itself of its universality and becoming an individual spirit. This is what Hegel meant by the Son in his Trinity. Every individual is an incarnation of the divine. Jesus is unique because of the quality of his realization of the idea, and not because of his essential difference from other human beings in virtue of his divinity. The answer given by the Hegelian Sir Henry Jones to the charge that he denied the divinity of Christ clearly illustrates this point. He stated that he denied the divinity of no man. The synthesis, the Holy Spirit, is the spirit returning to itself, having realized itself in and through its particularization. In short God evolves, or becomes fully 'himself' – it might be better to say 'itself' – through Man.[14]

For the student of religion, what is significant about this idea is that Hegel

---

[13] For brief outlines of Hegel's thought, see 'Hegel', in *Encyclopedia of Philosophy*, ed. P. Edwards, vol. 3 (New York: Macmillan, 1967), pp. 435–458; K. Barth, *op. cit.*, pp. 384–421; Reardon, *op. cit.*, pp. 59ff. Smart *et al.*, *op. cit.*, pp. 81ff.; C. Welch, *Protestant Thought in the Nineteenth Century*, vol. 1 (Yale: Yale University Press, 1972), pp. 86ff.

[14] Smart *et al.*, *op. cit.*, p. 100.

applies it to the historical religions, and thus becomes the first 'to articulate a history of religions based on the principle of development'.[15] He does this in his *Lectures on the Philosophy of Religion*.[16] The procedure followed by Hegel is somewhat similar to that followed by Schleiermacher in the introductory sections of *The Christian Faith*, in that the essence of religion is described first, and then it is shown how this essence relates to religion as found in its historical forms — what Schleiermacher called 'positive religion' and Hegel calls 'determinate religion'. The main difference between the two is that the former found the essence of religion in feeling, while the latter finds it in an idea or notion. Hegel also had a much deeper knowledge of world religions and was thus able to work out his idea of the development of religion more thoroughly.

The idea of development was not an invention of Hegel's, but it was he who made it into a controlling principle for understanding everything. The meaning of everything is to be found in its history, in the story of the way it has come to be what it is. It is as if one set out to write the biography of a famous man. The character and achievements might be well known but the subject's origins are not, so the biography begins, as actual biographies usually do, with some account of his parents and home and sometimes even of more remote ancestors. The purpose of this exercise is to show that certain characteristics of the famous man are an inheritance from his past, which go some way to explaining why he became the person who he was. This information, however, does not fully explain the famous person. What he did was to use his inheritance in a particular way which was unique to himself. So it is with Hegel's idea of the development of the human mind in general and of the development of religion in particular. The idea of religion is increasingly actualized in and through the various determinate religions that appear in the course of history.

What Hegel attempts in his *Lectures on the Philosophy of Religion* is to construct the family-tree of the concept of religion, which he believed he had discovered in his philosophical re-interpretation of the doctrine of the Trinity outlined above. He believed that the character of religion had become fully actualized in his philosophy, so that he was then able to trace the ancestry of the various traits of that character in the various religions of the world. As we would expect, given the all-pervasive triadic form of his thought, there are two main types or stages in the process of actualizing the notion of religion before it reaches its climax and

---

[15] *Ibid.*, p. 94.

[16] G. W. F. Hegel, *Lectures on the Philosophy of Religion*, trans. E. B. Spiers and J. Burdon Sanderson, 3 vols. (London, 1895).

fulfilment in what he calls the 'Revelatory or Consummate Religion'. The two preparatory stages are 'Natural Religion' and 'The Religion of Spiritual Individuality'.

To the stage of 'Natural Religion'[17] belongs the belief that all things are immediately indwelt by spirits. Included in this category are magic or shamanism, Chinese state religion, Buddhism, Hinduism, Persian (Zoroastrian) and Egyptian religion. What is common here is that there is no clear distinction between Spirit and nature, with the result that no clear notion of 'God' develops. However, the belief that the spiritual pervades nature proves that even Natural Religion is a moment in the process of the actualization of the notion of religion.

At the level of 'The Religion of Spiritual Individuality' we have Jewish, Greek and Roman religion. It is with the Jews that the idea of 'God' first becomes actual, though the emphasis here is on the otherness or transcendence and independence of God – the sublime Subject before whom all people bow. In Greek religion, on the other hand, the emphasis is very much on the immanence of the Spirit, but whereas in Natural Religion this immanence of Spirit develops into the amorphous pantheism of Hinduism and Buddhism, in Greek religion we have an anthropomorphous polytheism. Whereas in the Eastern traditions the Spirit has no definite shape, in ancient Greece the gods were given very definite human shapes, as can be seen from the many surviving statues of the gods. These gods in human form for Hegel are 'projections or representations of the *implicit* divinity of human spirit'.[18] Thus we come to the 'Revelatory or Consummate Religion', which is Christianity as interpreted by Hegel. The notion of Christianity, which is also the notion of religion as such, is that the Spirit which is absolute love divests itself of its transcendence and becomes actual in human experience and so, enriched, it returns to itself.

One final point needs to be made before we take our leave of Hegel, and that is to note the fact that, throughout his treatment of determinate religions, he is continually interpreting them in the terms of his particular philosophic terminology. This interpretative process is applied even in the case of the 'Revelatory or Consummate Religion'. What is implied in this approach is the idea that all religious language is in some sense symbolic or representational. The task of students of religions, therefore, is to discover the code which enables them to reduce the diversity of religious phenomena to some sort of order. In Hegel's case the key is the philosophical notion of religion which has been actualized in

[17] *Lectures on the Philosophy of Religion* , vol. 1, pp. 286ff.
[18] Smart *et al.*, *op. cit.*, p. 97.

and through the historical process of religious development.[19] As we shall see, the emphasis on religion as essentially a symbol generating activity has continued to fascinate students of religion up to the present, as has the quest for some general principle by which the meaning of religion in all its bewildering diversity may be understood.

Kant, Schleiermacher and Hegel laid the foundations for what might be called 'the idealistic approach' to religion in the modern period. We shall complete this introductory section on this approach by examining the work of Frederick Max Müller and Rudolf Otto. They are two of its most formative representatives in the area of Religious Studies.

F. MAX MÜLLER

F. Max Müller (1823–1900) was a German philologist who came to England in 1846 to edit a text of the Rig Veda for publication.[20] He never returned home but eventually became, successively, Professor of Modern Languages and of Comparative Philology at Oxford (1854–1875). Seeing language as the key to the understanding of religion, he became increasingly preoccupied with the latter. He published his *Introduction to the Science of Religion* in 1873, and in 1875 resigned his academic post to devote himself entirely to his new science. The main fruit of his efforts was his editing of the monumental fifty-volume *Sacred Books of the East* and his four series of Gifford lectures, *Natural Religion* (1890), *Physical Religion* (1891), *Anthropological Religion* (1892) and *Theosophy or Psychological Religion* (1893). It is with some justice that he has been called 'the father of Comparative Religion'.

On turning to his *Introduction to the Science of Religion*, one senses immediately that Müller belongs very much to the world of thought of Kant, Schleiermacher and Hegel. Religion means at least two different things to him. On the one hand, the historic religions with their specific teaching, traditions and dogmas; and, on the other, religion itself, that essential part of the human personality that is the source of all historic religion:

> If we say that it is religion which distinguishes man from the animal, we do not mean the Christian or Jewish religion; we do not mean any special

---

[19] See Bertrand Russell, *A History of Western Philosophy* (London: Routledge, 1991), p. 762, for a caustic onslaught on Hegel's approach.

[20] Müller came to England because India House, the headquarters of the East India Company, had a very fine collection of Indian manuscripts. The Rig Veda is believed to be the oldest Indian religious text.

religion; but we mean a mental faculty or disposition, which independent of, nay in spite of sense and reason, enables man to apprehend the Infinite, under different names, and under varying disguises . . .; and if we but listen attentively, we can hear in all religions a groaning of the spirit, a struggle to conceive the unconceivable, a longing after the Infinite, a love of God.[21]

In stating the case as he does in this quotation, Müller is adopting a similar approach to Schleiermacher and Hegel, that is, he begins by assuming that to be religious belongs to the essence of what it means to be human. There is something in humans which propels them beyond the limitations of nature and enables them to commune with the Infinite. That people have this ability, and that there is an Infinite to be apprehended, are the presuppositions of this type of idealistic approach. Having established this foundation, the next step is to come to the historic religions to try to make sense of them in the light of this primordial ability. The basic question is how the historic religions are related to the endemic religiousness of humankind.

Müller follows Hegel in seeking the answer in a comparative study of the world's literary religions in a historical context. His conclusion is that human religiousness has developed in and through the world religions, and that by a careful comparative study of the religions it is possible eventually to come to a clear conception of what religion actually is in its essence. He divided this whole exercise into the two main branches of Comparative Theology and Theoretical Theology, the two together making up the new Science of Religion. Comparative Theology is the historical part of the exercise in which, in Hegelian style, the ideas about God and the gods in the historical religions are examined to see whether any pattern will emerge to show how the ideas have developed. For this exercise, Müller was entirely dependent on a linguistic analysis of the ideas of deity found in the ancient scriptures of the world's religions. Having completed the preliminary work of Comparative Theology, the material gathered was then used to penetrate into the very essence of religion. This was the work of Theoretical Theology.

Müller made the most sophisticated statement of his position in the Gifford lectures,[22] which he delivered at Glasgow from 1888 to 1892, and which were

---

[21] *Introduction to the Science of Religion* (London: Longmans, [2]1893), pp. 13–14.

[22] Lord Adam Gifford (1820–87) was a Scottish judge who left a generous endowment for an annual series of lectures on natural religion at the four ancient Scottish universities. These lectures still continue, and have been delivered by many famous lecturers such as

THE CLASSICS

subsequently published in four substantial volumes. In the first, entitled *Natural Religion*, he developed his final definition of religion as 'the perception of the infinite under such manifestations as are able to influence the moral character of man',[23] which heralds something of a return to Kant. This is seen in the reference to morality and also in the somewhat nonsensical opening phrase 'the perception of the infinite'. What he means by this is that human access to the infinite can only be through sense experience — sense experience of the world external to them, and also of their own nature as human beings. Müller is also concerned to emphasize that sense experience can lead to an experience of a transcendent realm lying beyond sense, because, by the time he came to deliver his lectures, scientific materialism was gathering momentum with the general acceptance of the Darwinian idea of evolution.[24]

In the second series of lectures, *Physical Religion*, Müller discusses the search for something more than the finite in nature as an object. His argument is that, in the act of looking out on the world around them, human beings have sensed that the meaning of objective nature is not exhausted by what is apparent to the senses. They came to the conclusion that there must be something that transcends the simple appearance of nature external to them. Along this path they eventually fashioned the idea of 'God' as the source and life of the objective world.

The third series was entitled *Anthropological Religion*. Here Müller explores the idea of the divine that arose as a result of humans looking inwards into themselves. This is the story of the development of the idea of the soul or self. Here again people came to the conclusion that there was something in them which was more than just their physical being, that in some sense they could be identified with the divine that they had sensed in nature external to themselves. The conclusions of the second and third series of lectures can be viewed as the thesis and the antithesis of a Hegelian type of dialectic.

The synthesis comes in the fourth and final series, *Theosophy or Psychological*

Karl Barth, Emil Brunner, John Dewey, William James and Werner Heisenberg. Max Müller had the privilege of delivering one of the first series, and then the rare privilege of being invited back to deliver a second series. For a brief description of the lectures, see the article 'Gifford Lectures', in *New Dictionary of Theology*, pp. 268–269.

[23] *Natural Religion* (London: Longmans, ²1892), p. 188.

[24] Müller was already thinking of a conflict 'to the death' in 1878: 'The battle between those who believe in something which transcends our senses and our reason . . . and the surrender of the other party' (*Lectures on the Origin and Growth of Religion* [London: Longmans, 1878], pp. 30–31).

Religion. Here Müller seeks to prove that the climax of religious development occurs in the apprehension of the essential unity of the soul with the divine, which represents a transcending or synthesizing of the ideas of the infinite developed previously. He ends his lectures by arguing that this synthesis is best exemplified in the Christian mystical tradition and concludes that 'it was the chief object of these lectures to prove that the yearning for union or unity with God, which we saw as the highest goal in the other religions, finds its fullest recognition in Christianity'.[25]

Even when he published his lectures, Müller's influence was already waning, primarily, perhaps, because of his staunch opposition to Darwinism and the amateur anthropologist Andrew Lang's (1844–1912) demolition of his indefensible theory of the origin of mythology,[26] which Müller insisted on defending to the end. There are at present signs that another day is about to dawn for him, as students of religion begin to appreciate again his immense learning in the sacred books of the world and his spirited defence of spirituality in a materialistic age. His Gifford lectures can be described as the last comprehensive idealist study of religion in the Hegelian tradition which, though soon forgotten, have left a lasting legacy, not least in the continuing interest in mysticism in Religious Studies.

RUDOLF OTTO

As stated above, it was the study of religion in the Darwinian-inspired discipline of anthropology that sank Max Müller. But before we go on to look at some of the classics of this discipline, which has contributed so much to Religious Studies, we must look briefly at one more author who belongs very much in the idealist tradition. We refer to Rudolf Otto (1869–1937), whose famous volume entitled *The Idea of the Holy*, first published in English translation in 1923, has had a continuing influence in Religious Studies. It is significant that before publishing this volume Otto had already published a new edition of Schleiermacher's *Speeches*, a book on Darwinism and religion (1909) in which he

---

[25] *Theosophy or Psychological Religion* (London: Longmans, 1893), p. 583.

[26] See article 'Mythology', in *Encyclopaedia Britannica* (⁹1890), pp. 135–158, and in *Modern Mythology* (London: Longmans, 1897). Lang's most significant work, entitled *The Making of Religion* (London: Longmans, 1898), cut across prevailing anthropological theory by drawing attention to the fact that belief in 'high gods' was very common among so-called primitive peoples and could, therefore, be the primitive religion. In this he foreshadowed the work of Wilhelm Schmidt.

defended religion against the prevailing materialism of his generation, and a philosophy of religion (1909) in which he developed some of Kant's ideas as expounded by the neo-Kantian J. F. Fries (1773–1843).

Initially, therefore, Otto was an apologist for religion against materialism, who believed that religion could best be defended by a return to the thought of Schleiermacher and Kant. What Schleiermacher had done, in Otto's estimation, was to open up new avenues for the defence of religion against materialism and rationalism which could still be utilized at the beginning of the twentieth century. Like Schleiermacher, he believed that humans come into contact with that which lies beyond them on a deeper level than thought or action, a level which is real and inviolable to the chilling touch of scientific materialism.

But Otto was not an uncritical disciple of Schleiermacher. For example, he considered Schleiermacher's definition of religion as 'the feeling of absolute dependence' as too subjective. This definition does not make it clear that there is a numinous reality that is the cause of the religious experience. So Otto suggests 'creature-feeling' as an alternative, in order to emphasize that the source of religious experience is a wholly other numinous reality that exists over and above or beyond mere human experience.[27]

Following Schleiermacher, Otto also accepted Kant's two routes to knowledge by means of pure and practical reason, but he argued that the system needs to be completed by a third route to truth, the spiritual or the *numinous*. What he attempted in *The Idea of the Holy* was an evocation of this third type of human knowledge. The sub-title of the book gives us a helpful insight into its content: *An inquiry into the non-rational factor in the idea of the divine and its relation to the rational*. He does not dismiss the rational from religion, but sets out to discover the main characteristics of religious experience which he wanted to place side by side with pure and practical reason as a route to genuine human knowledge of that which is real. In attempting to do this, he realizes that he is not going to be able to describe the essence of religious experience, for to do so would reduce the experience to the level of the rational. That is why the word 'evocation' was used above. So, even though he criticizes Schleiermacher's subjectivism, like his mentor, he does locate the essence of religion in non-rational religious experience. The rational in religion is founded on the non-rational.

Otto's evocation of the essence of religious experience is embodied in his famous formula *mysterium, tremendum et fascinans*. He calls these terms a series of ideograms. They are terms which have a non-numinous meaning, but they can be used to 'stimulate into consciousness those uniquely religious feelings which

[27] R. Otto, *The Idea of the Holy* (Oxford: OUP, 1923), pp. 9–10.

they most nearly resemble'.[28] In religion, people come into contact, on a level beyond words, with a profound mystery which is both tremendous (in the sense of awesome) and fascinating.

A fine illustration of Otto's thesis can be seen in *The Wind in the Willows*, which, interestingly, was published some years before *The Idea of the Holy*. It comes from the account of Rat and Mole's adventure when looking for the lost baby otter, which they find eventually safe at the feet of Pan. When they land on the island in the river where Pan is,

> . . . suddenly the Mole felt a great Awe fall upon him, an awe that turned his muscles to water, bowed his head, and rooted his feet to the ground. It was no panic terror — indeed he felt wonderfully at peace and happy — but it was an awe that smote and held him and, without seeing, he knew it could only mean that some august Presence was very, very near . . . Trembling he . . . raised his humble head; and then, in that utter clearness of the imminent dawn, while Nature, flushed with fullness of incredible colour, seemed to hold her breath for the event, he looked in the very eyes of the Friend and Helper . . .
>
> 'Rat!' he found breath to whisper, shaking. 'Are you afraid?'
>
> 'Afraid?' murmured the Rat, his eyes shining with unutterable love. 'Afraid! Of *Him*? O, never, never! And yet — and yet — O, Mole, I am afraid!'[29]

In a sense, the details of Otto's theory are not relevant in this context.[30] What is relevant is his insistence that the experience of the holy or numinous is a genuine human experience that corresponds to something that exists in reality and that cannot be reduced to any other category.

CONCLUSION

In the light of the brief discussion of some of the chief classics of the idealist approach to religion, we can now summarize some of the main characteristics of that approach.

1. The demise of the traditional framework of Christian doctrine is assumed throughout. The advance in the scientific understanding of the world, which

---

[28] D. A. Crosby, *Interpretive Theories of Religion* (The Hague: Mouton, 1981), p. 132.

[29] K. Grahame, *The Wind in the Willows* (London: Methuen, 1978), pp. 134–136.

[30] For a slightly longer account of Otto's thought and a bibliography, see my article on him in *New Dictionary of Theology*, pp. 484–485.

includes the advances in natural science and in knowledge of non-Christian religions, was believed to have completely undermined the traditional picture of the origin and preservation of the world as recorded in Genesis. The idea that God had revealed himself exclusively to the Jews first, and then also to the Christians, was also considered to be untenable. In the light of science and history, it was believed to be impossible any longer to understand religion from the vantage-point of orthodox Christian dogma.

2. To understand religion, one must go to the religious phenomena in general and seek to discover what is essentially religious in them. By means of this procedure, the idealists believed that they could come to a scientific definition of religion. Generally speaking, they were not at all critical of their assumptions in coming to the religious phenomena, so more often than not their final definitions look very similar to their original assumptions.

3. The idealists thought of religion in terms of development. What they meant by this was that the idea of religion realizes itself in and through the historical forms of religion. Through religious history in general, the idea of religion which is there from the beginning becomes more and more explicit. Here a positive appreciation of non-Christian religion is emphasized, since every religion, to some extent or other, is an embodiment of what religion is in essence. However, this appreciation can refer only to non-Christian religions in the past, since all the idealist authors considered above believed that religion reached its most complete fulfilment in Christianity. The non-Christian religions are significant, therefore, up to the appearance of Christianity, and their persistence after that must be something of an anomaly. To complete the picture here, it needs to be emphasized that Christianity also developed. In Müller, for example, it reached its full development in medieval mysticism.

4. The idealist approach lays heavy emphasis on the value of religion. Religion is an essential element in human experience and corresponds to some transcendent reality which makes human life meaningful. That meaning may be discovered in morality, thought or feeling, but there is no doubt that it is there.

5. Every attempt to give verbal expression to the essence of religion from within a religious tradition is symbolic in some sense or other. Schleiermacher believed that it is impossible to go beyond the symbolism, so that his definition of religion is really a description of a psychological state which can be expressed in a variety of symbolic forms, though even he argues that Christianity possesses the best symbolic form. Hegel, on the other hand, attempts to reinterpret the symbolic language of religion into what he considered to be more precise philosophical language. But, for both, the understanding of religion is closely linked to the understanding of symbol.

2

the POSITIVIST CLASSICS

AUGUSTE COMTE

The term 'positivism' has its root in the philosophy of Auguste Comte (1798–1857), whose major work, *Cours de la philosophe positive*, was published between 1830 and 1842.[1] As with the idealists, Comte's thinking was dominated by the idea of development, and he also followed the idealists in his attempt to trace the development of human thought. His conclusions, however, were very different. He believed that human thought had passed through three main stages in its long history: the theological, the metaphysical and the positive. In the final stage it had become clear that belief in God was no longer needed.[2] The key issue in the whole process of development was the problem of causality. The way in which people have explained why events occur as they do determines to what stage they belong in the development of thought.

At the theological stage, all events were explained as the effects of supernatural beings. Because of people's inability to explain events in any other way, at this most primitive stage of intellectual development spiritual beings were postulated to solve the problem of causality. The clear implication is that at this stage people were rather poor natural scientists! In due course they passed to the next stage, which was the metaphysical. What happened at this stage was that thinking about the spiritual entities that cause events became more abstract and less anthropomorphic. The climax of this development was the abandonment of the gods in favour of the more abstract ideas of the idealist philosophers like

---

[1] English translation by Harriet Martineau, *Positive Philosophy*, 3 vols. (London, 1896).

[2] It is interesting that Comte did not foresee the demise of religion, because he devised a 'Religion of Humanity' with temples, priests and sacred literature – so that humans could worship themselves.

Kant and Hegel. But Comte believed that the metaphysical stage was, in his day, giving way to the final stage in the development of human thought, the positive.

At the positive stage, the question of the ultimate causes of events is put to one side as irrelevant and unanswerable, and humans become content with discovering the laws of nature by means of scientific observation. No causes other than those that can be observed are now considered relevant or real. Here Comte reflected the increasing confidence of the nineteenth century in science and in technology as being ways towards human progress and felicity that were superior to the traditional way of religion. As we shall see, Comte's idea of religion as bad science was to be an axiom for many students of religion until well into the twentieth century, the best example being the anthropologist Sir James Frazer.

It was Comte who devised one of the main methodological tools that was used by anthropologists such as Sir James Frazer. This was the 'comparative method'. Put simply, Comte held that the people who still lived at a low level of technological culture in the nineteenth century were living examples of humans at a lower level of intellectual development generally. In fact, from the positivist vantage-point, all who lived intellectually in the theological or metaphysical stages could be viewed as 'survivals' or 'living fossils' from man's infancy and early manhood as human beings. By comparing the ideas of contemporary 'primitives', such as the Red Indians or African tribesmen and also the rustic peasants of Europe, and then also utilizing evidence from the past history of human thought, the evolution of the intellectual life of humankind could be traced. Comte's conclusion, which was also his starting-point, was that the history of human thought was reaching its culmination in positivism, and many of the early anthropologists who turned their attention to religion agreed with this conclusion.

CHARLES DARWIN *and the* ANTHROPOLOGISTS

If it was Comte who provided much of the framework of thought for the positivist approach to religion, it was Charles Darwin (1809–82) who provided the greatest impetus. In 1859 he published *The Origin of Species*, in which he sought to establish his theory of the evolution of all organic life, and in 1871 he published *The Descent of Man*, in which he showed how his general theory applied to humans in particular. By 1871 Darwin's theory of evolution was being widely accepted, and the implications of his theory for the physical and cultural history of humankind were being vigorously developed into the new science of Anthropology,[3] by authors such as Herbert Spencer (1820–1903), Sir John

[3] See R. R. Marett, *Anthropology* (London, 1911), p. 8.

Lubbock (1834–1913) and E. B. Tylor (1832–1917). Traditionally, anthropology was the section of systematic theology which dealt with the origin, nature, primitive state, probation and apostasy of human beings. As the nineteenth century advanced, science claimed increasingly the right to speak authoritatively on many of these topics. The development of the idea of geological time in the first half of the nineteenth century had already put pressure on the picture of human origins in Genesis. Darwin's theory of evolution, which needed the vast aeons of geological time to be credible at all, made possible a severe challenge to the traditional picture.

Darwin's theory implies that it is impossible for human beings to have begun their history in a state of perfection, being fully endowed with all the potentialities that they now have. Evolution demands that humans began their history in a state somewhere akin to modern apes, and that all their exalted abilities were gradually evolved by means of natural selection. This process of development needed a time-scale that stretched far beyond the boundary of historical time – which is that time during which humans were able to leave some sort of record of their life to posterity. Comte's comparative method, as used by the anthropologists, was believed to be the answer to the problem of how to penetrate into prehistory. By studying what were called 'contemporary primitives', that is, people living in the nineteenth century on a low level of technological culture, it was believed that it was possible to describe the mental endowment of humans who had lived in prehistoric times. The anthropologist also believed that, by comparing the ideas and practices of the so-called 'contemporary primitives', they could discover how culture had evolved, just as Darwin's observations of physical variations had led him to construct his theory of organic evolution.

It is interesting to note in this context that the early anthropologists thought of themselves very much as natural or physical scientists. In 1868 we find E. B. Tylor reading a paper to the British Association for the Advancement of Science entitled 'On Language and Mythology as Departments of Biological Science',[4] and in the records of the Association papers on religion are found side by side with papers on 'The relative length of the first three toes of the human foot' and 'On the anthropological significance of ticklishness'! It was in the name of science that the anthropologists set out to fill the prehistoric vacuum that had been created by the rejection of the biblical account of human origins. Theoretically, religion should have occupied only a small part of their attention,

[4] *Report of the Meetings of the British Association for the Advancement of Science* 1868, Part 2, pp. 120f.

but the fact that they devoted much of their time and energy to it witnesses to the urgent need at the time to construct an alternative to the biblical picture of the early history of human beings.

Positivism was a belief in the ability of human beings to create a better world for themselves through science, without any reference to God. Maurice Mandelbaum's definition will serve as a conclusion to this brief introduction. According to him, positivism had three major characteristics: 1. 'Positivism rejects metaphysics on the ground that the questions with which metaphysics is concerned presuppose a mistaken belief that we can discover principles of explanation or interpretation which are more ultimate than those which are directly derived from observation and from generalisations concerning observations.' 2. 'The adequacy of our knowledge increases as it approximates the forms of explanation which have been achieved by the most advanced sciences.' 3. An advanced science is 'a science which has freed itself from metaphysical preconceptions' and which restricts 'itself to discovering reliable correlations within experience. To explain a phenomenon is to be able to subsume it under one or more laws of which it is an instance. A law, in its turn, is simply a well-authenticated general descriptive statement of uniformities which have been observed to occur in the past.'[5]

This definition highlights the fact that positivism was a faith commitment. It was an attempt to raise human ability to the place of God. This explains the circular argument. Humans can do without God (the rejection of 'metaphysics' in any form). Truth comes through 'advanced' science. An advanced science is a science that has nothing to do with any metaphysical explanations. We may not be quite so confident in the power of 'man' and science as we look forward to the third millennium since the coming of Jesus Christ.

SIR JAMES GEORGE FRAZER

The most eminent anthropologist of the first quarter of the twentieth century was Sir James George Frazer (1854–1941),[6] who devoted most of his active life to religious issues. He is also typical of the anthropological approach to religion in the positivist tradition of Comte and Darwin. His reputation was made by his

[5] M. Mandelbaum, *History, Man and Reason* (Baltimore: Johns Hopkins, 1971), pp. 10–11.

[6] For more details on Frazer's life and work, see R. A. Downie, *James George Frazer: The Portrait of a Scholar* (London: Watts, 1940), and *Frazer and the Golden Bough* (London: Gollancz, 1970).

THE POSITIVIST CLASSICS

The Golden Bough: A Study in Magic and Religion, which first appeared in two volumes in 1890, but was eventually expanded to the final edition of thirteen volumes published between 1911 and 1915. This was a very popular work despite its enormous bulk; a one-volume abridged edition was published in 1922 to accommodate the weaker brethren! Such was the popularity of Frazer that it is fair to say that what most informed people meant by Comparative Religion in the first quarter of the twentieth century was the kind of approach found in *The Golden Bough*. The term 'Comparative Religion' had become current in the last quarter of the nineteenth century but had been quickly assimilated to the 'comparative method' used in the positivist tradition. So, by the beginning of the twentieth century, Comparative Religion was commonly viewed as a branch of Anthropology.

Frazer inherited much from his predecessors in the tradition of Comte, and in particular from E. B. Tylor and Herbert Spencer. Like them, he was an evolutionist who believed that the task of the anthropologist was to discover the laws of cultural development. In doing this he also believed that he was operating scientifically, and that the 'history' which resulted from his enquiries was as true as any other scientific account of observable phenomena.[7] What he believed he could discover in the relationships between various aspects of religious life were 'laws of nature' as certain and clear as Newton's law of gravity. His method, like that of his predecessors, was the comparative method, which meant that most of his attention was directed to what he called 'savages' – and it is worth emphasizing that this term referred more often than not to peoples alive in Frazer's day. He states that,

> . . . as savage races are not all on the same plane, but have stopped or tarried at different points of the upward path, we can to a certain extent by comparing them with each other, construct a scale of social progression and mark out roughly some of the stages on the long road that leads from savagery to civilisation. In the kingdom of the mind such a scale of mental evolution answers to the scale of morphological evolution in the animal kingdom.[8]

The latter part of this quotation shows that Frazer was thoroughly intellectualistic in his approach to cultural evolution. What he attempted to do

---

[7] See *Psyche's Task* (London: Macmillan, [2]1913), pp. 160–161, 168; *The Belief in Immortality*, vol. 1 (London: Macmillan, 1913), p. 3; *The Worship of Nature*, vol. 1 (London: Macmillan, 1926), p. 9.

[8] *Psyche's Task*, p. 172.

was to delineate mental evolution. He also believed that this mental evolution, particularly in its early stages, was inextricably linked to religion. Like Comte he argued that there were three main stages in human mental evolution. The first stage was the Age of Magic, the second the Age of Religion, and the third the Age of Science. As with Comte, the problem of causality played a central role.

In their desire to discover the causes of natural phenomena, the first answer of primitive human beings was the belief that all natural phenomena are caused by similar natural phenomena. When the medicine man poured water on the ground as part of the rain-making ritual, he thought that to perform an action similar to raining would cause rain. This was the answer of magic to the problem of causality. In due course this answer was rejected by some in favour of a belief in the activity of invisible spirits. These spirits were thought to be superior to humans, so people were expected to present them with gifts and prayers in order to gain their favour.[9] At this stage the priest prayed to the spirit or spirits to send rain. This was the religious answer to the problem.

The appearance of religion did not lead to the immediate disappearance of magic, for both often co-existed in early history and still co-existed in many contemporary 'primitive' societies. Despite their co-existence, Frazer insisted that they were essentially different. But in some societies religion gained the upper hand and magic was suppressed. This move heralded the beginning of the development of religion from a belief in a multiplicity of spirits through polytheism to monotheism. The passage from polytheism to monotheism involved a process of secularization or despiritualization of the many gods and, according to Frazer, opened the door for the reappearance of magic. This time, however, magic played an important part in the development of modern science. 'Alchemy', he states, 'leads up to chemistry.'[10] So it seems that, for Frazer, the real evolution of human thought was from magic to science, with religion appearing as a temporary aberration in the process. Having made two unsuccessful attempts at solving the problem of causality in magic and religion, someone eventually found the right answer in science and, in so doing, opened the door to an unlimited progress for humankind. Frazer was very careful to avoid conflict with theologians and religious leaders, and insisted that his interest was exclusively in 'primitive' peoples and their culture. But it is difficult

[9] In *The Golden Bough*, vol. 1 (London: Macmillan, [2]1900), p. 62, Frazer defines religion as follows: 'By religion I understand a propitiation or conciliation of powers superior to man which are believed to direct and control the course of nature and of human life. In this sense . . . religion is opposed in principle both to magic and to science.'

[10] *Ibid.*, p. 130.

to avoid the obvious implications of his theory that religion belongs to a less advanced stage in the development of culture, and that it is destined to be eclipsed by the advance of science.

Frazer's theories sound very far-fetched to us today – and so they are! Attention has been drawn to them, not because of their intrinsic value, but rather to illustrate the difficulty of formulating a favourable view of religion when operating with positivist premises. It is difficult to see how a scholar who begins with a contempt for anything metaphysical can possibly do justice to religion. This point can be confirmed further by looking at Sigmund Freud's theories about religion, which have had a much more lasting influence than Frazer's.

SIGMUND FREUD

Sigmund Freud (1856–1939), the founder of modern psychiatry, is commonly regarded as one of the seminal thinkers of the twentieth century. Even though he came from a Jewish home, he became a militant atheist under the influence of materialistic science. 'I stand in no awe whatsoever of the Almighty',[11] he states in one of his letters. It is not surprising, therefore, when he had made his reputation as a scientist, that he considered himself 'one of the most dangerous enemies of religion'.[12] He not only rejected religion as a viable foundation for his own life but set out to discredit religion in the eyes of others also. It is important to approach his works on religion with this knowledge, because his theories are presented as unprejudiced attempts to explain the facts in a scientific way.

Freud's mature onslaught on religion came in his volume entitled *Totem and Taboo*, first published in German in 1913. The subtitle of this volume points clearly to its thesis: *Some Points of Agreement between the Mental Lives of Savages and Neurotics*. Writing as he did at the same time as the great positivist anthropologists, he could conveniently use their material, which was not very flattering to religion in the first place, to drive a few more nails into its coffin. Freud's basic thesis was that the symptoms of savage religion, which means religion in its origin, and mental illness are similar. Therefore they must come from a similar source in the unconscious. So, mental illness and religion can both be viewed in terms of a failure to cope with unconscious forces.

In constructing his theory, Freud attempted to marry some of his psycho-

[11] *Letters of Sigmund Freud*, ed. E. L. Freud, trans. T. and J. Stern (New York: Basic Books, 1960), p. 307.

[12] Ernest Jones, *The Life and Works of Sigmund Freud*, vol. 3 (London: Hogarth Press, 1957), p. 124.

analytical ideas with some highly speculative anthropological theories. He accepted the theory that totemism was the simplest and earliest form of religion, and that its main characteristic was two taboos: 'savages' were prohibited from killing their totem, and also from marrying within the same totem clan. These two prohibitions reminded Freud of the two basic elements of the Oedipus complex, which he believed he had discovered in his treatment of neurotic patients. The prohibition against killing the totem reminded him of the Oedipean desire to kill the father, while the prohibition against marrying within the clan reminded him of the desire to possess the mother. Then, two further anthropological theories were marshalled to complete the picture. The first theory was that originally the totem animal was sacrally killed and eaten in a solemn annual festival.[13] The second was that primitive human beings, as they emerged from the pre-human stage of evolution, were organized into hordes under the domination of one male.[14]

Freud was now in a position to re-create the primal drama. In the primal horde, the dominant male/father kept all the females to himself and either drove away or killed his sons when they became old enough to challenge him. Inevitably, in due course his strength waned, and some of his sons were able to rise in revolt against him. They killed their father and ate him! Unfortunately for them, after their dreadful deed, their remorse and rivalry hindered them from entering into the sexual heritage that they had craved. The end result of their deed was the founding of totemism. The renegade sons instituted a totem feast, in which they periodically ate the totem, which was normally forbidden them, in order to make atonement for their patricide. They also instituted the practice of exogamy, whereby they were forbidden to marry within the totem clan, which originally was a prohibition against marrying their sisters.

As stated above, Freud's theory − which is pure fiction as far as the facts go − was not just an attempt to explain 'savage' religion but to explain the origin and meaning of religion as such. For Freud, the Christian communion was a 'totem feast', and the law of consanguinity[15] the fruit of the unconscious horror of incest.

In one sense, it made no difference to Freud's theory of religion that the anthropological material that he used was completely unfounded, because the

[13] See W. Robertson Smith, *The Religion of the Semites* (Edinburgh: A. C. Black, 1927), p. 245.

[14] See Charles Darwin, *The Descent of Man*, vol. 2 (London: John Murray, 1871), pp. 362f.

[15] The law of consanguinity forbids marriage between certain categories of people. There is a list of some thirty such categories in the Anglican Prayer Book.

backbone of his theory was his psychoanalytic analysis of the person. Freud detected three areas of the personality: the id, ego and superego. The id is the area of the human genetic endowment, the repository of the biologically determined instincts. Though at the level of the subconscious, the sometimes fearful and imperious forces of the id have a tremendous influence over conscious life. The ego is the conscious mind, which attempts to reconcile the instinctual demands of the id with the realities of the external environment. The superego is that part of the ego that is developed during childhood as a sort of policeman who controls some of the more harmful products of the id. Unfortunately, in Freud's estimation, the policeman stays around into adulthood as some sort of god or authority image, limiting the person's freedom and filling life with guilt. 'God', according to Freud, is merely an image created by the superego during childhood, when the father's control of the child's instinctive sexual drives are projected into a non-human or celestial realm.

What Freud did in *Totem and Taboo* was to present a theory to explain the origin of the divine-father image and guilt in human history. It is not surprising that Freud finds no reality in the idea of God, since that was one of the assumptions with which he began his enquiry. But sadly, since there is no longer a loving heavenly Father to forgive us but simply a projection of our superego, we are left with our guilt, which is so vividly described by Freud and which is real enough whatever its source. As Marcel Vertes, the cartoonist, puts it so graphically: 'You mean to tell me that if Van Gogh had been psychoanalysed, he would not have cut off his ear?' 'Of course he would, but he would have known why!'[16]

The founding fathers of anthropological Comparative Religion focused their attention on the intellectual aspects of the origin and development of religion. They thought of religion primarily in terms of doctrines, and searched for the origin of religion in the intellectual processes which explained how the doctrines had arisen. They had the primitive philosopher always in view. This is not to say that they ignored the environment altogether, since they all believed that certain factors external to the individual had played a major part in shaping religious teaching. Climate, geography, political structure and the general level of intellectual and material culture were all considered to have played an important part in the development of religion. In the last analysis, however, the origin and development of religion was a matter of cognition, not of emotion or volition. Freud's theory that religion is a creature of the subconscious signals a departure

[16] Quoted by R. J. Rushdoony, *Freud* (Philadelphia: Presbyterian Reformed Publishing Co., 1965), p. 50.

from this approach. But the overall implications of Freud's theory are similar to that of the anthropologists: religion appears as a result of unhelpful developments in the human psyche that have been outgrown by modern scientific people.

We now go on to look at the theory of Emile Durkheim who, though he belonged in the positivist camp, argued that religion must correspond to something more meaningful in human experience than the intellectual error of the anthropologists.

EMILE DURKHEIM

Emile Durkheim (1858–1917), who is generally regarded as one of the founding fathers of modern Sociology, gave mature expression to his view of religion in *The Elementary Forms of the Religious Life*, first published in French in 1912. An avowed atheist in the Comtean tradition, he believed that 'sociology could not emerge until the idea of determinism, which had been securely estabished in the physical and natural sciences, was finally extended to the social order'.[17] What the sociologist studies are social facts that can be related to each other in terms of the law of cause and effect, just as in any other natural science such as physics or chemistry. Durkheim also believed that religion is essentially a social phenomenon, and that no true assessment of it is possible without taking this into account.[18]

Durkheim did not believe that the laws of nature simply emerge as a result of observing phenomena. Rather, they are imposed upon the phenomena as a result of scientific inquiry. One consequence of this idea is that those who are involved in religion cannot know what religion is really about. Knowledge is the prerogative of the scientist, and the scientist's knowledge of religion is very different from what the believer experiences. It is the scientist who is able to say what really happens in religion, and what really happens is not what the believer experiences.[19]

Durkheim could not follow the procedure of his predecessors, who merrily compared religious beliefs and practices from all over the world without any reference whatsoever to their social context. One obvious practical result of his

[17] K. H. Wolff (ed.), *Emile Durkheim 1858–1917* (Colombus, OH: Ohio State University Press, 1960), p. 376. *Cf. The Elementary Forms of the Religious Life*, trans. J. W. Swain (London: Allen Unwin, 1915), pp. 378, 418.

[18] *The Elementary Forms*, p. 94.

[19] *Ibid.*, pp. 417–418, 430.

emphasis on the social, then, was his concentration on a small number of religions, since each aspect of religion had to be viewed against its social background. In fact, in *The Elementary Forms of the Religious Life*, he concentrates almost entirely on one society, that of the Australian aboriginal, with the occasional glance at one other, the American Indian. He chose the Australian aboriginal society because he believed it to be the most primitive then existent[20] and the most likely, therefore, to provide the best evidence for the origin of religion.

This interest in origins betrays his evolutionary approach, even though he was very critical of the type of evolutionary schemes devised by Frazer and other anthropologists. He was also very critical of the anthropologists because of the unavoidable conclusion that one must draw from their theories that religion is basically an illusion. For Durkheim, religion must have a basis in reality, though by definition reality for him can include only that which can be observed in nature. He protests,

> How could a vain fantasy have been able to fashion the human conscious-
> ness so strongly and durably [as religion has] . . . Surely it ought to be a
> principle of the science of religions that religion expresses nothing which
> does not exist in nature, for there are sciences only of natural phenomena.[21]

The crucial question for Durkheim, then, is which part of nature to look to in order to find the basis of religion. His answer was society. He came to this conclusion as a result of his study of the totemism of the Australian aboriginals. We must therefore take a brief glance at some of his arguments.

Whereas anthropologists such as Frazer had argued that the basic element in religion is the worship of spiritual beings, Durkheim came to the conclusion that this was not in fact the case. For him, the basic element of religion was the division of the world into the two categories of the sacred and the profane.[22] The fact that everything aboriginals came into contact with was considered either sacred or profane, Durkheim argued, was more fundamental than any beliefs they might have in gods or spirits. The key question, then, is how primitives came to regard certain things as sacred. He discovers the answer in his study of aboriginal totemism.

When as a child one danced around an imaginary totem pole in some leafy glade in a world before television, where the Red Indian was still the hero, one had no idea then, mercifully, of the labyrinthine complexities of the ongoing debate about totemism. It remains very difficult to say what totemism is, in a

---

[20] *Ibid.*, p. 95.   [21] *Ibid.*, p. 70.   [22] *Ibid.*, p. 37.

nutshell, without being caught in the web of dissension. Suffice it to say that, in some tribal societies, the members of the various groups into which the tribe is divided are identified by certain signs or totems. These signs or totems can be anything from an animal to an unusually shaped stone. It is also undeniable that totems have something to do with the social organization of the tribe and with the foundation of the tribal traditions. It is at this last point that the religious dimension enters into the picture. Durkheim believed that the totem is in fact 'the very type of sacred thing', and that it is a symbol of the totemic principle which 'can . . . be nothing else than the society itself, personified and represented to the imagination under the visible form of the animal or vegetable which serves as a totem'.[23] If the totem as the very type of sacred thing is a symbol of the clan, then the spiritual authority represented by the totem and the clan or society must be the same. And if this is the case, according to Durkheim,

> Religion ceases to be an inexplicable hallucination and takes a foothold in reality. In fact we can say that the believer is not deceived when he believes in the existence of a moral power upon which he depends and from which he receives all that is best in himself: this power exists, it is society.[24]

In coming to this somewhat startling conclusion, Durkheim also shifted the emphasis in the study of primitive religion from belief to ritual. Frazer found the origin of religion in the cogitations of the individual primitive philosopher. Durkheim focuses on the primitive clan, meeting together periodically to celebrate their solidarity. As a result of the collective emotion generated by such meetings to express common relationships and common needs, religious beliefs were formulated to symbolize them. He called these symbols 'collective representations'. 'It is action', he states, 'which dominates the religious life, because of the mere fact that it is society that is its source.'[25]

The action of society creates religion so that the myths and doctrines which arise from the ritual are symbols of the social reality. This view of 'symbol' reflects Durkheim's overall method in his study of religion. As stated above, he believed that it was possible to discover 'laws of nature' operating in the cultural realm in exactly the same way as they were discoverable in the physical realm. What he meant by a law of nature was a uniform pattern of cause and effect which results from an objective observation of the facts. The law of nature that he discovered as a result of his study, at second hand, of Australian aboriginal religion was that it is society that is worshipped in their totemic rituals. Of

[23] *Ibid.*, pp. 119, 206.   [24] *Ibid.*, p. 225; *cf.* pp. 348, 387.
[25] *Ibid.*, p. 418; *cf.* pp. 403, 416.

course this is not a view that could be shared in any sense by the aboriginals themselves. As far as they were concerned, their totems and the rituals associated with them were sacred things handed down to them from the beginning of time. This belief, for Durkheim, bore no relation to reality. What he means, when he states that the totems and totemic rituals are symbolic, is that they represent a reality of which the aboriginals themselves are entirely ignorant. This highlights the gulf between the idealist and positivist view of symbolism. For the idealist, religious doctrines, rituals and so on are symbolic of some transcendent reality beyond nature. For the positivist Durkheim, they can only be symbolic of a natural reality. That natural reality was society.

the FUNCTIONALIST SCHOOL of SOCIAL ANTHROPOLOGY

Durkheim's significance in the anthropological study of religion has persisted, particularly since he was the fountainhead of the functionalist school of Social Anthropology, which dominated the anthropological view of religion in Britain until very recently. Starting from his view that religion can be explained in social terms, the functionalists emphasized the function of religion in the preservation of the social structure. A. R. Radcliffe-Brown (1881–1955), the founder of this school, states that 'the notion of function . . . rests on the conception of culture as an adaptive mechanism by which a certain number of human beings are enabled to live a social life as an ordered community in a given environment'.[26]

Radcliffe-Brown believed that, as one aspect of culture, religion contributes to the preservation of society. 'We may entertain as at least a possibility', he states in his Henry Myers lecture of 1945, 'the theory that religion is an important or even essential part of the social machinery . . . , part of the complex system by which human beings are enabled to live together in an orderly arrangement of social relations.'[27] What is interesting in Radcliffe-Brown here (and this is true also of Durkheim and Comte) is that, even though religion is emptied of all supernatural or transcendent meaning, it still seems to have a continuing validity. According to these positivists, there is no God in the sense in which Christians have traditionally believed, but the effects of such a belief on social existence is vitally important for the general well-being of humans in the world. The problem for the positivist is how to preserve the beneficial effect of religious

[26] *The Andaman Islanders* (Glencoe, IL: Free Press, 1964), p. ix. *Cf.* pp. 405–406 for the very Durkheimian conclusion to this anthropological classic.

[27] *Structure and Function in Primitive Society* (London: Cohen West, 1952), p. 154. *Cf.* pp. 175–176.

belief, having emptied it of all reality as religious belief. Comte's answer was his Religion of Humanity. He even attempted to set up an ecclesiastical institution with priests and temples for the worship of Man and his achievements, with himself as pope! Durkheim in his turn hoped 'that as spiritual religion declines a secularist religion of a humanist kind would take its place'.[28] For Radcliffe-Brown, the ideal was the rationalist and urbane religion of Confucius:

> The Confucians have shown us that a religion like ancestor worship can be rationalised and freed from those illusory beliefs that we call superstition. For in the rites of commemoration of the ancestors it is sufficient that the participants should express their reverential gratitude to those from whom they have received their life, and the sense of duty to those not yet born, to whom they in due course will stand in the position of revered ancestors. There still remains the sense of dependence. The living depend on those of the past; they have duties to those living in the present and to those in the future who will depend on them.[29]

CONCLUSION

From our brief look at some of its classical authors, some of the main characteristics of the positivist approach to religion can now be summarized.

1. The positivists were very impressed with the method used in the physical sciences such as Physics or Biology. They believed that, if the same method were applied to the various aspects of culture, including religion, a true understanding of such activity would be gained. What they meant by a scientific account of anything can be seen in Mandelbaum's description of the positivist approach. Any appeal to some supersensual or supernatural cause of an event is precluded from the discussion by definition as unscientific and a hindrance to knowledge.

2. Like the idealists, the positivists sought to discover the essence of religion and to fashion a general definition of religion on the basis of 'facts'. The difference between them was that the positivists precluded, from the beginning, the possibility of arriving at a definition which attributed reality to anything beyond nature. Their definitions, therefore, represent religion always as something different from that which the believers think it is. Durkheim in particular emphasizes that the religious person cannot possibly know what his or her religion essentially is, since that privilege belongs only to the scientist. Given

[28] *Elementary Forms*, pp. 430–431.
[29] *Structure and Function in Primitive Society*, p. 176.

THE POSITIVIST CLASSICS

their method, the positivists had to define religion in terms of a mistake of primitive man or as representing something which could be observed in nature. This approach is often called 'reductionist' by its opponents, because it reduces religion to something other than what it says it is. In fact, the danger of reductionism continues to be seen as a very real problem in those aspects of Religious Studies influenced by the social sciences.

3. It is not surprising, in view of its high regard for the physical sciences, that the positivist approach to religion has been dominated by the idea of evolution, as fashioned by Darwin and particularly the social Darwinists. Not surprisingly, the question of the origin of religion was paramount, and evidence for it was sought among the so-called contemporary 'primitives'. At first, tidy schemes of the evolution of religion were constructed, such as the ones devised by Frazer and Freud. Durkheim abandoned such simple unilinear schemes, although he continued to be very concerned with the origin of religion, which betrays his basic, evolutionary approach. However, his theory that society is the reality in religion opened the door to the study of the function of religion in society, which moved the discussion further away from questions of historical origin and evolution. But the concentration on 'primitive' societies in Social Anthropology after Durkheim's day witnesses to the fact that the evolutionary approach is not entirely forgotten.

4. In the case of some of the positivist classics at whom we have looked, it is obvious that religion was seen as more of a hindrance than a help to human progress. This was particularly true of Freud, who saw belief in God as an illusion to be rejected. Frazer, on the other hand, refused to draw the obvious conclusion from his theory that religion is something that is bound to be left behind as belonging to an earlier and inferior stage of mental development, and claimed that all he had done was to give an account of primitive religion. But Durkheim and Radcliffe-Brown, despite having emptied religion of all spiritual content, insisted on its permanent value. They believed that religion in some secular form would persist and that it was essential for the well-being of society. What is interesting here is that some, at least, of the positivists, were almost forced into admitting the value of religion, despite having emptied it of all its specifically religious content. This fact makes it less surprising that a number of scholars who were very much in the positivist tradition found it difficult to reject metaphysics altogether. These scholars, whose works must be included among the classics of Religious Studies, are the subject of the next chapter.

– 3 –

the AMBIVALENT CLASSICS

We have looked at two major streams of thought that have contributed to the modern study of religion. Generally speaking, they were also 'camps', and belonging to one camp meant exclusion from the other. But there were some who, though they seemed to speak the language of one camp, were obviously attracted by what was done in the other. This is why their work is described here as 'ambivalent classics'. Under this heading we shall look at the work of three scholars: the psychologist William James, the anthropologist R. R. Marett and the sociologist Max Weber.

WILLIAM JAMES, PSYCHOLOGIST

William James (1842–1910)[1] was an American psychologist. His most famous work on religion is *The Varieties of Religious Experience: A Study in Human Nature*. Originally delivered as Gifford Lectures[2] and first published in 1902, the fact that this volume has remained in print ever since witnesses to its popularity and influence. James classed himself with contemporary psychologists, such as J. H. Leuba (1868–1946), E. D. Starbuck (1866–1947) and G. A. Coe, who were seeking to apply scientific methods of research to religious experience. He regarded himself as a 'radical empiricist' and this is apparent, for example, in his acceptance of Starbuck's conclusion that 'conversion is in its essence a normal adolescent phenomenon', or in his suggestion that 'the whole phenomena of regeneration [may] . . . possibly be

---

[1] For some biographical information on James, see Eric J. Sharpe, *Comparative Religion: A History* (London: Duckworth, 1975) pp. 108–112.

[2] See ch. 1, 'The idealist classics', pp. 35–36, n. 22.

a strictly natural process'.[3] He also accepts the conclusion reached by Coe in *The Spiritual Life: Studies in the Science of Religion* that the principle of scientific predictability is valid for religious conversion. As James says,

> If you should expose to a converting influence a subject in whom three factors unite; first, pronounced emotional sensibility; second, tendency to automatism; and third, suggestibility of the passive type; you might safely predict the result: there would be a conversion.[4]

Again, in the conclusion of *The Varieties*, he argues that religious type is determined, it seems, by psychological type. He also endorses Leuba's positivist and pragmatic conclusion that 'God is not known, . . . is not understood; he is used',[5] and that, therefore, religious practices and doctrines are 'amongst the most important biological functions of mankind'.

However, James is at pains in his first lecture to deny that he is a materialist, even to the extent of ridiculing the type of materialism which 'finishes up Saint Paul by calling his vision on the road to Damascus a discharging lesion of the occipital cortex, he being an epileptic'.[6] His ultimate escape from the inevitable pressure of materialism on one committed to radical empiricism, that is, the positivist approach, is the subliminal or subconscious mind. Yet, when he first introduces his theory of the subconscious, he seems reluctant to leave his positivist moorings:

> Psychology and religion are thus in perfect harmony . . . since both admit that there are forces seemingly outside of the conscious individual that bring redemption to his life. Nevertheless psychology, defining these forces as 'subconscious' . . . implies that they do not transcend the individual's personality.[7]

Later on in the lectures, James seems to allow for the possibility of going beyond one's own individual personality to some transcendent realm by means of the subconscious:

> Just as our primary wide-awake consciousness throws open our senses to the touch of things material, so it is logically conceivable that *if there be* higher spiritual agencies that can directly touch us, the psychological condition of their doing so might be our possession of a subconscious region which alone should yield access to them.

---

[3] *The Varieties of Religious Experience*, rev. ed. (London: Longmans, 1907), pp. 199, 230.
[4] *Ibid.*, p. 241.   [5] *Ibid.*, pp. 506–507.   [6] *Ibid.*, p. 13.   [7] *Ibid.*, p. 211.

Even though he is prepared to go beyond the confines of the individual personality, James seems to balk at the truly transcendent, and ends his lectures still very much in the natural. The subconscious becomes 'the mystical region, or the supernatural region', that is, God. 'God', he states, 'is the natural appellation, for us Christians at least, for the supreme reality, so I will call this higher part of the universe [that is, the subconscious] by the name of God.'[8]

In view of this emphasis on the subconscious, it is not at all surprising that James's interest is primarily in individualist religious experience, and this is manifest in the central topics of his lectures – conversion, sainthood and mysticism. In this ascending scale of spiritual life, the affections are always to the fore, the height of religious experience being the ineffable vision of the mystics which takes humanity utterly beyond rationality. But if the affections predominate, their judge, according to James, is their effects. Religion is true or false to the extent that it works or not. James, more than any other, was responsible for the introduction of this pragmatic principle, which continues to be very influential in Religious Studies. He says:

> What I propose to do is . . . to test saintliness by common sense, to use human standards to help us decide how far the religious life commends itself as an ideal kind of human activity. If it commends itself, then any theological beliefs that may inspire it, in so far forth will stand accredited.[9]

Having studied a limited number of religious phenomena primarily from the Christian tradition, with the odd reference to other religions, in particular mystical Hinduism and Buddhism, James comes to the final conclusion that, whereas religious adherents differ greatly in their theories of the transcendent, their experiences and conduct are very similar. He looks forward to the day when all dogmatic theology will be buried and everyone will recognize that all their religious experiences come from the same subconscious realm – and that they should, therefore, be kind to one another! In fact, for James, the only hope religion has of survival depends on whether or not it can be emptied of its intellectual content. In a letter to a friend, he says that his aim in *The Varieties* was

> . . . first to defend 'experience' against 'philosophy' as being the real backbone of the world's religious life . . . and second, to make the hearer or reader believe, that I myself invincibly believed that, although all the special manifestations of religion may have been absurd [I mean its creeds

[8] *Ibid.*, pp. 515–516.   [9] *Ibid.*, p. 331. *Cf.* pp. 74, 211–212.

and theories], yet the life of it as a whole is mankind's most important function.[10]

James's mystical pragmatism has persisted, and his appeal to the subconscious or subliminal realm as the answer to the destructive implications of the positivist approach for religion has been greatly developed by C. G. Jung. Jung's views and significance will be considered in the chapter on the Psychology of Religion in the context of contemporary Religious Studies (see chapter 8).

R. R. MARETT, ANTHROPOLOGIST

R. R. Marett (1866–1943) was an Oxford anthropologist who had a great influence on the study of religion in the first quarter of the twentieth century. He has not received the recognition that is his due, especially since he developed an analysis of religious experience very similar to Rudolph Otto's some years before the latter published his *The Idea of the Holy*.[11] Marett was also one of the first Englishmen to recognize the importance of Emile Durkheim for the study of religion. In an article published in 1908, which was some years before Durkheim published *The Elementary Forms of the Religious Life*, Marett admitted that the approach of British anthropologists had been far too individualistic. He went on to commend Durkheim's idea of collective feelings as a fundamental source of religion.[12]

Durkheim's influence is apparent in Marett's emphasis on the primacy of ritual over myth, which he expressed succinctly in the memorable statement that 'savage religion is not so much thought out as danced out'.[13] He also accepted the sociological stress on the need to view any religious ritual or belief in its social context. But he was strongly opposed to Durkheim's reductionism. 'That religion is part of the social structure', he states, 'does not mean that it can be identified with it.'[14] But, however much he might have accepted a sociological approach with its attempt to discover the laws of social development and integration, Marett insisted that this could in no way undermine 'the functional independence of the spirit'. He also insisted that 'the ruling meaning and purpose of historical religion at its most essential . . . must be described in terms

---

[10] R. B. Perry, *The Thought and Character of William James*, vol. 2 (London: Oxford University Press, 1936), pp. 326f.

[11] R. R. Marett, *The Threshold of Religion* (1909; London: Methuen, [2]1914), p. xxvii.

[12] See 'A Sociological View of Comparative Religion', *The Sociological Review* 1 (1908), pp. 48ff.

[13] *The Threshold of Religion*, p. xxxi.   [14] *The Sociological Review*, p. 55.

appropriate to spirit, in terms of meaning and purpose'.[15] Here we have a clear rejection of the idea espoused by Durkheim that religion can be entirely explained in terms of natural law.

Marett had attempted to describe the essence and origin of religion as early as 1900 in an essay published in the journal *Folklore*. It was in this essay that his pre-animistic theory of the origin and essence of religion first saw the light of day, and much to his amusement it made him famous and the head of an anthropological school. Marett could see clearly that the views of anthropologists such as James Frazer, who saw the origin of religion in an intellectual mistake, could only lead to a rejection of religion, and so he argued that religion finds its origin not in thought but in feelings. This feeling he described as the feeling of awe, a feeling which arose at the point where the primitive's understanding broke down.[16]

From the beginning, humans have felt that there is something 'there' which is greater and more powerful than they, of which they were afraid but which also attracted them. The negative aspect of this emotion Marett called *tabu*, and the positive, attractive aspect he called *mana*. All religion developed from this basic emotional response to the supernatural as expressed in its social context. As an anthropologist dedicated to the natural science ideal, Marett did not believe that he could say anything about the supernatural but simply about its effects. But his definition of spirit as 'a Power that makes for righteousness'[17] witnesses to the difficulty of avoiding any definition of ultimate principles. The moral emphasis in this definition also brings us to the crux of Marett's objections to the implications of Durkheim's positivist explanation of religion.

For Marett, morality could mean nothing without the freedom to choose the good and reject the evil. He was prepared to accept physical evolution by natural law, and he was even prepared to accept that certain general patterns can be observed in human social behaviour. What he was not prepared to accept was that this meant that people were not free to choose a particular course of action in preference to another. He makes his point, as he so often does, forcefully and wittily: 'No system of external compulsion is likely to prove an attractive assumption when it is so much simpler to suppose that every creature with a tail is itself responsible for wagging it.'[18] Here Marett goes to the heart of one of the

---

[15] *Ibid.*, pp. 55–56.   [16] *The Threshold of Religion*, p. 28.

[17] *Psychology and Folklore* (London: Methuen, 1920), p. 166.

[18] *Head, Heart and Hands in Human Evolution* (London: Hutchinson, 1935), p. 31. *Cf.* Marett's statement on p. 33: 'If matter wins, mind will have endowed its own figment with the power of silencing all opposition by its grand incapacity for saying anything at all.'

THE CLASSICS

great dilemmas of modern thought: how to preserve human freedom and self-determination when faced with a science that explains everything in terms of deterministic natural law. The details of his philosophical arguments rejecting determinism are not relevant here; what is relevant is that he saw the implications of the positivist view of religion in these terms and insisted upon human self-determination. He argued that room must be made for the religious genius to bring about progress in human life, since progress occurs only in the moral and religious realms.

In another context, where he again discusses the tension between freedom and determinism, Marett argues that religion is the means by which this tension is transcended. To him, the scientifically insoluble philosophical problem of freedom versus necessity is lived out rather than thought out in religion. He states:

> Religion is 'teleo-practical'. Its function is to supplement 'why' theoretical with 'why' practical, to convert good as described by the mere intellect into such a form of good as may be absorbed into the economy of our thinking, feeling and willing soul-life as a whole.[19]

Marett's stress on the importance of the social dimension in the development of religion is, therefore, a stress on it as the sphere in which the fundamental spiritual and moral reality in religion realizes itself. True religion, or the end to which religion develops, is the realization of the Good, 'the Power that makes for righteousness', in the social sphere. It is in religion in this sense that people are able to assert their individuality for good over and above the forces of nature and society. It is not surprising that Marett does not envisage the disappearance of religion but, to the contrary, he believed it to be an essential aspect of human experience. 'The Power that makes for righteousness' will always be there for people to feel and express in acts of charity despite all the changes in the attempts to name it. In the last analysis, Marett fits into the idealist rather than the positivist mould, his emphasis on the primacy of emotion being reminiscent of Schleiermacher, and his emphasis on morality being reminiscent of Kant. His main significance for the understanding of Religious Studies is his highlighting of the tension between the positivist idea of the laws of nature and human freedom. This problem also occupied the third of our ambivalent classics, Max Weber.

---

[19] *Psychology and Folklore*, p. 154.

MAX WEBER, SOCIOLOGIST

Max Weber (1864–1920), who together with Durkheim is generally considered to be a founder of modern sociology, was bred in a German intellectual tradition heavily influenced by idealism. By the end of the nineteenth century, however, under pressure from positivist science, a very heated debate was going on in Germany concerning the status of the so-called human sciences such as history, sociology or economics. The main question was whether or not these human sciences should be assimilated to the physical sciences, as was the case in the positivist tradition.

Heinrich Rickert (1863–1936), a neo-Kantian philosopher who influenced Weber, argued that the human and physical sciences should be kept apart. However, since reality is one, he argued that the difference between them is not a difference of subject but simply a difference of method. The method of the physical sciences is generalizing in that they seek to establish general laws, while the method of the human sciences is individualizing in that they seek to highlight the unique or special aspects of a given phenomenon. For example, history as a human science is not concerned to describe general laws for the evolution of culture but to describe the unique character of some aspect of culture at a particular point in the historical continuum. Despite his respect for Rickert, Weber did not accept this analysis and held that the generalizing method is just as valid in the human as it is in the physical sciences. To adopt such a position could have been seen as a move in the direction of positivism on Weber's part. But what Weber attempted in fact was a synthesis of the two methods, as can be seen, for example, in his concept of the 'ideal type'.[20]

Weber's concept of the 'ideal type' has to do with the way in which the sociologist or historian seeks to understand the interaction between various social factors. In studying society one soon realizes that certain phenomena are similar, and by means of comparison it is possible to construct an 'ideal type' of these similar phenomena. This definition of a type, Weber emphasizes, is an abstraction which nowhere exists in reality, since what exist in reality are unique individual events. This concept of the 'ideal type', therefore, preserves the integrity of the individuals while providing a general principle for the convenience of understanding.

A fairly straightforward example of Weber's application of this procedure can be found in his famous volume *The Protestant Ethic and the Spirit of Capitalism.* The

---

[20] Max Weber, *The Sociology of Religion*, trans E. Fischoff (London: Methuen, 1965). Introduction by Talcott Parsons, p. xxiii.

THE CLASSICS

central thesis of the volume is that the ethic which arose from the Puritan development of Calvinism provided one of the main impulses in the creation of the spirit of modern capitalism. The development of this thesis demanded some discussion at least of the religious ideas or theology of the Calvinistic Puritans in particular. In coming to this discussion, Weber states:

> We can of course only proceed by presenting these religious ideas in the artificial simplicity of ideal types, as they could at best but seldom be found in history. For just because of the impossibility of drawing sharp boundaries in historical reality we can only hope to understand their specific importance from an investigation of them in their most consistent and logical forms.[21]

What Weber is saying is that no two statements of Calvinism, be they dogmatic statements by a body of divines such as the Westminster Assembly or statements by individual authors, are precisely the same, but that it is possible to abstract from a variety of statements an 'ideal type' which is the most consistent and logical form. Weber believed – wrongly as it happens – that the doctrine of predestination was the heart of Puritan Calvinist belief, and that it is in this doctrine that Calvinism finds its most consistent and logical form. Having isolated the typical idea, Weber then goes on to discuss the type of ethic that the idea creates, which brings us to the heart of his thesis.

The Calvinistic Puritans believed that the way in which they could prove that they were predestined by God to eternal life was by the manner in which they lived their lives in this world. Since they were precluded from using this world for their own enjoyment, the emphasis was on using this world to prove their faithfulness to God or to make the best of the gifts which God had given them. Every believer, whatever he or she does, is called by God to his or her work. Work thus becomes central, and success in work came to be seen as evidence of God's blessing, which in turn was evidence of predestination to eternal life. Success in work, however, in many cases was bound to lead to increase in wealth, but this wealth, once accrued, could not be spent on this-worldly enjoyment. Thus it became capital for re-investment, and so the Protestant ethic became one of the major forces in the creation of modern capitalism.

The details of Weber's argument, however interesting they might be, are not particularly relevant to our purpose here. What is relevant is Weber's attempt to show that an idea can influence social behaviour. This approach places him very

---

[21] *The Protestant Ethic and the Spirit of Capitalism*, trans. Talcott Parsons (London: Allen & Unwin, 1976), p. 98.

much in the idealist tradition. But in stating that this has been his approach in *The Protestant Ethic*, he is at pains to deny that this precludes him from approaching the issue from the other direction. He emphasizes that it is not 'his aim to substitute for a one-sided materialistic an equally one-sided spiritualistic causal interpretation of culture and history. Each is equally possible, but each, if it does not serve as the preparation, but as the conclusion of an investigation, accomplishes equally little in the interest of historical truth.'[22] It is just as possible, according to Weber, to show that material factors have an influence upon ideas as it is to show that ideas have an influence upon material factors.

In his *Sociology of Religion*, the emphasis seems to be on the more materialistic approach, and religious ideas are often presented as products of social or economic factors. It is also in the *Sociology of Religion* that we have the fullest development of Weber's typology of religion, and particularly his typology of religious leaders. It is here that he defines the characteristics of the magician, the priest and the prophet as the three main types of religious leader. In his examination of various paths to what he calls 'radical salvation', he lists two types of ascetic and two types of mystic paths. The ascetic types are the world-rejecting, such as the reclusive monk, and the inner-worldly, of which the Calvinistic Puritan is a good example. The mystic path is also twofold, the aim being identification with the divine as opposed to the ascetic quest for obedience to the divine. There is the world-rejecting mysticism, characteristic of the Hindu *sannyasin*, and the inner-worldly mysticism, of which Buddhist mysticism is a good example.

Weber's overall purpose in defining these ideal types is to show that certain types of religious leader appeal to different social groups, and to explore the mechanics of the formation of religious communities. Throughout this discussion the influence of social and economic factors on the ideas, leadership and organization of religious communities is highlighted.

The purpose of this section on Weber has been to emphasize the ambivalence of his approach to religion as a social and historical phenomenon. He seems to believe that religion can be understood from either a positivist or idealist point of view. The key to this seemingly self-contradictory position is his idea of 'understanding'. He believed that 'understanding' refers only to method and not to any ultimate reality. In fact, Weber held that to be agnostic with reference to ultimate reality is a prerequisite of any understanding of religion as a social fact. We shall return to Weber when considering the Sociology of Religion more specifically in chapter 7.

[22] *Ibid.*, p. 183.

— 4 —

CONCLUSION *to* PART ONE

We have come to the end of our parade of some of the classics of Religious
Studies. All of them belong very much to our modern age, and many have had a
profound influence on modern thought in general. The questions which they
raised in their attempt to understand religion in many cases continue to play a
central role in contemporary Religious Studies. Can God be known? Is there an
'essence' of religion common to all religions? And if so what sort of 'essence' is it?
If religion belongs to human nature as such, then what is its focal point? Is it in
the mind, emotions or will? How can religion be understood in the context of
modern science? Does modern science undermine the very basis of religion or
does it undermine only a certain type of religion? What is the place of the
unconscious in our understanding of religion? How are we to understand
religion as a social reality? These are some of the questions addressed by the
classics. Religious Studies continues to discuss them in a variety of contexts
which will be examined in due course.

Basic to the approach of almost every author considered in Part One was the
division of religion into its 'essence' and 'form'. This was true of both the idealists
and the positivists, and also of those who attempted some sort of mediation
between them. Of the idealists, Immanuel Kant distinguished between, on the
one hand, the dictates of the practical reason, which he considered to be the true
core of religion and, on the other hand, faiths or the historical forms of religion.
Friedrich Schleiermacher defined religion in its essence as 'the feeling of absolute
dependence' and distinguished this experience from what he calls 'positive'
religion.

Max Müller's 'Science of Religion' was divided into Comparative Theology,
which dealt with the historical forms of religion, and Theoretic Theology, which
'has to explain the conditions under which religion . . . is possible'. He further

states that the scientist of religion 'studies religions as they have been, and tries to discover what is peculiar to each and what is common to all, with a silent conviction that what is common to all religions . . . may possibly constitute the essential elements of the true religion'.[1]

The positivists also thought of religion in terms of its essence and form, although their ideas of the essence of religion were much less flattering to religion than was the case with the idealists. The positivists operated on the assumption that nothing can be known of any transcendent reality which corresponds to the religious experience of humanity, and that the source of that experience must be found somewhere in human nature. James Frazer found the answer in attempts to understand causality, and thus located the essence of religion in the primitive's mistaken belief that events are caused by supernatural beings who need to be propitiated.

Emile Durkheim could not accept that religion was simply the result of faulty reasoning, but insisted that there must be some reality in it although, as a positivist, he had to find that reality in nature. His conclusion was that the object of worship is, in fact, society itself as a power which imposes an external authority upon people. Here the form of religion is religion as viewed by the participant, while its essence is religion as viewed by the social scientist.

Whereas Frazer reduced religion to mistaken logic and Durkheim reduced it to social reality, Sigmund Freud reduced it to the operations of the unconscious, with its foundation in the biological make-up of the human being. For Freud religion, which he equates with belief in God, is essentially the result of certain operations of the unconscious resulting from the repression of sexual instincts during childhood. Here again, what religion is is apparent to the scientist, whereas what the religious participant believes bears no relation to any transcendent reality.

While admiring the achievements of empirical science and considering themselves scientific in their approach, the ambivalent classics were eager to avoid the more drastic consequences of the positivist approach. In some cases they returned to a position similar to that of the idealists. This was certainly the case with R. R. Marett, who saw the essence of religion in the transcending of the limitations of deterministic nature through moral action — a position very reminiscent of Kant.

In some ways William James came to a similar conclusion. His study of religious experience lead him to the conclusion that there must be some reality corresponding to such experiences. It is a matter of debate as to whether or not he

[1] Max Müller, *Natural Religion* (London: Longmans, [2]1892), p. 53.

identifies this reality with the subconscious or subliminal self. But whatever it is, it can be known only from its effects. Therefore, where human life is enriched and deepened by religion, whatever that religion may be, there we have the essence of religion.

With Max Weber we return to religion as a social reality. Unlike Marett and James, who attempted to accommodate the idealist perspective from a positivist base, Weber attempted to accommodate the positivist perspective from an idealist base. Of all the classics, Weber is the only one who is not concerned with the question of essence but simply with understanding the relationship between religious and other social institutions. His concern with 'ideal types' and with the meaning of religious acts is not a concern with ultimate essences or realities. This bracketing of the possibility of knowing anything of the truth in its ultimate sense was a characteristic of the positivist approach.

The difference between Weber and some other positivists is that, whereas he was agnostic about ultimate reality, they were atheistic. For Weber, since he did not know whether 'God' exists or not, he was forced to proceed in his attempt to understand religion on the assumption that he did not. What he discovered was a complex interaction between ideas and material factors – from one angle ideas influenced social and economic factors, whereas from another angle social and economic factors influenced religious ideas. Weber's theories were obviously relevant to both the history and sociology of religions, but it is only in the latter that his views have been developed. The lasting impact of Weber will, therefore, be considered in the chapter on religion and the social sciences (see chapter 7).

Despite all the differences between them as to precisely in what the essence of religion consists, all the classics constructed their theories in a historical framework. In the last analysis, all their theories attempted to explain the place and meaning of religion in history. In most cases, however, the definition of the essence of religion was not a matter of historical investigation, but rather of speculating about how a primitive human being *might* have reacted to certain phenomena, or in particular circumstances. But once the essence had been discovered, it was considered possible to explain the meaning of the history of religions as a whole.

Closely linked to the quest for the essence of religion in the classics of Religious Studies is the quest for the origin, or origins, of religion. What is at issue here is that first religious impulse which explains religion as it has appeared in history. This preoccupation is understandable in view of the rejection of the account of the origin of humans and their religion found in Genesis and other parts of the Bible, such as Paul's letter to the Romans.[2]

---

[2] See especially Romans 5:12–13.

According to the biblical account, humans were created by God in his own image as the crown of his creation. The glory of human beings was vested in their ability to communicate with their Creator, and in the mandate that they should rule the world which God had made. Sadly and mysteriously they fell from the original state of innocence and became alienated from God. Having rejected God's authority, they went and created gods for themselves. But God did not leave them in this state of alienation, but revealed himself to humankind through the family of Abraham. This revelation through the Jews reached its climax in the coming of Jesus, God's Son incarnate. Jesus claimed to be God's final revelation to all humankind and so, since his resurrection, Christians have claimed to be the bearers of God's final revelation.

This biblical picture of the origin of religion, and the meaning of religious history in general, was rejected by many in the nineteenth century and particularly so when Charles Darwin's theory of evolution came to be generally accepted. Darwin's theory of human evolution from a pre-human state as an ape-like creature was in stark contrast to the biblical account of the original setting of human beings in the paradisal Garden of Eden. In Darwin's theory the past history of humankind stretches back many millions of years whereas, traditionally, human life on earth was counted merely in thousands of years.

If Darwin's theory was accepted, then to say anything about the origin of any aspect of human culture meant penetrating into that enormous hypothetical period in history for which there is precious little evidence. Speculation on the basis of a study of human psychology, supplemented by a study of contemporaries living on a low level of technological culture, was the way in which the early anthropologists claimed to be able to fill this gap. The early anthropologists also concentrated very heavily on the intellect in framing their theories of the origin of religion. It was the primitive philosopher that they had always before their minds.

E. B. Tylor's animistic theory of the origin of religion, which was accepted in essence by James Frazer, imagined primitive human beings as they were just emerging from animality being puzzled by phenomena such as dreams, swooning, illusions and death. Thinking about these phenomena, they came to the conclusion that they were made up of at least two entities: a body, and a 'ghost soul', which was detachable from the body. What they experienced in dreams were the nocturnal peregrinations of this 'ghost soul'. By association souls or spirits came to be attributed to non-human phenomena as well, and so the spirit-world was born and with it, of course, religion. What Frazer does is to put this theory into the context of his three-age evolution of human thought and to emphasize more heavily the problem of causation. Both Frazer and Tylor thought that they were reconstructing what had actually happened in history, even though the evidence they marshalled owed more to imagination than to anything else.

In the case of the idealists, though they too were committed to the idea of development, the situation is different. Whereas for the positivists humans are just matter, for the idealists they are also spiritual beings. What this means practically is that human nature is much more of a constant in the idealist accounts of the origin and history of religion. What they looked for was that aspect of human nature through which they, as spiritual beings, come into contact with the Beyond. They found this crucial point in various aspects. Friedrich Schleiermacher and Rudolph Otto found it in feelings. Kant found it in the will, and G. W. F. Hegel in the mind.

Schleiermacher and Otto believed that people feel something out there which is greater than themselves and upon which they are absolutely dependent. Because they are also thinking and willing agents, they try both to describe that which they feel and to discover the right way to act in the light of their feelings. Kant on the other hand, in his analysis of human reason, argued that people are subject to a categorical imperative which overrides all other considerations and feelings. This inner command is intelligible only if humans are immortal and if there is someone there beyond us who can unite virtue and happiness. Thus morality demands the discipline of feelings and a belief in God and immortality.

For Hegel, the workings of the human mind individually and universally were in the last analysis the expression of the Absolute Mind. What happens in the story of human thought, despite all the contradictions and foolishness, is the self-realization of the Divine Mind in human history. All individual human beings as thinking creatures are divine, and the thought of humankind as expressed in religious and other institutions, such as the state, is the thought of the Absolute. It is obvious that thought takes the prime position in this system, closely followed by action or morality, with feelings coming a poor third in the list.

Müller attempted to combine these various idealist strands in his final definition of religion as 'a perception of the infinite that is able to influence the moral nature of man'. Having isolated the point at which people come into contact with the transcendent, the idealists then proceeded to show how this contact affected historical life. In these schemes the origin of religion is the same in every age, but differences arise in the expression of the original impulse. For example, the source of religion for Schleiermacher had always been, and always would be, the feeling of absolute dependence. Differences arose in the expression of this feeling. In the strict sense it is only the expressions that have a history at all, since the primal impulse remains constant. As we shall see, this view of the history of religions is very similar to the view espoused at present by Wilfred Cantwell Smith.

Interestingly, though firmly in the positivist tradition, Durkheim also traced the origin of religion to emotion, though in his case it was collective rather than individual emotion. Like earlier anthropologists, he denies by definition the possibility of the collective emotion bringing people into contact with a reality outside nature. The history of religion is thus the history of the way in which humans have responded to society as the authority external to them that overshadows every aspect of their life. As with other anthropologists and the idealists, Durkheim's idea of the origin of religion really determines the type of history of religion or religions that results. Weber stands alone among the classics, in that he gave up the quest for origins as hopeless and was content to try to understand history without any reference to ultimate origins or meanings.

The third general characteristic of the classics was their emphasis on the idea of development or evolution. Having divided religion into its essence and form and then identified the essence with the original religious impulse, the idealists believed that the essence was progressively manifested in and through the forms of religion. The history of religions is thus the opening-up process of the essence of religion through time. Individual religions could then be seen as manifestations of some aspect or other of the essence of religion. The Hegelian scheme is the paradigm for this approach, and the most sophisticated example of its outworking in the nineteenth century was Müller's four series of Gifford Lectures.

By the time Müller published his lectures, the idealist idea of development was being overshadowed by the positivist idea of evolution. It was Darwin who gave evolution its tremendous prestige, but it was positivist anthropologists, sociologists and psychologists who utilized the theory of evolution to prove that human beings had outgrown their need for religion and that religion belongs to a more primitive stage in their mental development. Frazer's three-age theory of intellectual evolution is a good example of such an approach. However, as we saw in the case of Marett, it was not long before the older idealist idea of development reasserted itself. Anthropologists and other students of the world's religions, though using the Darwinian terminology, became idealist in their philosophy of history. For example, Alan Menzies in his *History of Religion* states:

> It belongs to the very idea of evolution that the identity of the subject of it is not changed on the way up, but that the germ and the finished product

CONCLUSION TO PART ONE

are the same entity, only differing from each other in that the one has still to grow while the other is grown.[3]

What we have here is not a Darwinian or positivist, but an idealist, idea of evolution, since the principle ensures that the essence of religion is still there at the end of the process. This way of thinking has dominated the History of Religion throughout the twentieth century. We shall now turn in Part Two to the various ways of approaching religion that are current in Religious Studies.

[3] Alan Menzies, *History of Religion* (London: University Extension Manuals, 1895), p. 6.

II

VARIOUS APPROACHES TO RELIGION

– 5 –

the HISTORY *of* RELIGION

There was a time not so long ago when the discipline that is now called 'Religious Studies' was called the 'History of Religions'. One of the main international institutions which seeks to bring together scholars who study the world's religions is still called the International Association for the History of Religions. This reflects a reaction against the general theories of religion that were formulated by the classical authors already considered. The real task of the study of the world's religions was to tell the story of individual religions and not to formulate a theory of religion as such. The reaction was particularly strong against the unilinear evolutionary theories of anthropologists like James Frazer. With the influence of Emile Durkheim and others, the focus in anthropology and sociology was more on the role that religion has in society than on how religion had evolved. But what was being offered by this new stage in the study of religion was still a general theory, even if the evolutionary perspective had become somewhat muted.

E. O. JAMES'S COMPARATIVE RELIGION

The dominant figure in Britain (in this 'history of religion' in the singular) for much of the twentieth century was the Anglican clergyman E. O. James (1888–1972). His intellectual roots were in theoretical social anthropology,[1] so he preferred to call his discipline 'Comparative Religion'. Reflecting these roots, he believed that it was as a result of the 'great revolution in knowledge initiated in

---

[1] E. O. James is described as a 'theoretical social anthropologist', because he had no field experience of his own. Another popular way of describing his type would be 'an armchair anthropologist'. Emile Durkheim and James Frazer also belonged to this type.

1859 by Charles Darwin that Comparative Religion became established as a scientific discipline'.[2] Yet despite his preference for anthropology, which had its roots in Darwinism, he rejected the evolutionary schemes developed by his predecessors. He did not believe, for example, that cultural and intellectual development could be explained in terms of three clear-cut stages as Frazer had contended. But accepting — what he considered a Darwinian idea — that we live 'in a dynamic universe continuously undergoing change', he set out to discover and describe some of the mechanisms which explain such change in the realm of the human spirit.

The mechanism that James concentrated on tended to reflect his preference for the theories of social anthropologists such as A. R. Radcliffe-Brown, with his emphasis on the function of religion as a force for social integration. But, in concentrating on certain details of evolution, he did not forget the wider canvas, believing that 'in its broadest sense "history" presupposes that there is something happening having some permanent value and significance in relation to the totality of events'.[3] History is not simply a story of change, but a story that in its totality is going somewhere. There is a purposeful transcendent dimension to history, and the task of Comparative Religion, according to James, is to discover what this purpose is. The emphasis is on *Comparative* Religion because he believed that the overall direction of the development of religion as such would become clear only with the comparison of the histories of various religions. The study of one religion would not yield the secret of the overall direction of the evolution of religion.

A brief account of James's study of sacrifice will clearly illustrate his method. He begins by dividing sacrifices into two main categories, blood offerings and bloodless oblations, and argues that the former were the first to appear because of the evolutionary commonplace that 'man' was a hunter before he was a farmer. The fundamental idea of sacrifice, even at the earliest stage, was the idea of giving a life in order to promote life. At the lowest level of the so-called Palaeolithic hunters, this fundamental idea did not get 'beyond the awareness of a vital relationship existing between themselves and certain animal species on which they depended for their food supply'.[4] This vague feeling eventually developed into a more specific technique of sacrificing a life in order to ensure fertility.

A further development came with the mystery religions of classical antiquity.

[2] 'The History, Science and Comparative Study of Religion', *Numen* 1 (1954), p. 92.
[3] *Ibid.*, p. 96.
[4] *The Origins of Sacrifice* (London: John Murray, 1933), p. 34.

THE HISTORY OF RELIGION

In the initiation ceremonies of these mystery religions, the novice sacramentally died and was raised to life again in communion with the god. At this stage, the process of sacrifice becomes symbolic for the first time. This symbolic idea of sacrifice reached its apex in the Christian eucharist. The sacrifice of the mass is, therefore, the culmination of the evolution of the idea and practice of sacrifice. What James says is that the fundamental idea of sacrifice, the giving of a life to promote life, has been operative in the various forms of sacrifice that have appeared in history. These forms of sacrifice, when compared with each other in the light of the basic idea, can be arranged in an evolutionary order, the principle of ordering being the increasing realization in history of the idea of sacrifice. Since he was a devout Anglo-Catholic, it is not surprising that this evolution reaches its culmination in the sacrifice of the mass.

For James the mass, as the ultimate form of sacrifice, was much more than a ritual form; it was an expression of the essential 'ritual' of human life as a whole. As an Anglo-Catholic, he believed that in the incarnation of God in Jesus Christ that which is true of every human being was manifested. This truth is that we are all partakers of the divine nature. Since New Testament times, the reality of the incarnation, of the birth, life, death and resurrection of Jesus Christ is actualized in the mass:

> The ancient death and resurrection culture pattern centring in the divine Kingship and expressed in the Mystery cults acquired its true meaning as seen in its fulfilment as part of the redemptive process made actual throughout the ages in the Eucharistic drama, as the central act of worship of redeemed humanity.[5]

It was convenient for James the Anglo-Catholic that the social anthropology of his mentors, such as R. R. Marett, emphasized the central importance of ritual in the history of religion. 'The history of ritual', states James, 'is the history of religion.'[6] As a functionalist, he was convinced that religious rituals were the main integrative force in society, that it was religious rituals that kept societies from disintegrating into chaos. Like many other intellectuals in his day, he felt that Western culture was facing a tremendous crisis as a result of the severe blow dealt to progressive evolutionism by the First World War. For James, the main cause of the crisis in Western civilization was the rejection of religion. He

[5] *The Social Function of Religion* (London: Hodder & Stoughton, 1940), p. 292. *Cf. The Origins of Sacrifice*, p. 183, and *The Origins of Religion* (London: John Heritage, 1937), p. 142.

[6] *The Origins of Sacrifice*, p. 289.

believed that modern society's only hope was the rediscovery of the meaning of religious ritual as the key to social integration. In England's case, this could only mean, as far as James was concerned, a rejuvenation of the Church of England on Anglo-Catholic lines, with its heavy emphasis on the centrality of the ritual of the mass.

As for those countries where religions other than Christianity were dominant, he would have rejoiced to see the re-awakening of the non-Christian religions because, though imperfect, their rituals pointed forward to the perfect ritual found in Christianity. The naturalistic ritual patterns of the non-Christian religions, though inferior to the revelatory ritual of the mass based on the historic fact of Christ, could yet save their societies, to an extent at least, from the disintegrating effects of secularization. Claiming to be an anthropologist before all else in his approach to religion, and as such an objective scientist, it is interesting to note that the fruit of his objective study is very much shaped by his Anglo-Catholic theology. One thing is very clear, and that is that his idea of the ultimate meaning of religion did not come to him as a result of an objective study of the facts of religious history. On the contrary, the facts were made to fit his theory.

History of religions and/or history of religion

We have discussed some of James's ideas about religion and the way in which the history of religion should be approached, but not because of their intrinsic value. James's ideas are now universally considered to be old-fashioned and his whole approach is generally deprecated. He does, however, remain instructive as an example of the difficulty of being objective in the study of religion, despite all claims to objectivity. This is not a problem that has disappeared from Religious Studies. But whereas James attempted to write the history of religion in the singular, the emphasis is now very much on the plural, and it is commonly held that only individual religions have a history. Any consideration of religion in the singular is reserved to another discipline, the Phenomenology of Religion, which, it is argued by some, has nothing to do with history.

It must be admitted that this emphasis has been beneficial for Religious Studies in some respects and makes possible a right appreciation of the valuable scholarly work that has been done since the middle of the nineteenth century in opening up the stories of the great religions of the world. Without the detailed linguistic and historical work of scholars on individual religions, there could be no Religious Studies in any sense, and our understanding of human history in general would be greatly impoverished. It is questionable, however, whether one can be fully satisfied with a history of individual religions. More general questions inevitably arise even for the historian. After all, the individual religions must be types of the one *genre* 'religion', and religious activity everywhere is a human activity. As Ursula King puts it:

> The permanent dilemma of historical enquiries consists in the fact that history does not know 'religion' in the singular but knows only a plurality of religions, and yet it requires a unitary concept of 'religion' to look at religions in the plural.[7]

E. O. James, who was living in the shadow of the Darwinian revolution, was not greatly concerned with this dilemma but believed that, as a result of a scientific study of religions, what religion is, and how it came to be what it is, would become apparent enough. What is striking for us, looking at James from an intellectual context not quite so dominated by Darwinism and positivism, is his inability to see that his whole effort in the history of religion was very much conditioned by his own religious convictions. Since James, scholars have been much more reticent about making claims to scientific objectivity as well as being reticent about writing histories of religion in the singular,[8] but the dilemma emphasized above by King remains and continues to condition the work of historians of religions. At some point or other, they all seem to be forced to think about the whole story of religion and its meaning as opposed to the stories of the individual religions. In the end, it seems very difficult to escape the realm of ultimate meanings, and this is particularly true in the case of religion because by definition religion, in whatever form it is found, has to do with ultimate meanings. This will become very apparent when we examine the work of Wilfred Cantwell Smith, who is generally considered as one of the most eminent contemporary historians of religion and religions.

WILFRED CANTWELL SMITH

Wilfred Cantwell Smith (1916–) was, on his own admission, brought up in a theologically conservative Presbyterian home in Canada. He spent eight years in Lahore from 1941 to 1949, where he laid the foundations of his understanding of Islam. He was ordained as a Presbyterian minister in 1943, though he has never served as a parish minister. In 1949 he became a Professor of Comparative

---

[7] Ursula King, 'Historical and Phenomenological Approaches', in F. Whaling (ed.), *Contemporary Approaches to the Study of Religion*, vol. 1 (Berlin: Mouton, 1983), p. 74.

[8] Trevor Ling, however, did so as recently as 1968 in his *A History of Religion East and West* (London: Macmillan, 1968).

Religion at McGill University, and in 1951 established the McGill Institute of Islamic Studies. He moved to Harvard in 1964 as Director of the Harvard Center for the Study of World Religions. In 1973 he went to Dalhousie University, Nova Scotia, but returned to Harvard in 1978. Smith is unquestionably one of the leading authorities in the field of Religious Studies today. He made his name as an Islamicist, but has gone on to consider more general questions of the nature of religions and the relationship between them. He considers himself first and foremost a historian of religion, and his contribution to the more general questions is made explicitly from that perspective. It is by means of a historical approach that he seeks to find that elusive unitary concept of religion which is to make the study of religions meaningful.

Cantwell Smith's The Meaning and End of Religion

A good example of Smith's historical approach is his study of the concept 'religion' in *The Meaning and End of Religion*.[9] He begins this volume with a historical analysis of the term 'religion'. Here he argues that it is only in the last two hundred years or so that the term has come to mean a system of beliefs and practices that may be distinguished from other systems of beliefs and practices, which led to the classification of religious phenomena into a series of '-isms', such as Hinduism, Confucianism, Buddhism and so on. Smith argues that to describe religious phenomena in this way is modern, and is alien to the way in which religious people have viewed their beliefs and practices. Religious people have traditionally thought of what they believe, and what they do in the light of their beliefs, in terms of their personal relationship with 'God' or the transcendent.

For example, what John Calvin meant by the title of his famous work *Institutio Religionis Christianae* was not, as often understood, *The Institutes of the Christian Religion*, as if 'Christian Religion' was some sort of entity that could be defined and comprehended in a book, but rather something like *A Handbook of Christian Piety*. According to Smith, Calvin did not write his famous book in order to mark out the boundaries of the territory possessed by 'Christianity' so that it could be distinguished from the territory possessed by other 'religions'. In other words, the Christian 'religion' is a matter of a relationship with God, and not a matter of rehearsing beliefs and practices which exclude from the fold those who refuse to adhere to them. For Calvin, according to Smith, the word 'religion' meant 'piety'. Religion is an attribute and not a thing.

Reference has been made to Calvin simply to illustrate the type of evidence to which Smith appeals. He argues that the same is true in other 'religions' as well —

---

[9] First published in New York by Macmillan, 1962.

either that they have no term at all corresponding to our term 'religion', or that the term or terms that they have always refer primarily to a relationship to the transcendent and not to some body of doctrine and ritual which sets the believers apart from those with different doctrines and rituals. He argues that this is true even in the case of Islam, even though it is most strikingly true in China and Japan where various 'religions' have co-existed happily for centuries. It is in the case of the Eastern 'religions' that Smith finds the most convincing proof that 'religion' was not something exclusive until around two hundred years ago.

On the basis of his analysis of the term 'religion' in the Western tradition and similar terms in other traditions, Smith argues that we should now abandon the term, since it has come to mean something that it never meant in the 'religions' themselves until relatively recently. In its place, he suggests that we should adopt two new terms, 'faith' and 'cumulative tradition'.[10] Faith refers to that relationship to the transcendent or piety which Smith sees as the core idea of the term 'religion', and 'cumulative tradition' refers to the doctrines, rituals, and ethical practices that cluster round the 'faith' in the course of history. What we have here, in fact, is yet another version of the old 'essence' and 'form' division of religion, with 'faith' as the essence and 'cumulative tradition' as the form; and, just as in the older theories, the essence remains constant while the form is in a constant state of flux. The History of Religions, strictly speaking therefore, is the history of the 'cumulative traditions'.

The thinking that underlies Smith's theory is fairly easy to detect. Like many theologians who belong to the liberal Protestant tradition, the exclusiveness of the gospel became something of an offence to him. He rejects the belief that Jesus is the only way to God and that religion apart from Jesus is idolatry. But, if all religions lead to God, one is left with the problem that the religions often contradict each other. Smith's ideas about religion reflect his assumptions perfectly. He argues that 'religion' as a term never meant anything exclusive. Religion is in fact made up of the two distinguishable aspects of 'faith' and 'cumulative tradition'. 'Faith' never changes, while 'cumulative traditions' do change from age to age. It is 'cumulative tradition' that differs from one religion to another, while 'faith' remains constant. It follows that if something in one 'cumulative tradition' contradicts something in another, this in no way undermines the unity of 'religion', since unity exists at the level of 'faith'.

Since Smith launched his theory of 'religion' in 1962, some evidence has emerged which casts doubt on his main conclusion. Peter Biller, in an article

---

[10] See *The Meaning and End of Religion* (London: SPCK, 1978), pp. 170–192, for Smith's definition of 'faith', and pp. 154–169 for his definition of 'cumulative tradition'.

entitled 'Words and the Medieval Notion of Religion',[11] has produced evidence showing that 'religion' was thought of as a body of doctrines and of practices founded on them as early as the thirteenth century CE. Biller provides evidence for the transition from using the word 'religion' to mean an attitude (*i.e.* worship, or worshipful attitude) to using it to mean a thing (*i.e.* a religion, or one system as opposed to another system) as taking place in the period from the eleventh to the thirteenth centuries. This undermines Smith's theory that this transition occurred in modern times. What is more significant, however, is Biller's examination of the use of terms such as 'faith', 'law', 'sect' and 'heresy', to which he appeals to show that, even in the eleventh century, the idea of 'religion' as a system existed even though the word 'religion' was not used to express it.

Biller does not develop this point, though he has touched on a major weakness in Smith's theory – his overemphasis on the meaning of the term 'religion'. It might very well be that the original meaning of the term 'religion' was 'worshipful attitude' and that at some point it came to mean 'a system of belief', but that in no way makes it impossible for the idea of 'a system of belief' to have existed long before the idea became linked to the term 'religion'. In fact, the whole history of religions witnesses to the fact that the religious mind has always operated with systems of belief which exclude other systems. This is as true of the Eastern religious traditions as it is of the Semitic. A good example is the detailed treatment of 'pernicious views' in the Tipitaka,[12] the scriptures of Theravada Buddhism, or in the correction of false ideas in the Hindu Upanishads and Bhagavad-gita.

The Buddha seems to have been in no doubt whatever about the way to release from the round of rebirth, and thus about the ideas that had to be held in embracing that way, and the moral and meditative practices to be built on the foundation of the ideas. As far as the Buddha was concerned, any other way just would not do. It is very difficult to deny that the Buddha was exclusive after

---

[11] *Journal of Ecclesiastical History* 36 (1985), pp. 351ff.

[12] The Tipitaka is the canonical scripture of Theravada/Southern Buddhism. The term means 'three baskets', which refers to the three sections of the scriptures: the Vinaya Pitaka, which deals with the monastic life; the Sutta Pitaka, which contains the discourses attributed to the Buddha; and the Abhidhamma Pitaka, containing the supplementary teaching of various schools. In the Sutta Pitaka, the Buddha deals with a whole range of what are called 'pernicious views', and distinguishes his teaching from that of others. A good example would be the 'Greater Discourse on the Destruction of Craving', from *Middle Length Sayings*, vol. 1, trans. I. B. Horner *et al.* (Pali Text Society, 1954), pp. 311–324.

reading the Tipitaka. This is not to deny that the Buddhist system, particularly as developed in the Mahayana tradition, became more inclusivist. The way in which Buddhism has co-existed with the indigenous traditions of China witnesses clearly to this fact. But, even in China where it is possible for an individual to observe Buddhist, Confucian and Taoist practices, Buddhism in particular has preserved its individual identity. There have always been Buddhist experts in China since the religion was first introduced there by the end of the first century CE.

'Cumulative tradition'

Having examined briefly some aspects of Smith's treatment of the term 'religion', we must now examine his alternative terminology: 'faith' and 'cumulative tradition'. He defines 'cumulative tradition' thus:

> By 'cumulative tradition' I mean the entire mass of overt objective data that constitute the historical deposit, as it were, of the past religious life of the community in question: temples, scriptures, theological systems, dance patterns, legal and other social institutions, conventions, moral codes, myths, and so on; anything that can be and is transmitted from one person, one generation, to another, and that an historian can observe.[13]

This 'cumulative tradition' is the visible form of the essential faith that underlies it. Smith says that it

> . . . crystallises in material form the faith of previous generations, and it sets the context for the faith of each new generation. A man's faith is what his tradition means to him. Yet it is further, what the universe means to him, in the light of that tradition.[14]

It is in the 'cumulative traditions' that the differences and contradictions appear in the history of human religious life. However, in a later volume entitled *Towards a World Theology*,[15] Smith sets out to argue for a unity in humankind's religious history as well as in the 'faith' that underpins it. Given Smith's presuppositions, this has to be. He believes that there is only one 'transcendent', with which the pious in every 'cumulative tradition' have dealings which bring them salvation and/or fulfilment. If 'faith' is one, then in some sense the history

---

[13] *The Meaning and End of Religion*, p. 156.

[14] *Ibid.*, pp. 158–159.

[15] The full title of this work is *Towards a World Theology: Faith and the Comparative History of Religion* (London: Westminster Press, 1981).

of that 'faith' in the 'cumulative traditions' must also be one. In this context Smith does not resort to an evolutionary theory but to a theory that is somewhat akin to 'diffusionism'.

Diffusionism was a theory developed early in the twentieth century as a reaction to the evolutionary theories then current which argued that culture emanated from certain centres by means of historical contact. A good example of this theory at work is the argument that the world's largest pyramid, which is found in Mexico, was in fact built on the pattern of the pyramids of Egypt. That is, there must have been some historical link between the builders of the Mexican pyramid and the Egyptian pyramid. It is this idea of a historical link between the 'cumulative traditions' of the religious world that Smith emphasizes in arguing for a unity in the religious history of humankind. Religious traditions, he claims,

. . . have interacted with the same things or with each other, or that one has 'grown out of' or been 'influenced by' the other; more exactly, that one can be understood only in terms of the context of which the other forms a part.[16]

This statement deserves careful analysis.

What does Smith mean when he says that the religious traditions 'have interacted with the same things'? He does not, in fact, specify what these 'things' are. It could mean, first of all, the physical environment. But it says nothing about the unity of religious traditions to say that religious people everywhere are concerned with their natural environment – with its origin, control and life-giving provision.

Secondly, it could mean that all religious people are concerned with the common human experiences of birth, growth to maturity and death. Religious people are indeed united in their concern with these fundamental human experiences, but what is really significant is the different responses in the various 'cumulative traditions'. Then again he could be thinking of the disorder in human existence and in the world around us – sickness, misfortune, disasters, death. But, here again, what is really significant is the differing responses and not the common experience. It is difficult to see how interaction 'with the same things' highlights the overall unity in religious history as he suggests.

Smith seems to be on much safer historical ground at least in suggesting that the interaction 'with each other' is some basis for arguing for a unified religious history. There is plenty of evidence of the interaction of religious traditions though, generally, the interaction has been somewhat localized. Yet no-one can doubt the link between Judaism, Christianity and Islam, or between Hinduism

[16] *Ibid.*, p. 5.

and Buddhism, or between Buddhism, Confucianism and Taoism, and so on. However, there is not much evidence of close interaction between the religious traditions of the West and those of the East. It is this lack, maybe, that causes Smith to give such a prominent place in his discussion to what he himself recognizes as the somewhat trivial Christian story of Barlaam and Josaphat, which he found originally in one of Tolstoy's works. The story's 'central theme is the renunciation of worldly power and wealth by a young prince, Josaphat, who under the influence of the preaching of an other-worldly hermit, Barlaam, is baptised a Christian, abdicates his throne, and goes off into the wilderness in ascetic piety'.[17]

The career of this story as told by Smith is indeed fascinating. Beginning with Tolstoy, he traces its source to the monks of Mount Athos; from Mount Athos its source is traced to Islam, and then finally to Buddhism. In its origin, Josaphat was a Bodhisattva who left his princely life at the instigation of the Buddha. This enthralling case of the diffusion of a story leads Smith to the somewhat startling conclusion that, 'The historical fact is that, through this story, for a thousand years the Buddha *was* a Christian saint.'[18] But it is very doubtful whether he is justified in coming to such a conclusion. All that can be said is that, by a very circuitous route, a Buddhist story came to be utilized by Christians to illustrate the Christian truth that it is a virtuous thing to abandon wealth and worldly ambition in the pursuit of spiritual reality. This idea has been an aspect of the Christian 'cumulative tradition' from the beginning, though Christians have differed as to the precise meaning of such ascetic renunciation. It so happens that ascetic renunciation is also an important aspect of Buddhism, so that a story about such a renunciation in Buddhism could easily be utilized in a Christian context. The meaning of the acts of renunciation in the two cases, however, is radically different, so much so that it is nonsense to suggest that for one thousand years the Buddha was a Christian saint. The story of Barlaam and Josaphat provides precious little evidence for the overall unity of the history of the various religious traditions.

The third point which Smith makes in justifying his thesis is that, in some cases, at least one religious tradition has grown out of another. There is undoubtedly plenty of evidence of interaction here. Buddhism appeared in the context of Hinduism; the Madhiyamika school of Mahayana Buddhism developed in conscious and detailed interaction with Hindu schools of thought; Christianity sees itself as a continuation of Judaism; Islam also, in its origin, had close links with Judaism in particular, and, again within the Christian tradition,

[17] *Ibid.*, p. 8.   [18] *Ibid.*, p. 20.

its theology was developed particularly in the Middle Ages in close contact with Greek philosophy. But, does saying that one religious tradition has grown out of another mean the same as saying that both are part of a larger history, which contains not only them but also every other religious tradition as well? A brief look at the way two religious traditions relate to each other in this way might help to clarify the issue.

The example that is most accessible to us is that of Judaism and Christianity. Consider Jesus' view of the Jewish religious tradition, as understood in the Christian tradition before the modern period. Jesus in no way saw himself as standing outside the Jewish tradition, even though what he said and did was introducing a radically new element into the tradition as it stood in his day. As Messiah, he saw himself as destined to become the focal point of the tradition of revelation stretching back to the patriarch, Abraham. However, the Jews as a nation rejected Jesus' claim – and continue to do so today. What this rejection has meant historically is that there have been two major ways of understanding the Jewish tradition, as embodied in the Old Testament, since the time of Jesus. The Christian way sees the Old Testament as culminating in Jesus and witnessing to Jesus as the Messiah. The Jews see the Old Testament as a body of law and revelation pointing forward to a Messiah who is yet to come.

We may bemoan the historical consequences of this bifurcation but, while being very conscious of the guilt of Christians in their treatment of the Jews, it does not seem to make much sense to say that the two religious traditions that have developed from the Old Testament are in some sense part of a greater religious tradition. Both traditions are obviously part of the history of humankind as a whole, but to say this in no sense does away with the differences between them. And if this is true of traditions that have a common scripture, it must be doubly true of those traditions that have developed in relative isolation from each other.

The fourth way in which Smith would have us believe that there is an overall unity in the development of religious traditions is that 'one can be understood only in terms of a context of which the others form a part'. Here again his meaning is not immediately evident. Is he saying that if we focus on any one religious tradition then, in order fully to understand that tradition historically, we must inevitably become conscious of other religious traditions? On one level this is a rather obvious thing to say, since there is no religious tradition that has developed in total isolation from all others. Smith, however, seems to mean much more than this by this statement:

THE HISTORY OF RELIGION

. . . the Christian idea of God in its course over the centuries has been, the historian can now see, a part of the world history of the idea of God on earth, Christians receiving from, contributing to and participating in that total history.[19]

Here he takes the very big step from observing historically that there are interconnections between religious traditions to believing that there is a transcendent referent in the various religious traditions that is constant. Every religious tradition, therefore, tells us some small part of the total story of the 'idea of God on earth', because what happens in the world's religious traditions is the cumulative revelation of the meaning of the 'transcendent' for humanity. This view cannot possibly be the result of a historical enquiry, but it raises the important question of the relationship between 'God' or the transcendent and the process of history in Smith's thought.

For Smith history, by definition, is process. There is no unchanging ground; all in the religious traditions is in a state of flux. What it means to be a Muslim is not a matter of accepting a body of truths as an unchanging foundation to life, but participation 'in the Islamic process, as the context of one's religious life'.[20] What happens is that the Muslim 'cumulative tradition' is accepted and used to reach out to the transcendent. Nothing other than this is possible for Smith, since history contains no certainty other than the certainty of change. Is he content, then, with an absolute relativism and individualism where the history of religious traditions is concerned, since he lays such emphasis on what the individual makes of a religious tradition that is continually changing as a result? At the beginning of his chapter on 'Religious Life as Participation in Process', he seems to recoil from such absolute relativism.

When discussing the elements of the historical pattern Smith states: 'Of the elements out of which the pattern is formed some transcend the disparate religious traditions, historically; while others emerge and disappear within each other.'[21] It seems, then, that there are certain elements in individual religious traditions that are found in other religious traditions which suggest that there is some constant factor even in the history of religions. But to appreciate fully what he means here, we must consider the second aspect of what he considers to be a more adequate way of thinking about religion. We refer to his idea of 'faith'.

[19] *Ibid.*, p. 16.   [20] *Ibid.*, p. 31.   [21] *Ibid.*, p. 21.

Cantwell Smith's idea of 'faith'

The first thing to be said about Smith's idea of 'faith' is that it is intensely personal. 'Men's faith', he states, 'lies beyond the sector of their religious life that can be imparted to an outsider for his inspection.'[22] In *The Meaning and End of Religion*, he discusses the various ways in which 'faith' has been expressed, such as through art, community, ideas, words and belief. It might be surprising to some that he argues that 'faith' is essentially different from 'belief', belief being just one of the ways in which faith is expressed. Belief, according to Smith, belongs to the world of the relative and the mundane, that is, to the world of history. Faith, on the other hand, is a human being in the presence of the transcendent or trans-historical. Like Schleiermacher, he believes that his experience can never be captured in words, or as the Tao Te Ching puts it, 'The truth that can be told is not the eternal Truth.' Individuals or communities can attempt to express their 'faith' in words – in fact their humanity sentences them to attempt the task – but they will never capture the transcendent in words. Unlike the Unchangeable with which 'faith' deals, words change. An unbridgeable gulf is opened between faith and belief, and Smith's attempts to describe 'faith' must be seen in the context of this gulf.

In *Faith and Belief*, Smith describes 'faith' as 'a quality of human living', which

. . . at its best has taken the form of serenity and courage and loyalty and service: a quiet confidence and joy which enable one to feel at home in the universe, and to find meaning in the world and in one's own life, a meaning that is profound and ultimate, and is stable no matter what may happen to oneself at the level of the immediate event.[23]

In *Towards a World Theology*, he describes faith as

. . . an orientation of the personality, to oneself, to one's neighbour, to the universe; a total response; a way of seeing the world, and of handling it; a capacity to live at a more than mundane level; to see, to feel, to act in terms of a transcendent dimension. The early Christians proclaimed that in Christ faith had become available to man, so that a new life thereby became possible.[24]

---

[22] *The Meaning and End of Religion*, p. 170.

[23] *Faith and Belief* (Princeton, NJ: Princeton University Press, 1979), p. 12.

[24] *Towards a World Theology*, pp. 113–114.

Consistent with his basic view of 'faith', these attempts to describe it are really attempts to describe its effects without any reference to belief.

Smith's distinction between faith and belief has been subjected to critical analysis by William J. Wainwright in an article entitled 'Wilfred Cantwell Smith on Faith and Belief'.[25] Wainwright rightly contends that the heart of Smith's position is his conviction that assurance of the truth of certain propositions is not essential to faith. Wainwright examines the various arguments put forward to justify this belief.

The first argument to support the contention that assurance of certain propositions is not essential to faith is that the importance of doctrine varies from one religious tradition to another. In some religious traditions, such as Christianity, doctrine or belief is very important, whereas in other traditions, such as Zen Buddhism, doctrine or belief is not important. That belief is important in some religious traditions and not in others proves to Smith that it is not essential. What we have here is a modern version of the essence and form analysis of religion developed in the nineteenth century. The assumption is that 'faith' is essential to religion but that belief belongs to the form, or the non-essential, aspect of religion. Because faith is something that by definition is found in every religious tradition, it is described in very abstract and general terms such as 'serenity', 'courage' and so on. Wainwright argues, however, that it is very doubtful whether there are any religious traditions where belief is entirely unimportant, and he charges Smith with failure to distinguish between a formal system of doctrine and being convinced of the truth of certain propositions. It is true that a formal system of doctrine is unimportant in some religious traditions, but it does not follow that the adherents of those traditions have no convictions that certain propositions are true. To the contrary, Wainwright would argue that it is very unlikely that one could find a religious believer who does not believe in the truth of some proposition or other.

A second argument put forward by Smith to justify opening a gulf between 'faith' and belief is that, whereas belief varies from age to age and person to person, faith remains constant. What he means by this is that beliefs or doctrines change from age to age in response to various historical pressures, but authentic 'faith' can be found everywhere in every age. Beliefs, therefore, are not essential to 'faith'. But, as Wainwright points out, Smith assumes here the correctness of his idea of faith as the foundation for his argument. He builds his case on his unproven conviction that there is something essential that is of vital importance for humankind at the root of the diversity of the religious traditions. This essence

[25] *Religious Studies* 20 (1985), pp. 353–366.

he assumes cannot be subject to change and must, therefore, differ from anything that does change. Doctrines and beliefs change and so they cannot belong to this essence – which brings us back to the beginning of the circular argument.

Another assumption underlying Smith's argument, according to Wainwright, is that the objects of 'faith' as expressed in belief are unimportant. In other words, what 'faith' is and does can be divorced from its object as expressed in doctrines, so that it does not really matter whether one believes in Christ, Buddha, Allah or any other object of 'faith'. These names in which millions have trusted are, in the last analysis, attempts to express in words the essential reality at the core of religion; they are merely shadows of the ultimate reality that lies beyond them. As Wainwright says, this 'argument's premise will only be granted by those who are antecedently convinced that the nature of one's doctrinal convictions is only peripherally related to the authenticity of one's faith'.[26] In other words, it could be accepted only by a 'Christian' who sees his or her belief about Jesus as peripheral to the essence of faith. It is difficult to understand how anyone who knows anything about the actual religion of real believers could suggest such an untenable idea. Real religion of any sort just does not operate in this way.

A third assumption underlying Smith's thesis is that belief presupposes faith. He assumes that faith is primary and belief secondary or derivative. Wainwright questions the possibility of having any religious experience or experience of faith that is 'logically prior to any sort of conceptual articulation'. His analysis of the illustrations which Smith uses to support his point of view proves the justice of Wainwright's criticism here. What Smith claims to contrast is what he calls 'insight' (knowing the truth of something, or recognizing it and 'propositional knowledge' (knowing that something is true). 'Faith', he claims, has the quality of 'insight'. He illustrates this point by comparing 'insight' to seeing what is funny in a joke, a 'seeing' which, Smith argues, is quite separate from the telling of the joke. Wainwright points out quite rightly that there would have been no 'seeing' without the 'telling'. 'Propositional knowledge' must be, therefore, at least a part of the process of 'seeing'. This does not mean that 'propositional knowledge' and 'faith' are identical, but what it does mean is that there is a much closer relationship between them than Smith is prepared to admit. He fails to see that to say that A cannot be identified with B is not the same as saying that A is unlike B. In other words A (belief) might correctly represent B (the truth/God) though only partially. If this is so where two beliefs contradict each other, both cannot be true. That is a conclusion which Smith seeks to avoid at all costs.

It is interesting how very suspicious Smith is of propositions, propositional

[26] *Ibid.*, p. 357.

truth or propositional knowledge. He possesses almost the same fervour as an eighteenth-century revivalist in his insistence that religious head knowledge is not enough and that there is no authentic 'faith' without a commitment of the heart. The great difference between them, of course, is that for Smith head knowledge is ultimately unimportant. In this context it is possible to explain him in terms of the modern search for some final experience beyond understanding; some solid ground underneath the tumult of the conflicting and contradictory voices of our pluralist society; some island of hope beyond the horizon towards which one can sail blindfolded without any knowledge that the island is there at all!

Another way in which Smith expresses this same point is his statement that 'the object of faith's cognitive attitudes is the transcendent, not propositions or statements'.[27] Here again he seems to misunderstand the basic mechanism of faith. No-one who says that he believes the Apostles' Creed is saying that the Apostles' Creed is the object of his faith. God is the object of the believer's faith, the God who is described in the creed. A similar mistake is made by those who charge 'fundamentalists' with bibliolatry or worshipping the Bible. To believe that the Bible is the very word or words of God is not the same as worshipping the Bible, and to suggest that it is is illogical.

Faith and tolerance

Smith's view of 'faith' belongs to his broader humanistic emphasis, which he sets in opposition to the dehumanizing objectivity of some modern study of human beings. In this broader context it is difficult to disagree with some of his views. One feels a certain sympathy with his attack on what he calls 'objectivism' in the academic world and especially as a method applied to the study of people. One deplores with Smith the action of the social anthropologists, who study 'primitive' people in order to communicate their findings to the select *coterie* of their discipline, in order to find acceptance, promotion and so on. This type of approach to human beings is unquestionably immoral exploitation. It is also true that over-specialization has created such a fragmented picture of the person that it is easy to push love, understanding and other moral virtues to one side. In this context, one sympathizes with Smith's call to a more holistic approach to people, with his emphasis on faith as a personal matter and with his contention that any statement about persons must be acceptable to 'both outside observer and participants'.[28]

It is doubtful, however, whether Smith has been able to live up to the latter

[27] Quoted by Wainwright, *ibid.*, p. 359.
[28] *Towards a World Theology*, p. 59.

ideal, since to plead for this type of tolerance while insisting that there is an essential difference between faith and belief is like tugging away furiously at the mat on which one is standing. Smith says that 'no observer's statement about a group of persons is valid that cannot be appropriated by those persons. In the history-of-religion instance, this applies to faith, if not to tradition [which latter can be known objectively].'[29] This statement gives with one hand while taking away with the other. Take the case of an evangelical committee member of a Christian Union, affiliated to the Universities and Colleges Christian Fellowship (UCCF). The ideal for historians of religion studying the group to which this committee member belongs is that they should say nothing which the committee member himself or herself could not accept as statements about himself or herself. There is a caveat, however, and that is that, in the case of the historian of religion, this applies to faith and not to belief.

What this means practically is that the historian can say that what this group believes – the doctrinal basis of the UCCF – is a historically conditioned declaration of belief which bears no essential relation to the reality of faith. To say this, according to the historian of religion, is not to undermine the 'faith' of the Christian Union committee member, because there is no essential link between faith and belief. This is all very well, but does saying this to any of our committee members tell them something about themselves which they can accept as true of themselves? And if this assessment of the situation were accepted, would that leave our committee members in exactly the same position as they were before? The answer to both these enquiries has to be 'Obviously not.' In fact, if any of them accepted Smith's position, there would be no alternative but to resign, which leaves his ideal of making statements that are acceptable to 'both outside observer and participants' in ruins.

Another problem with the gulf which Smith opens between faith and belief is that, according to his own assumptions, this idea itself must belong to the realm of beliefs. After all, what he says about 'faith' – that it is 'a quality of human living' and so on – is a series of propositions, which once made are sucked inexorably into the flux of human history. One is reminded here of Wilhelm Dilthey's statement that 'the relativity of all human concepts is the last word of the historical vision of the world'. It is not difficult to extract a creed from Smith's writings but, according to his own approach, there is no reason why one should accept his creed rather than any other, since all creeds are relative in the last analysis. If one did extract a creed from Smith's writings it would go as follows:

[29] *Ibid.*, p. 97.

THE HISTORY OF RELIGION

I believe,

1. in 'God', the transcendent reference-point of human experience;
2. that this 'God' is worshipped in all the religious traditions of the world;
3. that, where authentic existence is found, this transcendent reference must be at work;
4. that the universe bears witness to the fact that this transcendent reference is love.[30]

For anyone familiar with the history of theology since the nineteenth century, this creed has a strangely familiar ring, and its offering as a novel approach to the question of the relationship of the essence of faith and the history of religions is somewhat surprising. All that Smith does really is to sing again what is by now the somewhat worn-out tune of liberal Protestantism. It looks very much as if the contemporary history of religion in the singular, as opposed to the history of religions in the plural, has not left the ground occupied by the classical idealist authors of the nineteenth and early twentieth centuries.

[30] For the various clauses of Cantwell Smith's creed, see *The Meaning and End of Religion*, p. 184; *Faith and Belief*, p. 12; *Towards a World Theology*, pp. 103, 151, 164–165.

– 6 –

the PHENOMENOLOGY *of* RELIGION

INTRODUCTION

Those who are experts in the study of religion agree that phenomenology is an important contemporary approach to the subject. They also agree that defining this particular approach is very difficult. Phenomenology, like existentialism, is one of those terms that is very difficult to pin down. Some have suggested that there are as many phenomenologies as there are phenomenologists. This may be true. But before we look at the work of some self-confessed phenomenologists, it may be helpful to review those points in the story of Religious Studies which will help to explain their appearance.

Every 'new' approach to a subject inherits something from the past. Intellectual history can be compared to travelling somewhere by train. The scenery can change from moment to moment. The change in scenery can be quite dramatic but the train is still running on the same track. Changing track or even mode of transport altogether is only a rare occurrence in intellectual history. Phenomenology is definitely only a change of scenery on the intellectual track of the study of religions on which we have been travelling so far.

The track on which Religious Studies has run was laid in the eighteenth-century Enlightenment. The authority of the Christian tradition was rejected in favour of autonomous reason. Belief in God was no longer the truth because it was revealed in the Bible, but because reason demanded it. The gulf which was opened at this point between Christianity as a historical religion and what human beings can discover by themselves has developed into a fundamental principle in understanding religion ever since. This is the root of the 'essence' and 'form' dichotomy that has been discussed in the previous chapter.

During the nineteenth century, tremendous work was done in uncovering the history of the various religions. Christianity, for obvious reasons, received the greatest attention, but by 1900 there was also an increasing body of literature on other traditions. Running parallel with this growth in information about religions, and intertwined with it, went the growth of theories about religion. Philosophers, theologians, anthropologists and sociologists all had their theories of religion. By the end of the century the idea of evolution was dominant. In the idealist tradition, it meant the increasing realization of the essence of religion in and through its many forms while, in the positivist tradition, it meant the desacralization of the world through the development of scientific understanding. By 1900, particularly in the English-speaking world, the positivist approach was dominant.

It was inevitable that the proliferation of different theories of religion should lead to a questioning of the whole exercise, particularly since the theories often contradicted each other. There was obviously a need to look at the way in which general theories of religion were formulated and at how the data of religion were handled in the process. It became clear that many of the theories that had been proposed were, in fact, not the result but the starting-point of the study of religions. The whole exercise was then reduced to an attempt to justify subjective opinion, as we have seen already in the case of many of the major figures in the history of Religious Studies. Phenomenology of religion is an attempt to go back to the drawing-board in the wake of the perceived failure of general theories of religion by the beginning of this century. It does not mean that the hope of finding an adequate general theory is abandoned. That is kept as the ultimate goal, but the focus moves to the way in which religions are studied and how aspects of religions can be compared. The emphasis is now on the process of understanding and the classification of religious phenomena.

GERARDUS VAN DER LEEUW *and his* PHENOMENOLOGICAL METHOD

Since there is no agreement as to what phenomenology of religion is, the best way to proceed may be to look at the way in which a few self-confessed phenomenologists define their approach. Although Gerardus van der Leeuw (1890–1950) did not invent the term 'the phenomenology of religion', it was almost exclusively associated with his name for many years after the publication of his *Phenomenologie der Religion* in 1933.[1] He gives an outline of his method in an Epilegomena at the end of the book, where he states:

[1] The English translation is *Religion in Essence and Manifestation* (London: Allen & Unwin, 1938).

The phenomenon is not produced by the subject, and still less substantiated or demonstrated by it; its entire essence is given in its 'appearance', and its appearance to 'someone'. If [finally] this 'someone' begins to discuss what 'appears', then phenomenology arises.[2]

The aim of discussing what is actually there, without any imposition upon what is observed from the experience of the observer, seems simple enough. But, sadly, life is not that simple.

Van der Leeuw uses the term 'phenomenon' in its basic dictionary sense of 'a thing that appears', but his statement presupposes a lot of philosophical discussion about scientific method, in particular the method to be employed in the human sciences (history, sociology, etc.), as opposed to the natural sciences (physics, chemistry, etc.). He believes that the human sciences are concerned with 'phenomena' whereas the natural sciences are concerned with 'facts'. For the natural scientist a 'fact' is there to be dissected and experimented upon, so that the various elements of which it is made up can be isolated and then the relationship between those elements described. In this process the idea of causation is crucial. What the natural scientist aims to observe is a chain of cause and effect, the overall aim being not simply to explain what is happening but to gain control over it. This whole exercise, according to van der Leeuw, does not take the scientist nearer to what is actually there. Empirical analysis does not bring us to the 'phenomenon'.

It so happens that this type of empirical analysis had been applied increasingly in the study of religion in the half century or more before van der Leeuw's time. The animistic theory of the origin of religion associated with E. B. Tylor and James G. Frazer is a good example of this type of approach. The theory itself is simple. It envisages primitive 'man' emerging from pre-human animality being puzzled by sleep, dreams, hallucinations and death. In his dream he was able to wander far and wide, while some part of him remained in its primitive bed. He came to the conclusion that he must have a part of him which can live apart from the body. So, when death occurred, this 'soul' left the body but did not return. The anthropologists who accepted this theory treated religious phenomena as facts in natural science. They boasted that they were natural scientists and that their theories had the same status as formulae in chemistry or biology. What they did was arrange facts from the many accounts

---

[2] These quotations are from an extract of *Religion in Essence and Manifestation* in J. Waardenburg, *Classical Approaches to the Study of Religion*, vol. 1 (Berlin: Mouton, 1973), p. 413.

of the religion of peoples who were on a low level of technological development, so as to support their theory.

Emile Durkheim's theory of the social origin and Sigmund Freud's theory of the psychological origin of religion, and many others, could be placed in this category. Religion is seen as a collection of facts that can be analysed according to the method of the natural sciences and then explained in terms of causation. Following this method, earlier anthropologists saw bad reasoning as the cause of religion: for Durkheim it was collective emotion, and for Freud unconscious psychological forces at work during childhood. According to van der Leeuw, what religion is in its essence never 'appeared' to these scholars. So how should we approach religion so as to make sure that what is there actually appears?

First of all, we must realize that there are three levels of phenomenality. The first is the level of relative concealment. In our ordinary everyday experience, phenomena do not appear. We do not understand our experience. What is essential in all our experiences has 'passed irrevocably away by the time our attention is directed towards it'.[3] When we begin to reflect, we are forced to reconstruct the past in our minds in some way or other. In this process of reconstruction we move on to the second level of phenomenality. Through the process of reflection the phenomenon is gradually revealed, and we move to the third level of phenomenality, which is the level of understanding. The aim of phenomenology is to get to this level.

Understanding, as used in this context, cannot mean subsuming what appears under some causal law or other. It is not a question of discovering causes by empirical research but of seeing patterns in the chaotic maze of things. The pattern of relations that appears is called a 'structure', and where a structure is repeated, a 'type' or 'ideal type' appears. The gate into this exercise as a whole is the pursuit of meaning. So the phenomenologist sets out in search of meaning, and observes structures which eventually appear as ideal types. When this happens, understanding is achieved, the essence has appeared, and the phenomenon has been seen.

Van der Leeuw lists seven stages in the process that leads up to the phenomenological vision. Before listing these stages, it may be helpful to emphasize the claim that phenomenology is simply a method of studying religion and not a theory of religion. The attitude which one has in coming to the 'facts' or 'things' is what is in view. The temptation to seize the 'facts', to dissect them and subsume them under some natural law or other, must be positively rejected from the start. It is only where there is a commitment to 'meaning' that there is any

[3] *Ibid.*, p. 413.

hope of understanding and thus of seeing the phenomena. But, if the commitment to meaning is there, it is possible to talk about the appearance of the phenomenona right from the beginning of the process.

At the first stage of the process, van der Leeuw says that 'what has become manifest . . . receives a name'.[4] What he means here is the classification of religious phenomena into distinct categories such as cosmology, belief in gods, sacred places, sacred time, sacrifice and so on. The next stage is the 'interpolation of the phenomenon into our own lives'. This is the exercise of *empathy* (*Einfuhlung*). In explaining what he means by this, he quotes G. K. Chesterton's statement that 'when a professor is told by the barbarian that once there was nothing except a great feathered serpent, unless the learned man feels a thrill and half a temptation to wish it were true, he is no judge of such things at all'.[5] To empathize successfully means bringing the experience of the stranger within our own experience. For this interpolation to occur, what was in our mind or heart before must be pushed to one side in some way or other. This brings us to the next stage, which involves the bracketing of one's own experience in order to assimilate the experience of another. This is the exercise of *epochē*, which is fundamental to phenomenology. Van der Leeuw had a very high opinion of this human capacity to bracket one's own existence. Here phenomenology is

> . . . man's true vital activity, consisting in losing himself neither in things nor in the ego, neither in hovering above objects like a god nor in dealing with them like an animal, but in doing what is given to neither animal nor god; standing aside and understanding what appears into view.[6]

Bracketing makes possible the next stage in the process, at which the structural relations of the phenomena become apparent. The first four stages together then make possible the fifth stage, which is genuine understanding of the phenomena when they appear in the form of ideal types. This fifth stage is the *eidetic vision* of the phenomena. 'The chaotic and obstinate "reality"', states van der Leeuw, 'thus becomes a manifestation, a revelation.'[7] The type of understanding that is achieved at this point has nothing to do with the position in time of the phenomenon that is being observed. This type of understanding is just as difficult to achieve in reading a colleague's letter as it is in reading

---

[4] *Ibid.*, p. 415.   [5] *Ibid.*, p. 416.

[6] *Ibid.*, p. 417. *Cf.* E. Sharpe, *Comparative Religion: A History* (London: Duckworth, 1975), p. 224, for a brief and helpful discussion of *epochē*.

[7] *Ibid.*, p. 417. 'Eidetic' is derived from the Greek noun *eidos*, meaning 'that which is seen', 'shape' or 'essence'.

Egyptian hieroglyphics. It has nothing to do with the mechanics of language or the historical context. Van der Leeuw is not saying that there is no need to learn how to read Egyptian hieroglyphics in order to understand them, but that learning to read is not the same as understanding. If one wants to understand the letter from a colleague or the Egyptian hieroglyphics, one must go beyond the words on the page or the symbols on the rock and penetrate to their meaning. It is only when one has entered into the mind and heart of the writers, or stood in their shoes, that one can make any claims to understanding. In this sense, time or history is not important to the phenomenologist.

This emphasis was very radical in 1933, since it cut across the evolutionary way of thinking which was dominant at the time in the study of religion, as it was in most other disciplines. For the evolutionist, the meaning of something was determined by its place in a process of evolution or by its position in a time sequence. Polytheism was understood as a stage in the evolution of religion from a belief in a multiplicity of spirits (animism) to a believe in one supreme God (monotheism). For van der Leeuw to place a religious phenomenon in such a time sequence is not to understand its meaning, and does not help the phenomenon to reveal itself. It is rather a case of imposing an alien theory on to the phenomenon, which obscures its meaning. He does not deny the possibility of an evolutionary pattern emerging as a result of a phenomenological study. What he rejects is the imposition of such a pattern on to the phenomena from the beginning. 'History' has to be bracketed in coming to the phenomena.

We are still only at the fifth stage of the phenomenological process when understanding in this trans-historical sense occurs. There are two stages yet to go. The sixth stage is the correction of phenomenological conclusions as a result of new discoveries. Interestingly, having insisted on the non-historical nature of the eidetic vision, van der Leeuw immediately emphasizes the fundamental link between phenomenology and the history of religions. The phenomenologist can do nothing without the historian, since it is the historian who provides the phenomenologist with raw materials. Religious texts are one fundamental source of material. It would be vain for the phenomenologist to suggest an understanding of a particular phenomenon if it were based on a reading or translation that has been proved to be erroneous. Historians are also all the time bringing to light new material, which demands the continual testing of any phenomenological understanding.

The seventh and final stage of the phenomenological process is the review of the whole exercise in the light of its ultimate goal, which is 'pure objectivity'. Van der Leeuw states:

THE PHENOMENOLOGY OF RELIGION

Phenomenology aims not at things, still less at their mutual relations, and least of all at the 'thing in itself'. It desires to gain access to the facts themselves; and for this it requires a meaning, because it cannot experience the facts just as it pleases. This meaning, however, is purely objective: all violence, either empirical, logical or metaphysical, is excluded.[8]

This seventh stage takes us on to the third level of phenomenality, which is the '[relative] transparency' of the phenomena. Phenomenology denies all subjective imposition and claims to be simply a matter of testifying to what has been seen.

The terms which van der Leeuw used in explaining his phenomenological method were not original to him. Terms like '*epochē*', 'empathy' and 'eidetic vision' were taken from the philosophical phenomenology of Edmund Husserl (1859–1938). Scholars disagree as to the extent to which van der Leeuw adopted the underlying philosophy as well as the terminology of Husserl. But, like Husserl, he belongs to a generation of scholars that had become dissatisfied with the prevailing scientific method of their day. He was not satisfied with the idea that science is a matter of arranging objects or facts on a bench and then noting the causal connections between them. It had become very obvious, particularly in the human sciences, that the scientist is much more involved in the process than that. Objectivity in science is not rejected as an ideal. What is called for is a recognition of the scientist's subjective involvement, so that strategies can be put in place to mitigate its distorting effect. So, in coming to the facts, the scientist must first sort out in his own mind those things which could obscure their true meaning. Just as a gardener weeds his flower border before putting in bedding plants, so the phenomenologist has to put her own opinions or theories to one side if phenomena are to be revealed to others through her mind.

Philosophically speaking, the phenomenologist is concerned with the old problem of the relationship between particulars and universals. Looking at this issue used to be a popular way of introducing students to the whole discipline of philosophy, with Plato as the starting-point. Plato posed the problem like this: Why is it that a whole range of different actions can be described as 'good' or 'just'? They can be described as this, according to Plato, because they partake of 'the good' or 'the just'. An action 'X' can only be called 'good' or 'just' because it partakes of the *form* of goodness or justice. This form really exists in an eternal world beyond the empirical.

Particulars are intelligible to Plato because universals exist. The ideal realm makes the realm of particulars meaningful. This world of change and diversity is

[8] *Ibid.*, p. 418.

but a shadow and memory of the unchanging and real world of the ideals. The particulars find their meaning in the universals. While I am not suggesting that van der Leeuw and other phenomenologists were Platonists, they do belong to that tradition of thought which attempts to go back to meaning, essence, or the universal, in opposition to the perceived emphasis on the particular, in the anthropological study of religion which dominated the scene in the first quarter of the century.

These universals that the phenomenologist seeks do not reveal anything of the Object of religious experience. Phenomenology is concerned with the essence of the human experience of 'God' and not with the being of 'God'. To put it in Kantian terms, it is concerned with phenomena and not noumena. The noumena are the concern of theology. The existence of the noumena, however, is vitally important to phenomenology, because it makes it impossible to explain the phenomena away in terms of poor reasoning, society and so on. The noumena or noumenon is the guarantee of the integrity of the phenomena.

The content of Religion in Essence and Manifestation

Having outlined van der Leeuw's method, it may be helpful to look at something of the content of his *Religion in Essence and Manifestation*. The section and chapter headings themselves convey something of the flavour of the phenomenological approach. He begins with 'The Object of Religion', which is discussed under the headings of 'Power', 'Sacred Environment', 'Archetypal Figures' and 'Power and Will'. The next section is 'The Subject of Religion', which is divided into 'Sacred Man', 'Sacred Community' and 'Soul'. The third section, 'Reciprocal Action', is further divided into outward and inward action. The first part of this section looks at 'Sacrifice', 'Divination', 'Sacred Time', 'Sacred Space', 'Sacred Word', 'Myth' and 'Sacred Writing', while the second part considers 'Religious Experience'. The fourth section, 'World', deals with 'Ways to the World' and 'Goals of the World'. The final section is 'Forms', which is divided into 'Forms of Religion' and 'Sacred Persons'.

In the chapter on 'Forms of Religion', van der Leeuw divides the religions into the following types. (A historical example of each type is noted here in brackets.) There are religions of remoteness and flight (Confucianism), struggle (Zoroastrianism), repose (mystical), form (classical Greek), infinity and asceticism (Hinduism); nothingness and compassion (Buddhism), will and obedience (Judaism), majesty and humility (Islam) and, finally, love (Christianity).

PETER MCKENZIE'S *THE CHRISTIANS*

Van der Leeuw's type of approach has not become very popular in the English-speaking world. It may be because of the fact that it sounds too reminiscent of the sort of idealist analysis associated with philosophers like G. W. F. Hegel, which are anathema to the strongly empiricist bent in British thought. Phenomenology does, however, have its advocates in Britain.

One such British advocate is Peter McKenzie, who published a substantial volume entitled *The Christians: Their Practices and Beliefs* in 1988. This book is, to quote its title page, 'An adaptation of Friedrich Heiler's *Phenomenology of Religion*'. Heiler's *Erscheinungsformen und Wesen der Religion (Manifestations and Nature of Religion)*, first published in 1961, was a massive volume of general phenomenology in a form similar to that of van der Leeuw. What McKenzie did was to take Heiler's categories and much of his Christian material and create a volume on the phenomenology of Christianity. So what we have is a study of an individual religion, using a method and categories formulated in the process of studying a plurality of religions.

McKenzie explains that the categories used by Heiler may be

> . . . arranged within three concentric circles: the outer circle represents the world of religious *manifestations*. Its categories include the sacred object (both natural and made by hand), sacred space, sacred time, sacred number, sacred action (purification, sacrifice, unification), the sacred word (from and to the Deity), sacred silence, sacred writing, sacred person and sacred community. An inner circle of religious *concepts* follows: the concept of Deity (or lack of it), creation, revelation, salvation and eternal life. Inside that circle is another, that of religious *experience* (both in its normal and supranormal forms).[9]

Though the multiplication of examples gets rather tedious at times, what results from putting Christianity into Heiler's categories is often fascinating and instructive. But the volume also suffers from the common weaknesses of the phenomenological method.

Fundamental to phenomenology is the claim to objectivity. By bracketing his or her opinion, the phenomenologist allows the phenomenon to appear. The problem comes in choosing what facts to focus on while *en route* to the phenomenon. Here the phenomenologist is dependent on the historians. That historians can deal with the same facts and come to different conclusions suggests

[9] *The Christians* (London: SPCK, 1988), p. 3.

that even in their case something more than just the objective arrangement of facts is taking place. McKenzie's material on the Lord's Supper will illustrate this problem very clearly.

The essence of the Lord's Supper

At the beginning of his discussion of 'The sacramental meal', McKenzie notes that 'it occupies a special place in the Greco-Roman mystery religions, whose proximity to early Christianity we have already had occasion to refer to'.[10] One of his assumptions, then, is that because there is some similarity between Christianity and the mystery religions, the latter must have influenced the former in some way. His theory is that the Lord's Supper started off as a common meal which Jesus shared with his friends, with the possibility that there might have been some eschatological meaning to it. It may have prefigured the glorious feast in the kingdom of God. Then Paul came along, and because he had 'grown up in an atmosphere of mystery cults which were familiar with the sacred drama in the form of the sacred communion',[11] he transformed the eschatological meal into a sacramental meal re-enacting the drama of the dying redeemer. Crucial to this theory is the absence of the reference to the cup in Luke 22:19b–20, and the belief that Paul's account of the Lord's Supper is the earliest and that it influenced the accounts in the Gospels. The words in dispute in Luke are, 'This cup is the new covenant in my blood, which is poured out for you' (Lk. 22:20, NIV). If these words were not there, then a case could be made for the absence of any concept of a dying redeemer in the original institution of the Lord's Supper. Unfortunately for McKenzie, textual critics are now fairly certain that these words are a genuine part of Luke's Gospel and not the result of emendation under Pauline influence. The weight of opinion is also now in favour of Mark as including the earliest account of the Lord's Supper. This means that the idea of a dying redeemer was very much part of the Lord's Supper from the beginning, and that the historical context for this element in it was not the mystery religions but the Jewish Passover. If this is true, McKenzie's case for closing the gap between New Testament teaching and Greek mystery religion, which makes the development of the ritual of the mass a natural development of what was there from the beginning, is very much open to question.

If this is the case, then it is fair to ask questions about the objectivity of McKenzie's choice of historical facts as well as about the claim to phenomenological objectivity in penetrating to the meaning of those facts. To put the matter into the best possible light, we may say that he has not examined

[10] *Ibid.*, p. 121.   [11] *Ibid.*, p. 123.

the evidence thoroughly enough. On the other hand, we could say that his presumption that the Christian tradition has been shaped by the Greek mystery religions led him to find the facts that support that presumption. There is quite a lot of evidence in the volume to suggest the second as the more plausible alternative. Each way, confidence in his conclusions about essences and meaning is undermined.

It may be of interest to examine one of McKenzie's general conclusions about the essence of a religious phenomenon. Sacrifice is a good example. He makes the following statement about this phenomenon:

> And yet prior to, and above all human sacrifice, is the divine sacrifice. Man is not in a position to present a sacrifice to God. God himself is in the final analysis the power of sacrifice and even the sacrifice itself. This was seen long ago in ancient India where Prajapati is both creator and also sacrificial victim; and it is as we shall now see no different in the Christian tradition.[12]

What McKenzie claims here is that the essence or meaning of sacrifice is found in the idea of the sacrifice of God. This is proved by the fact that this idea can be found in a number of religious traditions, and he refers particularly to the Indian idea of the sacrifice of Prajapati as evidence of his insight.

Prajapati, which means 'lord of creatures', was in the first place a description of some of the early Aryan gods, such as Indra. Eventually he became a 'creator' god in his own right and was identified with Purusha, the primal Man.[13] In a late poem in the Rig Veda (10.90), there is an account of 'creation' in terms of the dismemberment of Purusha. Purusha, the primal Man, grew by some mysterious 'food' to an enormous size. 'All creatures are a quarter of him; three quarters are what is immortal in heaven.'[14] Mysteriously the gods, which must belong to the immortal three quarters of the Man, sacrifice him. Out of this sacrifice various things come into being, such as beasts, the verses and chants and poetic meters, domestic animals and the four Indian classes (varnas) – *brahmin, kshatriya, vaisya* and *sudra*. Added to this, the moon came from his mind, the sun from his eye, the gods Indra and Agni (Fire) from his mouth and wind from his breath. Then the middle realm of space came from his navel, the sky from his head, and the earth from his two feet. In the Brahmanas, Purusha-Prajapati is described as generating tremendous heat (*tapas*) through his ascetic and erotic practice. He got so hot that

---

[12] *Ibid.*, p. 103.

[13] See Mircea Eliade, *The History of Religious Ideas*, vol. 1 (London: Collins, 1979), p. 277.

[14] Purusha-Sukta, vs 3, *The Rig Veda* (Harmondsworth: Penguin, 1981), p. 30.

VARIOUS APPROACHES TO RELIGION

he immolated himself and out of the sacrifice *brahman*, the sacred word, was born, and then the various parts of the divine and human creation.[15] In the *Satapatha Brahmana*, this myth is the justification for an annual sacrificial rite for the preservation and continuation of the earth with its animals and human society. This reflects a period in India's religious history when the priests claimed tremendous power as the guardians of the sacrifice, but it also shows a religion that is well on the way to the monism of the Upanishadic period that was to follow that of the Brahmanas. If the world and everything in it is a part of the god Prajapati, then it is a short step to believing that in the last analysis there is nothing but Prajapati, and that the diversity of the world is ultimately an illusion. Already in the Brahmanas, one of the Prajapati sacrifices was seen as a way of identifying with him and thus gaining immortality.[16] What the sacrifice of Prajapati means, then, is that everything in the last analysis is a part of 'god', and that by re-enacting his primal sacrifice it may be possible to achieve his immortality.

The Christian idea of sacrifice is very different. Here there is no suggestion of creation by means of the dismemberment of the deity. Creation is by the command of a transcendent God. Sacrifice is seen as an important element in the way in which humans relate to their creator after their rebellion against him. It is an expression of thanksgiving but it is also a way of removing guilt. It is this latter idea that became central in the Christian view of sacrifice. Because of the depth of human sin and rebellion, God the Father eventually sent his own Son to become incarnate as Jesus Christ. As a real and perfect human being, Jesus offered himself to God as a sacrifice in the place of sinful humanity. So he went to the cross willingly to suffer the punishment of sinners and pay the price of their release. The Lord's Supper is a continual reminder for Christians of what Jesus has done for them — of the way in which he established a new covenant or agreement between God and human beings through his blood (*i.e.* his death). As the hymn-writer Mrs C. F. Alexander puts it:

> There was no other good enough
> To pay the price of sin;
> He only could unlock the gate
> Of heaven, and let us in.

As Christianity developed, the Lord's Supper eventually came to be seen as a re-enactment of the sacrifice of Christ, but it is very clear that the New Testament writers did not view it in this way. To them it was a simple but profoundly

---

[15] *Satapatha Brahmana*, 6.1.1.8ff.

[16] Eliade, *op. cit.*, p. 230.

meaningful reminder of what Christ had done for them in dying on the cross. The essence of the Christian view of sacrifice, then, is the belief that God was prepared to become incarnate in order to pay the price of human guilt. By believing in the dying and risen Lord, Christians can be forgiven their sin and have eternal life.

It seems very clear that the essence of the Indian idea of the sacrifice of Prajapati and the essence of the Christian idea of the sacrifice of Jesus Christ are very different. The difference comes into focus when the concepts are seen in their contexts. McKenzie's problem is that he has ignored the context in order to come to his conclusion. This illustrates very clearly one of the shortcomings of the phenomenological approach. If the context of any phenomenon has to be taken into consideration, deciding what is the essence of anything that appears in a large number of different religious traditions becomes a very laborious process. But if the laborious process of contextualizing is not done, there is always the danger of making superficial comparisons which are unfounded — as McKenzie has done in his comments on the essence of sacrifice.

Underlying his conviction that there is one essence of various religious phenomena, such as sacrifice, is McKenzie's conviction that the essence of all religion is one. He makes this quite explicit in his conclusion:

> Thus the nature of religion, including Christianity, is fellowship of men and women with transcendent reality, a fellowship which flows out of divine grace, which is accomplished in worship and sacrifice and leads to the blessedness of men and women and of humanity . . . God's Kingdom, which forms the content of Jesus' gospel, is greater than all the religions, including Christianity, in that it signals their final fulfilment . . . In the state of fulfilment . . . fellowship with God in worship, praise and thanksgiving . . . continues for all eternity.[17]

So there is only one 'God' who is worshipped and experienced under many different names. This is the true meaning of Jesus' teaching about the kingdom of God.

This sort of statement illustrates the difficulty in defining phenomenology. If this is the conclusion of his phenomenological journey, we can ask what happened to the ideal of empathy, of standing in the shoes of the religious adherent in order to understand. There is nothing in this description of the essence of religion to which a Theravada Buddhist monk could relate. What this statement highlights is the tension between the desire to understand, which is

[17] *The Christians*, pp. 311–312.

fundamental to the phenomenological approach, and the desire to go beyond the diversity of phenomena to the truth — not only to explore religious experience, but also the reality that underlies it. This raises the fundamental question of whether it is possible to isolate the phenomena from the noumena.

NINIAN SMART: PHENOMENA *and* NOUMENA

Ninian Smart (1927–) deals with the question of phenomena and noumena in *The Phenomenon of Religion*.[18] In order to find out what it means to treat religion as a 'phenomenon', he takes the eucharist as an example. Since phenomenology claims to enter into the experience of the participant, Smart asks what it means to enter into the experience of Christ who is the Focus of the eucharist. He suggests four possibilities. The first is the experience of each individual attending the eucharist. It is probably true to say that, in any congregation, the picture of Christ which each individual has does differ. But even if this is true, the eucharist is not an individualistic activity, so there is no need to attempt to reconstruct the eucharistic experience from an analysis of the experience of all the individuals involved — which would be a well-nigh impossible task anyway. Smart's second and third possibilities are somewhat similar — that the Christ experienced is the 'typified Focus' either of one congregation, or of a wider group to which the congregation belongs, such as a denomination or a sect. Here, in the case of Anglicanism, the liturgy as performed would be a good pointer to what is meant by the 'Focus' of the eucharist. Phenomenology has to do primarily with the third of these possibilities.

However, there is a fourth possibility, according to Smart, and that is that 'the Focus is the "real" Focus, transcending the pictures found in the preceding, but recognized in principle by the participants, and by the community at large'.[19] What he says here is that phenomenology may also have to do with a real something that corresponds to the experience of those participating in the eucharist. This is obviously a reference to 'the noumena'. Smart's reasoning is very difficult to follow when he comes to discussing the role of this 'noumena' in understanding religious experience, but it seems that what he says at this point is fundamental to his whole thinking about religion. It is worth trying to grasp it, since he has been such an important figure in Religious Studies for many years.

Fundamental to Smart's thinking here is his conviction that the noumenal Focus 'can have no particular purchase on the world, for it lies beyond

[18] *The Phenomenon of Religion* (London: Macmillan, 1973), ch. 2, pp. 53ff.
[19] *Ibid.*, p. 64.

particularities and so in an important sense beyond the world of our experience'.[20] One problem in trying to understand what he means by this is whether this is a statement about our knowledge of the Focus, or a theological statement about the nature of the Focus. If the first, then he is saying that nothing happens in our experience to which we can point and say that this has been caused by God or some other supernatural being. If the second, then he is saying that the Focus in its essence is unknowable – a view held by many mystics. On balance, the first alternative is more likely. Behind this view is a long history of theological debate in the Western Christian context about divine causation, miracles and prophecy. The development of science eroded the possibility of divine intervention in many situations, and gave confidence to those who believed that there was no need of God's intervention in any situation. Part of this process was the denial of the historicity of the miracles of the New Testament, or of the relevance of the prophecies of the Old Testament to future events. The last step in this development was to question the historicity of the picture of Jesus that we have in the New Testament. Smart accepts the theory of Rudolf Bultmann (1884–1976) that we can learn hardly anything at all about the historical Jesus from the New Testament. All we really know is that Jesus existed; everything else is an account of the experience of the early church.[21] That experience was mediated through concepts and traditions which are no longer tenable for those living in a scientific age. As far as Smart's phenomenology is concerned, even if the noumenon has some relevance, it cannot be supernatural.

Having ruled out of court the possibility of explaining or understanding religious phenomena in terms of the Focus intervening from outside, Smart also rejects the idea that if one does this then all one is left with is nature. Phenomenology must somehow try to chart a course between supernaturalism and naturalism.[22] He does not think that Rudolph Otto's argument that there is a type of unique human experience of the holy is the answer. Otto's argument is still really an argument for the existence of 'God' and is, therefore, theological and supernaturalistic. All that the phenomenologist can claim is that there are religious experiences to describe and classify, and that, as things stand, they cannot be fully explained in terms of psychology or sociology or any other 'ology'. They can also be explained within their own context, so that Hindu devotion can be explained in terms of the bhakti tradition in India, and so on.[23]

Smart also says in an earlier part of the book that 'the noumenal Focus' is necessary for the phenomenologist 'because a noumenal outreach is itself typically built into [the Focus] and its analogues in other religions; and second

[20] Ibid., p. 65.   [21] Ibid., p. 127.   [22] Ibid., p. 140.   [23] Ibid., pp. 140–141.

because it expresses the openness and dynamism of a religious tradition'.[24] What he means by 'noumenal outreach' here is not at all clear. As stated above, the context of this part of the volume is his discussion of what it would mean to explain the eucharist phenomenologically. In coming to consider the object of worship, Jesus Christ, he has said that the phenomenologist is concerned with the Christ who is defined for the congregation in its denominational tradition. This is the Christ who is the Focus of the congregation in the eucharistic rite. So what does it mean to say that a 'noumenal outreach' is necessary to the phenomenological understanding of what the Anglican experiences in the eucharist? Is Smart saying something more than the very obvious point that the worshipper believes that the Christ whom he worships in the eucharist is something much more than the emblems or what is said about him in the liturgy?

Smart's second reason for the noumenal Focus being a necessity for the phenomenologist is even more puzzling. He expands on it as follows:

> The conception of a noumenal Focus transcending the pictures presented is a regulative device suggesting the construction of new pictures to replace the old. A new picture itself is not noumenal, for the transcendental Focus still serves the same function, namely to suggest that the new picture itself may be replaced.

Is he saying that it is an essential part of the experience of the worshipper in the eucharist, as mediated through the denominational tradition, that the object of worship is unknowable in itself, and that this is an intentional aspect of the experience, since pictures of the mystery inevitably change? That this is the explanation for the Christian belief and experience that Christ transcends our understanding is open to question. It seems to reflect more strongly Smart's fundamental approach to religion. It is axiomatic for him that God cannot be known. In Kantian terms the noumenon or thing-in-itself is beyond knowledge. But 'God' can be felt or intuited. Here he stands firmly in the intuitive tradition of Friedrich Schleiermacher.[25] The original religious impulse is intuition, and all religious language is an attempt to verbalize that intuitive experience. The moment anyone attempts to make a religious experience public property, it becomes something observable – a phenomenon. But an account of a religious experience can never be the religious experience itself, so the noumenon witnesses to the possibility of change in the phenomenon.

[24] *Ibid.*, pp. 66–67.
[25] See 'Our Experience of the Ultimate', *Religious Studies* 20 (1985), pp. 19–26.

That Smart has passed way beyond objective observation at this point is obvious. What we have here is a theory of religion with its roots in Schleiermacher, the father of the Western liberal theological tradition. Smart is theologically committed. As we saw above, he has argued that phenomenology must operate without the assumption that there is something there which evokes the religious experience. But he himself believes that there is something there, and the way he understands religion is profoundly influenced by that belief. In *Beyond Ideology*, he describes himself as a 'transcendental pluralist': transcendental 'because the sorrows and happinesses of humans, the quest for identity in individual and in group, are illuminated by what lies Beyond', and 'pluralist' because 'All religions are true but the most true is that which recognizes . . . this truth. If Christ is divine so also is Krishna and so in the last resort are all human beings.'[26] It is sufficient at this point to place Smart theologically. He obviously belongs to the idealistic stream.

There is one more aspect of Smart's phenomenology which needs to be highlighted. I refer to the bracketing of emotion and attitude as well as belief. It is not surprising that, since the modern study of religion was born in a Protestant context, the emphasis has been on the intellectual and doctrinal aspects of religion. The Scriptures were central to the Protestant tradition, so comparison with other traditions tended to focus on their sacred writings. *Epoche* primarily meant bracketing one's own religious ideas in order to understand the religious ideas of others. But religion includes feelings and attitudes which are generated as much by rites as by words. So phenomenological bracketing should include bracketing of feelings and attitudes, and seeking to interpolate into one's own experience the feelings and attitudes of other religions. In the context of classical phenomenology, this was seen very much as an imaginative rather than a practical proposition. Phenomenology was a comparative exercise which drew on a whole host of religious phenomena from all periods of history. Taking part in the rituals of various religious groups in order to understand was not really on the agenda. In fact, this was more on the agenda of anthropological field-workers, as we shall see in the next chapter.[27]

The phenomenology of religion is a very complex subject. What has been attempted in this chapter has been a brief description of this approach, taken from the work of self-confessed phenomenologists, with some indication of the

---

[26] *Beyond Ideology* (London: Collins, 1981), pp. 14, 28.

[27] When the phenomenological method was applied to teaching religion in schools, the re-enactment of religious rituals became popular for a time. Educationalists, however, are now having second thoughts about this approach.

difficulty in carrying out their programme. Historically there is no doubt at all that the approach of van der Leeuw, Heiler or W. Brede Kristensen (1867–1953)[28] is superior to that of James Frazer. They do not set out to debunk religion while claiming to be objective scientists just letting the facts speak for themselves. In contrast, recognizing the existence of presuppositions, the phenomenologists tried to devise a strategy to deal with them so that they could be really objective. They did not succeed, because they operated on the assumption that history can deliver objective facts whose meaning can be penetrated by using the phenomenological method. The multiplicity of views based on the same historical facts indicates that their confidence in historians is not well-founded. Historians come to facts with presuppositions. So, if the historical facts of religion cannot be known objectively, the phenomenological method of penetrating their meaning cannot even begin.

[28] Kristensen's magisterial volume *The Meaning of Religion* (The Hague: Martinus Nijhoff, 1960) has been admired by many. He is less prone to sweeping statements than most.

– 7 –

the SOCIAL DIMENSION

That religion has a social dimension is beyond dispute. The question is: How shall we understand its nature and significance? In the last century or so, two disciplines have developed specifically to explain how societies work. They are Anthropology and Sociology. Up to this point in our consideration of Religious Studies, religion has been centre stage. We now move to disciplines where religion is not the only preoccupation.

ANTHROPOLOGY

Introduction

The dictionary definition of 'Anthropology' is 'the study of humankind, especially of its societies and customs; the study of the structure and evolution of humans as animals'.[1] Traditionally, Anthropology was the branch of theology that dealt with the origin, nature, primitive state, probation and fall of human beings. During the nineteenth century, science increasingly claimed the right to speak authoritatively in this area, particularly on the matter of origin, nature and primitive state. This development reached its culmination after Darwin had published his *Origin of Species* in 1859. The idea of evolution came to rule the roost. Human beings were now placed firmly among the 'animals' that had emerged during the aeons of evolutionary time. There were some scientists at the time, as there are today, who saw no essential contradiction between the theory of evolution and the biblical picture of human origins. They saw evolution as the way in which God had created. The Genesis account of human origins can then

---

[1] *The Concise Oxford Dictionary* (Oxford: OUP, [9]1995).

be slotted into the appropriate point in evolutionary history. There were others, such as Herbert Spencer and T. H. Huxley (1825–95), who passionately believed that evolution provided a scientific and superior alternative to the Bible. They were positivists, and the discipline of Anthropology was very much the child of this philosophy.[2]

It is axiomatic to the positivist that the biblical picture of human origins is inadequate. It belongs to the most primitive – *i.e.* the theological – stage in the development of human understanding. At that stage it was thought that a supernatural God was responsible for what happens in the world. The biblical account of the origin of religion would be an example of this kind of thinking. God makes human beings and places them in an idyllic setting, where he appears to them and speaks with them. They reject him and are driven away from his presence. The memory that they once knew their creator in an intimate way remains with them and causes them to seek him. This is the origin of religion. For the positivist, the kind of supernatural God who figures in this story was an explanatory tool of a more primitive way of thinking which is no longer necessary. By the nineteenth century, understanding of causation had left the theological, passed through the metaphysical, and reached the positive level. At this level there was no need to resort to any form of supernatural causation. Science could find the natural laws to explain everything.

Having jettisoned the biblical picture, the positivist anthropologists set about filling the gap that had been left behind. Their methodological tool was the 'comparative method' devised by Auguste Comte. They believed that contemporary peoples living at a simple level of technological development, who were regularly referred to as 'savages' or 'primitives', provided evidence which could be used to construct an evolutionary scheme of all human institutions. Using this method, Anthropology claimed to provide a more adequate explanation of prehistory than that provided by Christianity, which had dominated Western European understanding for 1,500 years. Not surprisingly, when E. B. Tylor came to outline its scope in the tenth edition of the *Encyclopaedia Britannica* (published in 1910), it had become somewhat ubiquitous. In the strictest sense, Anthropology 'has as its object to study man as an unit in the animal creation'. In the broader sense, it draws on ethnology, ethnography, anatomy, physiology, psychology, philology, ethics or moral science, archaeology, geology, sociology, and finally the science of culture, which is 'concerned with the origins and development of arts and sciences, opinions, beliefs, customs, laws, et cetera'. It needs to be emphasized that the material

[2] See the section on Auguste Comte, in ch. 2, 'The positive classics', pp. 41–42.

which was drawn into the anthropologists' mill from this very long list of disciplines would be relevant to re-creating human prehistory. It also suggests that, in considering human origins, we engage with a very fundamental issue in our attempt to understand ourselves, so it is not surprising that just about every conceivable way of looking at a human being is considered relevant. The subject here is a fundamental philosophy of human nature which has a bearing on everything that can be said about us.

In Tylor's long list, it would seem that religion plays a very minor role, as one aspect of the science of culture. Yet anthropologists seem to have devoted much of their time and effort to it in the late nineteenth and early twentieth centuries. Two thirds of Sir John Lubbock's *Origin of Civilization*[3] was devoted to religion, as was the bulk of Tylor's monumental *Primitive Culture*.[4] Sir James Frazer's whole life as an author was taken up with the study of religiously related questions, beginning with his study of totemism and culminating in the vast third edition of *The Golden Bough: A Study in Magic and Religion*, which was published in thirteen volumes between 1911 and 1915. This created the impression in Britain that Comparative Religion was in fact a branch of Anthropology. Outside Britain, Emile Durkheim, who is generally regarded as one of the few creative thinkers in sociological theory in the twentieth century, devoted much of his energy to understanding religion. *The Elementary Forms of the Religious Life* (1912) is his biggest and most important work. This preoccupation with religion is understandable, because Anthropology was seen very much as an alternative explanation of human nature to that found in religion. Religion as the embodiment of a spiritualistic philosophy of life had to be discredited if positivism was to gain the upper hand – even if Comte and his followers believed that the triumph of positivism was an evolutionary certainty.

This material on the origins of Anthropology has been included in order to emphasize the point that one of the disciplines that has focused on the social dimension of religion was born out of a philosophy that was very negative towards its subject. Its aim, originally, was to discredit religion, to prove that it was an aspect of human experience that was a hindrance to enlightenment, and that it was destined to disappear before the advancement of science. Interestingly, the early anthropologists claimed to be working as objective scientists. It was the facts and nothing but the facts that they presented. They argued that their theories were as valid as any formula in physics or chemistry. It was recognized in due course that there is a difference between formulae in the

[3] London, 1870.
[4] Published in two vols. (London, 1871).

'natural' sciences and theories in the 'human' sciences, but the 'scientific ethos' so-called, with its claim to objectivity, is still thought to be crucial by anthropologists and sociologists, as we shall see later in this chapter.[5] It will also be interesting to see to what extent the negative attitude towards the subject has persisted.

The natural science ethos of Anthropology is very apparent in the 'physical' branch of the subject. The emphasis of Anthropology in the United States even today is more on the physical side than on the cultural. Physical Anthropology is very much wedded to evolutionary theory, and especially to the prehistory of *Homo sapiens*, where the fundamental building-blocks of social behaviour are said to have been laid. The effect of the theory of evolution on people's perception of themselves in the nineteenth century has been described as a change from seeing themselves as a little lower than the angels to having to accept that they were just a little higher than the apes. In this tradition, Physical Anthropology looks to primatology – the study of primates – for information that will tell us something about human prehistory. The assumption here is that, if we have evolved from ape-like creatures, then we may be able to learn something about ourselves by studying apes. The gorillas can dispel the mist of our prehistory! Some anthropologists argue that the physical aspect is the foundation of the science and that everything else must be built on it. An understanding of culture or society built on foundations laid by ethology (the science of animal behaviour), genetics and cybernetics ('the science of systems of control and communications in animals and machines'), they believe, will be more fruitful in coming to a scientific understanding of ourselves. Most anthropologists may not be so closely wedded to this natural science model, but it is helpful to remember that it is there at the theoretical roots of the discipline, particularly since all types of anthropologists often speak as if they were still natural scientists.

Almost up to the end of the nineteenth century, anthropologists were not particularly interested in the social dimension of religion. The fathers of anthropology, such as Tylor and Frazer, had no firsthand experience of the 'primitive' societies they wrote about. The depended on accounts of peoples with a preliterate culture, written by travellers and missionaries. These were then supplemented by their knowledge of the classics, European folklore and

---

[5] Alfred Radcliffe-Brown, *Structure and Function in Primitive Society* (London: Cohen & West, 1952), pp. 188–189: 'I regard Social Anthropology as a branch of natural science . . . I conceive of Social Anthropology as the theoretical natural science of human society, that is, the investigation of social phenomena by methods essentially similar to those used in the physical and biological sciences.'

some information from the major historical religious traditions. Towards the end of the nineteenth century in the United States there was a move, associated with the name of Franz Boas (1858–1942), for anthropologists to study preliterate societies at first hand. This led to the formation of what is called 'Cultural Anthropology' in the States. In the first decade of the twentieth century, the English anthropologist Alfred Radcliffe-Brown (1881–1955) went to study the Andaman Islanders, armed with Frazer's theories of religion. He found that those theories just did not work. After returning home he discovered Durkheim's work, and found that he could make more sense of his data with the latter's theories. The ensuing volume marked the beginning of British 'Social Anthropology'.[6]

Social and Cultural Anthropology

Cultural Anthropology in the States and Social Anthropology in Britain are parallel developments. A key concept in both movements is that the meaning of any cultural fact or phenomenon can be grasped only when it is seen in its social context. In the States this led to describing the very coherent cultural systems of various Native American tribes. This material was used by some to argue for diffusion, as opposed to evolution, as the best explanation for cultural development – which includes religious development. In Britain, under Durkheim's influence, the focus moved to the *function* of various cultural aspects in the social coherence. As a positivist, Durkheim could not accept that there is any spiritual reality in religion, but he was impressed by its universal and enduring occurrence. He could not believe that there was no reality in such a common and lasting fact. His conclusion was that the reality in religion is society itself. It is a mechanism for objectifying what is essential to the society's well-being and survival. It functions, therefore, as a means to preserve a society. Radcliffe-Brown took the data that he had gathered while with the Andaman Islanders and used Durkheim's theory to illustrate how religion functioned as a means to preserve the social life of the Islanders. As a result, 'functionalism' became a dominant theory in Social and Cultural Anthropology.

One inevitable outcome of the positivist roots of Social Anthropology is the distinction that has to be made between the way the religious participants view their religion and the scientific view of the anthropologist. Positivism decrees that there can be no validity in the participants' explanation. If there is any reality in religion, it must be different from the participants' view of it. The first phase of Anthropology, which focused on the cognitive aspect of religion, came

[6] *The Andaman Islanders* (London, 1922).

to the conclusion that belief in God or gods — which anthropologists considered as a fundamental principle of religion — was in fact the result of a misguided process of reasoning. Their attack on religion as such was indirect, because they limited their attention to what they called 'primitives' or 'savages', but they were in fact saying that all religious beliefs are the result of muddle-headed thinking. They were really saying that there is no reality in what the participants say about their religion. But, as we saw above, Durkheim, even though a positivist, came to the conclusion that there is reality in religion even if it is different from what the participants think it is.[7] In coming to this conclusion, he focused on the emotional rather than the thinking or cognitive side of human nature. Rites, feasts and public ceremonies are more important to understanding religion than beliefs. As R. R. Marett, who was an admirer if not a disciple of Durkheim, put it, 'religion is danced out rather than thought out'. And this dance is never a solitary, but a social, affair.

There is no need to go into the intricacies of Durkheim's theories here, but what he focused on has been the preoccupation of Social and Cultural Anthropology ever since. He is also seen as a key figure in the development of Sociology. Kinship and economic survival were fundamental to his theory. He focused particularly on the aboriginal societies of Australia, and he believed that their totems were the original type of sacred object. Durkheim argued that, since the totems are linked to social relationships and the food on which the society depends, they are really representations of the society. This being so, when the tribe got together for their totemic rites, what they were really doing was celebrating their society. The collective emotion generated in the rites and festivals was a means of confirming and preserving community. The details of Durkheim's theory may have been questioned, but the understanding of the way in which relationships of kin are worked out in 'primitive' and not-so-primitive society has been crucial in anthropological field-work ever since. It is estimated that around 50% of the enormous output of Social Anthropology has been about kinship.

With kin relationships, the relationship of a community to the natural world from which it gets its sustenance, but which can also be very threatening, has also been important in the development of social anthropological theory. This is particularly so in the development of theories about religion. There is a tradition going back to Radcliffe-Brown which sees religious ritual as a way of translating 'uncontrollable natural forces into symbolic entities which, through the

[7] *Elementary Forms of the Religious Life*, trans. J. W. Swain (London: Allen & Unwin, 1915), p. 417.

performance of ritual, can be manipulated and dealt with'.[8] The use of the term 'symbol' for what one finds in religion brings us back to the crucial point that Social Anthropology is committed to reducing religion to something other than that which the participants believe it to be. Because religion is symbolic, the language of the believer cannot be about the essence or reality in religion. The task of the anthropologist is to show what the religious symbols symbolize, which is what they are really about and not what the believers think they are about. This point may have been laboured somewhat, but it is crucial to any understanding of the approach of Social Anthropology. The following quotation from J. Beattie's volume, first published in 1964 but reprinted in 1989, shows that Durkheim's basic approach is very much alive:

> To say that religious symbols are man-made is not to decry the validity of religion, for ritual is a statement about something, not just about itself. But the comparative study of the religious beliefs and practices of other cultures may suggest that in religion, reality is misrepresented if the symbol, and not the often indefinable thing that it symbolises, is taken to be the ultimate truth.[9]

Claude Levi-Strauss

There is one movement in contemporary Anthropology which focuses very much on symbols but which signals a clear break from the Durkheimian tradition. The movement is called 'structuralism', and its prophet is Claude Levi-Strauss (1908–). A Belgian by birth, he was educated in Paris, graduating in Law and Philosophy before developing an interest in Sociology. He was a Professor of Sociology at the University of São Paulo, Brazil, from 1934 to 1937. During this time he had about five months' experience of 'primitive' societies. He did no field-work in the accepted anthropological sense that calls for an extended stay, involving total immersion into a society and including learning its language. He began writing from a structuralist point of view in 1945 when living in the United States, where he had formed a close association with the structural linguist Roman Jakobson (1896–1982). The works that have made him the head of a school were published in the 1960s – *Totemism* and *The Savage Mind*,[10] and the massive four-volume *Mythologiques*.

---

[8] J. Beattie, *Other Cultures: Aims, Methods and Achievements in Social Anthropology* (London: Routledge, 1964), p. 239.

[9] *Ibid.*

[10] Both published in Paris in 1962, with English translations in 1964 and 1966.

Any attempt to describe Levi-Strauss' anthropology is doomed to appear superficial, given the immense complexity of his thinking. Some autobiographical comments will give us some indication as to his general view of reality. He confesses that he had three intellectual mistresses – geology, psychoanalysis and Marxism.

Marxism seemed to me to proceed in the same way as geology and psychoanalysis . . . All three showed that understanding consists in the reduction of one type of reality to another; that true reality is never the most obvious of realities . . . in all these cases the problem is the same, the relation . . . between reason and sense-perception . . .[11]

This quotation shows that his roots were very firmly planted in the positivist tradition as represented by two militant atheists, Sigmund Freud and Karl Marx. He is nowhere concerned with any reality that may transcend the human mind. Such realities do not exist. What he is concerned with is the way in which the human mind, which is a function of the brain, deals with the stimuli it receives by means of contact with the external world via the senses.

Levi-Strauss's interest in religious or any other phenomena is simply in order to find evidence for the way in which the human mind works. As an atheist, he assumes that nothing exists outside nature which includes 'man' and everything external to 'man' with which contact is made through the senses. Non-inclusive language is used deliberately at this point, because Levi-Strauss distinguishes between 'man' and 'human being'. 'Man' is what belongs to the world of nature; 'human being' is what results when the brain has processed the stimuli that come into it via the senses. The activity of the brain is an individualistic natural process characteristic of 'man'. Levi-Strauss wants to get beyond this to the characteristic process of the 'human being' which he calls the 'human mind' or the 'human spirit' (l'esprit humain). This is very much in the essence and form tradition of Western intellectual history since the Enlightenment. Levi-Strauss also wants to get to the universals. He wants to say something that is universally true about humankind. In the context of Anthropology, his approach is reminiscent of earlier exponents such as Tylor or Frazer. Like them, his approach is intellectualist. He is concerned with the way in which the human mind works, and he ignores the role of emotion which had become important in Social Anthropology. Where religion is concerned, he is much more interested in myth than in ritual.

---

[11] Quoted from *Tristes Tropiques* (1955) in E. Leach, *Levi-Strauss* (London: Fontana, 1970).

The model which Levi-Strauss uses to approach his ambitious task is the linguistic. Language is crucial in our understanding of 'man' because it is what distinguishes 'man' from the animal. We would expect, therefore, that our understanding of the way in which language works will tell us something about the way in which the human mind works. Levi-Strauss believed that Jakobson's structural analysis of language provided the answer. According to Jakobson, a child learns to speak by learning to contrast vowels and consonants. This basic opposition of sounds (phonemes) is then developed by means of a whole series of other contrasts such as loudness/pitch, compact/diffuse, grave/acute. So language learning proceeds by means of *binary pairs* or *binary opposition*. This linguistic idea was taken up in genetics and computer science with dramatic results, which have helped to boost the prestige of structuralism. If the structure of language is binary, its purpose is communication. A *language* is a sort of *code* from which I select certain elements or *speech* in order to convey a *message*. But language is not the only code that humans use to communicate with each other. Dress and food are examples of non-linguistic codes. Levi-Strauss attempts to read off the message inherent in various codes, believing that the human mind works everywhere by means of binary pairs.

We can now turn to Levi-Strauss's analysis of mythology, which is really his analysis of religion. His task is to read off the message that is buried in the code of mythology. What he means by making sense, or reading off the code, of the weird and wonderful things that go on in myths, is earthing them in the very real world of human experience. Fundamental are those binary pairs which are essential even to the survival of animals – the ability to distinguish between my own and other species, dominance and submission, the difference between sexual availability and non-availability, and between what is edible or not. But if the understanding of such oppositions are adequate for animal survival, they are not adequate for human survival. In the case of human beings, survival is dependent on the ability to understand the place of fellow humans in the social structure. This is done by transferring the universal structural characteristics of the brain, which man shares with the animals, to the universal structural characteristics of the human mind, which is unique to man and expressed in language. What Levi-Strauss ends up with is a theory that is very reminiscent of Freud. In primitive society, survival and continuity are dependent on alliances between small kin groups, which are cemented by gifts of women. Because society is dependent on giving away the daughter/sister, incest is severely banned. Exogamy, or marriage outside the kin group, is practised and the daughters/sisters are given away. This original binary opposition between sexual availability and unavailability is a fundamental message in the mythological code. It also explains the contradictions in myths of origin. If the sister/daughter is unavailable, where did the kin group or society come from? In some myths one of the original pair is non-human, whereas in others society begins as a result of an incestuous relationship. The whole of mythology, in fact all the paradoxes of the 'primitive' mind, can be boiled down in the last analysis to this paradox which is generated by the unavailability of the daughter/sister/cousin.

> All the paradoxes conceived by the native mind, on the most diverse planes: geographic, economic, sociologial, and even cosmological, are, when all is said and done, assimilated to that less obvious yet so real paradox which marriage with the matrilateral cousin attempts but fails to resolve. But the failure is *admitted* in our myths, and there precisely lies their function.[12]

It is interesting that this grand theory in the Freudian tradition, which was constructed as an alternative to functionalism, ends up speaking about the function of myth.

Levi-Strauss has built a massive castle in the process of explaining the logic of myth, but the assumptions on which it is built are very debatable. Most fundamental is the assumption that there is no God, so that in the realm of culture, which includes religion, there is nothing but the creations of the human mind. But even if the existence of God made no difference – which it certainly does – his reasoning is circular. The existence of binary pairs in cultural phenomena proves that the human mind works in terms of binary oppositions, while the belief that the brain works in binary oppositions justifies the search for binary pairs in cultural phenomena. Linguistics has now moved on and sees the brain as operating in a much more complex way than in terms of binary oppositions, which justifies the feeling that much of Levi-Strauss's analysis seems terribly forced and artificial. As with Freud, it seems that the big castle has been built in the air. But as happened with the Emperor's new clothes, there was a time when everyone stood back and admired and, for fear of being considered odd, praised the beauty of the non-existent cloth. Structuralism is a technique that has been much admired, but as a major theory for explaining cultural reality, and religion in particular, it is just another atheistic attempt in the Freudian mould to explain religion away. This is not surprising, because if there is no God, then any talk about him must really be talk about something else.

---

[12] Leach, *ibid.*, p. 58, quoting Levi-Strauss's study of 'The Story of Asdiwal'.

Edmund Leach

It is probably true to say that Levi-Strauss's influence on Anglo-American Social Anthropology has not been very significant. Edmund Leach (1910–), one of Britain's leading social anthropologists since the 1950s, has been an enthusiastic advocate of Levi-Strauss's structuralism, but, even though Levi-Strauss himself sees his theories as an alternative to functionalism, Leach does not believe that welcoming structuralism involves abandoning functionalism. The quotation from Levi-Strauss above where he writes of the function of myth shows that his ideas could be fitted into a functionalist mould. This is precisely what Leach seems to be doing in his description of Kachin cosmology in his *Social Anthropology*.[13] Leach describes his discipline as a 'detailed study of the network of relationships operating within a single small scale community'.[14] The aim of doing this is to discover principles that are true for everyone, including the anthropologist. As they do this, they must distinguish between 'what people actually do and what people say that they do'.[15] The anthropologist's task is to interpret the way in which the three fundamental aspects of society are interrelated. 'The basis of everything, the "infrastructure", is the mode of subsistence . . . At the other end is the cosmology . . . the "superstructure" which serves as a justification for everything that goes on. And in between, but permeating both, is the dimension of kinship.' Here, what Leach means by 'cosmology' is 'religion'. Religion or cosmology is 'the creation of the imagination'.[16] Though described in structuralist terms, it is still seen as a function of social integration in the tradition of British functionalism. Nothing else could be expected from a convinced atheist like Leach. What is frustrating is the tired old claim that all this is done in a fair, objective and scientific way.

The myth of scientific objectivity

There is, however, in current anthropological writing, some evidence that the myth of scientific objectivity is being questioned. An interesting article by Katherine P. Ewing, Assistant Professor in the Department of Cultural Anthropology at Duke University, is a case in point.[17] The title of the article is 'Dreams from a Saint: Anthropological Atheism and the Temptation to Believe'. What she means by 'anthropological atheism' is the methodological atheism with which an anthropologist has traditionally been expected to approach the

[13] Oxford: OUP, 1982, pp. 213ff.   [14] *Ibid.*, p. 127.   [15] *Ibid.*, p. 130.
[16] *Ibid.*, pp. 212–213.
[17] K. Ewing, *American Anthropologist* 96.3 (1994), pp. 571–583.

people being studied. The anthropologist goes as a neutral observer. But at the root of this approach is the conviction that the scientific way of understanding the world developed in the West is true. By definition, therefore, it is denied that 'the subjects of one's research may actually know something about the human condition that is personally valid for the anthropologist'.[18] It is assumed that to accept the beliefs of the natives would be to move from rationality to irrationality. So the method is really a way of shielding the anthropologist from the 'natives' so that their experience can be fitted into Western stereotypes. In this way, the superiority of the Western way of understanding the world and its meaning is confirmed. But in doing this, the anthropologist is left standing outside, unable really to understand the folk that are being studied.

Some anthropologists, according to Ewing, have cut the Gordian knot of this dilemma and 'gone native'. She refers to a number of studies, among them that by Favret-Saada of witchcraft in rural France. Favret-Saada came to the conclusion that 'it was only by believing that she was able to see the practice at all',[19] so she became personally involved in the practice. Ewing does not say whether this involvement was temporary, in the interests of research, or not. She just refers to the case as an example of believing in order to understand. Ewing herself sees dreams as a possible halfway house between anthropological atheism and 'going native'.

Ewing came to this conclusion as a result of her field-work among Pakistani sufis.[20] Dreams are important in the relationship between sufi masters and their devotees. In one of her meetings with a sufi master, he told Ewing that he would come to her in a dream. That night she had a very vivid dream in which she saw a white horse coming towards her and felt something touching her thumb. Having woken up startled, she immediately began interpreting her dream experience in Freudian terms as a case of suggestion. She became troubled, however, when she came into contact with a number of educated Pakistanis who were also sufis. Among them was a psychiatrist, who accepted scientific psychology but still held the sufi belief that masters are able to come to their disciples through their dreams. This led her to go to a sufi master, approaching 'the whole encounter as a personal experience rather than as anthropological research'.[21] The result of this visit was another very vivid dream, in which the sufi master seemed to be uninterested when she next met him. He just said that she would come to know her teacher (murshid) in due course.

[18] Ibid., p. 571.   [19] Ibid., p. 573.
[20] Sufism is a Muslim type of devotional mysticism.
[21] Ewing, op. cit., p. 575.

THE SOCIAL DIMENSION

In processing these experiences, Ewing still struggled with the seeming contradiction between the 'scientific' interpretation of dreams in the Freudian tradition and the sufi interpretation. At the most fundamental level, they seemed to represent different value systems. In Freudianism, independence is seen as a sign of maturity, whereas in sufism it is quite the opposite — total dependence on the master is the aim. But some psychologists have questioned the validity of the Freudian ideal and claim that the most mature human beings need the support of others. So, the sufi and the psychologist may not be so far apart after all. Ewing concludes:

> Dreams are one of the places where we, both anthropologists and the people we study, struggle to create new meanings that transcend differences. Instead of bracketing these sources of significance . . . we should take them seriously and allow them to play a role in shaping what are ultimately realities we share as participants in a global human community.[22]

This brief outline of Ewing's article is included not so that it may be criticized in detail, but rather as an illustration of an anthropologist questioning some of the fundamental shibboleths of her discipline. She herself admits to be still sitting on the fence. Yet those who value religion must welcome the recognition that to be religious is not necessarily to be irrational and unscientific and primitive. Yet a very big question remains. Religious people believe that they are in contact with a reality that transcends our mundane existence. This is as true of an evangelical Christian as it is of a sufi or a Hindu village priest or a witch. If there is such a variety in the conceptions of the transcendent reality, do we just accept that the variety is underlain by the same reality, or must we take the conceptions seriously? It is understandable, when anthropologists bred in the Western tradition of contempt for religion come up against what seems to be religious reality, that they should be impressed. The realization that there may be something in this 'spiritual' business after all must come as a tremendous shock to the system. But there is a danger of not realizing that, like the human world, the spirit world may not be uniformly good. There may be a need to prove the spirits and to hang on to that which is good. We shall return to this crucial issue again in chapter 9. Meanwhile, we turn our attention to the other closely related discipline which is concerned with the social dimension of religion, Sociology.

[22] *Ibid.*, p. 579.

SOCIOLOGY

Sociology and Social Anthropology are really two branches of the same tree. They trace their roots to the same place in Comtean positivism, and as far as the twentieth century is concerned they look to Durkheim and Max Weber as their seminal thinkers. The major difference between them is that Social Anthropology has tended to concentrate on small communities living at a simple level of technological development, while Sociology has concentrated on contemporary Western European society. It is also probably true to say that, while recognizing the contribution of Durkheim, the shadow of Weber can be felt more heavily in the Sociology of Religion. In Social Anthropology, Durkheim has been the greatest influence. This is not surprising, since Durkheim focused on Australian aboriginal society while Weber focused primarily on society in the modern world.

Max Weber and Karl Marx

An outline of some of the significant contributions of Max Weber (1864–1920) has already been provided in chapter 3 in the section on the classics. The typology which he developed continues to be used and refined. His thesis in *The Protestant Ethic* seems to have been the source of endless fascination and debate.[23] A very significant fact, which was not highlighted in the earlier section but which is crucial in the development of Sociology generally, is that Weber was developing his theories in relation to the teachings of Karl Marx (1818–83).

In Marx, sociologists were faced with a theory of society that claimed to be scientific in the positivist sense. But this theory was not something to be discussed by genteel professors in the comfortable common rooms of ancient universities, but a political programme for the freeing of the oppressed working-class from their economic thraldom. It was as much of a faith to be preached and put into practice as the faith of any 'evangelical' preacher. Put very briefly, Marx believed that class conflict was the key to understanding history. The conflict is over access to material goods. Throughout history, certain groups in society have claimed the right to enjoy the lion's share of the goods available. Social institutions were devised to preserve this privileged position, which was buttressed by a system of ideas about the nature of 'man' and society called 'an ideology'. Religion is significant as an instrument of class ideology. It is one of the means used by 'the haves' to keep 'the have nots' in their place. Religion was not very important to Marx. That it was without substance had been conclusively

---

[23] See the current debate in *The British Journal of Sociology*, *e.g.* the issue dated Dec. 1994.

proved, as far as he was concerned, by L. A. Feuerbach (1804–72).[24] What was important was for the proletariat to realize this, to reject the bourgeoisie ideology to which it belonged, and bring about the revolution that was destined to happen in obedience to the dictate of 'historical materialism'.

Sociologists could not ignore Marx, because he claimed to be scientific in the way in which they claimed to be scientific. On this plane he claimed to have discovered the law of historical social development, and believed that the victory of the proletariat was as certain as any observable event in the natural world. He was just an objective scientist, observing what was happening in society. But there is something of a contradiction in Marx. His economic analysis, despite the claim to scientific objectivity, had a political purpose. That the proletariat were destined to take over the means of production was as certain as any other scientific law, yet the Marxist ideology was an incitement to the proletariat to grasp the fruit that was denied them by the oppressive capitalist system. The inevitable revolution could be helped along by political action. Sociologists have lived with this tension ever since. It is not surprising that a great many sociologists have been decidedly left-wing politically, despite the constant claim to scientific objectivity. This also explains why conservative establishments are very suspicious of sociology.

From the more academic perspective, Weber's response to Marx was fairly typical. He accepted much of Marx's framework but questioned his conclusions. The role of economic interest, class relationships and in particular class conflict takes centre stage. He admits that social or economic circumstances do shape the view of salvation of the 'non-privileged group'. 'Since every need for salvation is an expression of some distress, social or economic oppression is an effective source of salvation beliefs,' he states. But he immediately adds, 'though by no means the exclusive source'.[25] He even argued that certain types of belief were characteristic of certain social classes, which seems to support Marx's view of ideology.[26] His study of Chinese Confucianism is presented as an illustration of the way in which a belief system and a social structure fit together.[27] On the other hand, the central thesis of *The Protestant Ethic* is that ideas can have a social

[24] Feuerbach was a convinced pupil of Hegel for some time. He eventually came to the conclusion that Hegel's idealist 'god' did not exist and that all gods were the creations of human aspirations, names for human ideals. His influence on twentieth-century thought has been immense.

[25] Max Weber, *Sociology of Religion* (London: Methuen, 1965).

[26] *Cf. ibid.*, pp. 20, 56.

[27] *The Religion of China* (Glencoe, IL: Free Press, 1951).

and economic impact.[28] By arguing that religious ideas can shape economic circumstances, he cut right across Marx's view that religious ideas are always determined by economic circumstances.

Where Weber stands, in the last analysis, will remain a mystery, as he probably intended. Unlike Marx, his aim was to understand, not to change, society. Marxist cynicism would say that this was not surprising, because he belonged to the privileged class who enjoy talking to each other about all sorts of things, and who have set up all sorts of organizations in order to be able to do so. It may be very interesting to understand that there are different types of religious leaders or that religious organizations can be described as churches, sects, denominations or cults and so on. But then, what is the point of it all? At least we know where we stand with Marx. If he had his way, religion would soon disappear.

Sociology of Religion which has been shaped by Weber leaves us in doubt as to the purpose of the whole exercise. Interestingly, when trying to give some point to their work, sociologists of religion seem to revert to a Durkheimian perspective. Much of R. L. Johnstone's *Religion in Society* is a development of Weberian themes. But when he comes to discuss 'The Future of Religion', he reverts to Durkheim. Religion will persist because of its function. It reinforces social norms, it integrates people into 'meaningful relationships', it helps people to adjust to crises in their lives and so on. Religion 'has a future to the extent that humanity has a future, because religion is an expression of the confrontation of people with their environment, both physical and social, and with each other'.[29]

There can be no doubt that Weber, even though he wrote at the beginning of the twentieth century, has been the dominant force in shaping the Sociology of Religion. From around 1920 to 1959, sociology was dominated by the Marxist agenda and religion was generally ignored. But since around 1950, there has been a renewed interest in religion, fuelled primarily by religious renewal particularly in the United States. Weber's works were translated into English at the beginning of this period and provided a methodological framework for this renewed interest. Up to now most of the work done has concentrated on Christianity, with very little reference to other religions except where they appear in new religious movements in the West. Sociologists of religion have been slow to follow Weber in his study of the sociology of some of the world's major religions.

[28] *The Protestant Ethic and the Spirit of Capitalism* (London: Allen & Unwin, 1930).

[29] *Religion in Society: A Sociology of Religion* (Englewood Cliffs, NJ: Prentice Hall, [3]1988), p. 288.

Scientific objectivity and the Sociology of Religion

We have seen that the claim to scientific objectivity was fundamental to the method of Social Anthropology but that some practising anthropologists are beginning to question it. The same principle holds in the Sociology of Religion. We shall end this chapter by looking at Bryan Wilson's defence of scientific objectivity,[30] David A. Fraser and Tony Campolo's sociological analysis of this claim,[31] and Peter Berger's attempt to affirm religion despite his acceptance of this method, which he describes as 'methodological atheism'.[32]

Bryan Wilson (1926–) begins by accepting that, though religion was very significant to sociology from the beginning, the founders of the discipline saw it as an outmoded way of seeing the world which needed to be displaced by the scientific approach. He also accepts that this very negative view of religion has persisted in sociology. This is true of the Marxist tradition and of sociologists like Kingsley Davis,[33] who considered religion to be false but socially valuable, or Charles Glock,[34] who saw religion as nothing more than a compensatory response of deprived people. It is obvious that Wilson himself does not go along with this negative view of religion. Yet he firmly believes that the sociology of religion is a science and that scientific objectivity is absolutely essential for this claim to have any integrity. In explaining this approach he makes the following statements:

> He [the sociologist] is not going to become a disciple. Were he to do so he would necessarily cease to be a sociologist . . . This is not to say that a sociologist of religion cannot be personally a religiously-committed man; clearly that is a possibility. But in his sociological work he must adopt the professional stance of the detached, neutral and objective investigator; and this we may take as a necessary qualification.[35]

[30] Bryan Wilson, 'The Sociology of Religion as a Science', in *Religion in Sociological Perspective* (Oxford: OUP, 1982), pp. 1–26.

[31] David A. Fraser and Tony Campolo, *Sociology Through the Eyes of Faith* (Leicester: Apollos, 1992).

[32] Peter L. Berger, *A Rumour of Angels* (Harmondsworth: Penguin, 1970).

[33] Kingsley Davis, *Human Society* (New York: Macmillan, 1949).

[34] Charles Y. Glock, B. B. Ringer and E. R. Babbie, *To Confront and to Challenge* (Berkeley, CA: University of California Press, 1967). Their theory is called the 'relative deprivation thesis'.

[35] Wilson, *Religion in Sociological Perspective*, pp. 13, 23.

This fundamental methodological principle, that it is impossible to practise Sociology of Religion as a religious believer, deserves exploration.

We are back really with the dilemma of the social anthropologist Katherine Ewing – that of the profound taboo against 'going native'. Why should this be? The most superficial examination of religious belief of any sort would soon prove that it is in fact a world-view. Religious belief is the platform from which the world is understood. This 'world' obviously includes society. So for a religious believer it is impossible to divorce faith and understanding. For believers, what they believe is like the wearing of spectacles by a severely short-sighted person. What they see without the spectacles is a muddle of shapes and colours. The spectacles bring things into focus so that they can be seen as they really are. The point being made here is not a claim that Christianity is the only belief system that gives access to the truth – that is, to things as they really are. Rather, what is being argued is that it is of the essence of religious belief of any sort to provide a way of seeing the world. If this is so, sociology according to Wilson's definition is impossible for a religious believer.

The Christian's situation will illustrate this point very simply. A Christian believes that the world and everything in it has its origin in the creative act of God. The nature and destiny of human beings as individuals and in their various relationships are included in God's purpose, particularly as it is revealed in his Son, Jesus Christ. There is a great variety of commitment to this fundamental belief among Christians, but it is very generally the case among them that their belief does condition the way in which they relate to family, to the communities in which they live and work, and also in many cases to the wider community of the state. God has much to say about the way in which humans are to relate to each other, which is not surprising, because he created them in the first place. But what Wilson says is that if any of these Christians really want to understand how society works, they must banish God from the equation. That is impossible for the Christian, because without God there can be no meaningful equation.

Scientific objectivity explained: Fraser and Campolo

This fact, that 'scientific objectivity' as defined by sociologists like Wilson excludes Christians, and any other religious believer, from practising sociology, reminds us of the anti-religious roots of sociology in a positivist world-view. In their *Sociology Through the Eyes of Faith*, David A. Fraser and Tony Campolo[36] have

[36] See note 31 above.

subjected this positivist sociological tradition itself to sociological analysis, with some interesting results.

Sociology is now represented by an established academic community of professionals. In the United States there are some 20,000 professional sociologists teaching in universities. The situation is not so flourishing in Europe, but even in the United Kingdom there are chairs of Sociology in many universities and just about every university will have someone teaching Sociology. In surveys that have been made of the religious beliefs of academics in the United States, the sociologists have consistently come out as the most antagonistic towards religion. Interestingly, the lowest incidence of atheism among American academics is found among the natural scientists. Those working in the humanities come somewhere between the natural and social scientists. These statistics raise some intriguing questions. Why is it that sociologists who claim to operate on the same principles as the natural scientists are more atheistic than they are? Fraser and Campolo offer an answer to this question.

Fraser and Campolo argue that one reason for the difference is the way in which the sociologists have responded to modernity. Modernity can be defined in various ways. One way is to define it as a movement in the direction of pluralization, privatization and secularization.

Pluralization means the development of a whole range of institutions that take over functions that were previously performed by one institution. Whereas at one time the church was responsible for, say, education and healthcare, pluralization means that those functions are taken over by other bodies – in the case of education by the government, Local Education Authorities and teachers' unions and, in the case of healthcare, by the government and various professional bodies such as those of the doctors and nurses. Pluralization also means the undermining of the close link between religion and the state, so that the existence of a whole range of religious institutions becomes possible.

This leads to the second characteristic of modernity, that of privatization. With the disintegration of a unified Christian world-view, unification was sought on the level of scientific, rather than religious, truth. Many came to believe that science could provide a body of truth on which everyone could agree. The facts speak for themselves. Religion on the other hand, since it belonged to the world of values about which no unanimity was possible, was consigned to the realm of private opinion. Faith of any sort is a private matter, which cannot provide principles that can be applied to society generally.

Closely linked to this move towards the privatization of religious faith was the belief in secularization. It was believed that, as a result of pluralization and privatization, the significance of religion in a modern society would inevitably diminish. The destiny of religion was to wilt under the corrosive influence of modernity.[37] Sociology claims to belong to this idea of modernity. But then the question can be asked as to how this view came to be embodied in its professional ethos.

To answer this question, Fraser and Campolo looked at three factors that led to the birth of Sociology as a profession. The first factor was the dramatic success of Newtonian science. John Newton's theories made the industrial revolution possible, and created the impression that science could solve all human problems. If the facts were known, life on earth could be utopian. The second was the development of capitalism and the bourgeoisie. The success of the industrial revolution, driven on by capitalism, put tremendous power into the hands of the bourgeoisie. They came to direct the social agenda. Not surprisingly, they placed the highest value on what they considered the more precise natural sciences, which laid the foundation for technological developments. They also considered economics to be a precise science. Moving from this foundation to social or political issues was a move in the direction of decreasing precision and factuality and an increasing value content. The third factor was the development of centralized government to serve the bourgeois agenda. The development of universities was important here, with science, technology and economics taking the first place. Sociology, on the other hand, took a long time to gain proper recognition in the universities. This development took place in the first half of the twentieth century in America, whereas in the United Kingdom many sociology departments were not established until the 1960s.

Fraser and Campolo suggest that the reluctance of the bourgeois establishment to accept Sociology explains the anti-religious ethos of the discipline. The insistence on being a science is really a cry for acceptance, and explains why Sociology ignores the fact that many sociologists who contributed to the formation of the discipline were committed Christians. This claim to be scientific which, in the positivist tradition, is closely related to a very negative attitude to religion, became part of Sociology's image in creating a professional niche for itself in bourgeois academia. Being anti-religious is seen, therefore, as part of what Peter Berger calls the 'plausibility structure' of the community of sociologists. Like every other community, in order to survive, the community of sociologists or the profession of Sociology needs a structure of ideas and practices that give it its identity. The development of Sociology has meant that a negative

---

[37] For a definition of secularization, see S. Bruce (ed.), *Religion and Modernization* (Oxford: OUP, 1992).

attitude to religion has become a part of that structure. Being negative to religion is therefore part of what it means to be a sociologist.

Scientific objectivity and Peter Berger

What Fraser and Campolo do is show that the theory of Sociology, like the theory of any other discipline, or even the theory of religion, is a world-view from which reasoning proceeds. The theory of religion itself is just one option among the ever-increasing range of options that is available to us in our pluralistic world. The sociologist Peter Berger (1929–) had made a similar point some twenty years ago in his book *A Rumour of Angels*.[38] Berger emphasizes that to discover the sociological foundations of why people believe as they do does not settle the question of truth. He does not ask sociologists to put aside their problems with the supernatural, for he himself has their 'methodological atheism' as his starting-point. He just asks them to suspend their belief that there is no supernatural, and to look again at human experience with an open mind. If they did this, they would see what Berger calls 'signals of transcendence' in everyday human experience.

Berger discusses five possible signals: order, play, hope, damnation and humour. What he says about 'damnation' will serve as an example of his type of argument. He says that there are certain types of gross evil that are the subject of unqualified condemnation. Even objective sociologists suspend all relativizations when faced with the type of monstrous evil perpetrated in a place like Auschwitz. There is no doubt that those who perpetrate such evil should be punished and that no human punishment can be sufficient. Is there not a signal of transcendence here? If no earthly punishment is adequate, justice is not vindicated. This situation demands a hell. This is very similar to Kant's argument for the existence of God, that, since earth is not an adequate scene for the reward of obedience and the punishment of disobedience of the moral imperative, there must be a God and heaven and hell to accommodate it.

On the basis of such signals of transcendence, Berger hopes to build a more adequate theology for the modern world, based on induction rather than deduction. As he says, 'Inductive faith moves from human experience to statements about God, deductive faith from statements about God to interpretations of human experience.'[39] This is not the place to discuss the theological method which he develops in order to do this in his book *The Heretical Imperative*.[40] It is enough at this point to see Berger as an example of a sociologist trying to escape from the strait-jacket of his discipline's negative attitude to religion.

[38] Berger, *op. cit.*, p. 57.   [39] *Ibid.*, p. 76.   [40] London: Collins, 1979.

– 8 –

PSYCHOLOGY *and* RELIGION

INTRODUCTION

Psychology is a very pervasive fact of our modern life. If a child is being rather a nuisance at school or having problems with learning, the child psychologist is called in. If a company wants to appoint a senior manager or set up a new production line, the industrial psychologist is called in. If the police want to catch a criminal and have no real leads to go on, they call in a criminal psychologist to construct a 'psychological profile'. If one is finding life difficult to cope with for a whole host of different reasons, it is getting more and more likely that a counsellor will be called in, and a counsellor without psychology is a contradiction in terms. If a Christian mission agency wants to send someone to work overseas, the final decision as to whether or not a person is fit to go will depend on the opinion of a psychiatrist – and a psychiatrist operates at the clinical end of psychology. The list could go on.

From one point of view, this development can be seen as the erosion of a Christian way of seeing human beings by the modern psychological way. As far back as 1966, an American psychologist Philip Rieff was saying in *The Triumph of the Therapeutic*[1] that 'psychological man' was in the process of replacing 'Christian man'. What he meant by this was that psychological ways of understanding how a human being works and acts are fast replacing the Christian way. This assumes, of course, that the two ways are alternatives, that what we have here is a case of either/or. That there are many Christian psychologists and psychiatrists, and that Christian counselling is becoming a very big movement indeed, seem to give the lie to this contention. On the other hand, it may be that Christians have welcomed a Trojan horse into their city. The

[1] New York: Harper & Row, 1966.

clock must be turned back a bit once more before we can hope to say anything definite about this situation.

'Psychology' is defined as 'the scientific study of the human mind and its functions, especially those affecting behaviour in a given context'.[2] The word itself is a combination of the two Greek words *psychē* ('soul') and *logos* (which basically means 'word', but in this context means something like 'knowledge of the soul'). The two terms were brought together in modern and not classical times to refer to the study of the way in which the human mind works. To someone committed to a religious or even specifically Christian way of viewing human beings, that aim seems unobjectionable in itself. But if this aim is combined with the Enlightenment creed that 'man is the measure of all things', then the situation changes. What this means is that the traditional Christian way of seeing things is turned upside down. The meaning of human existence is not explained by divine revelation any more, but divine revelation is inferred from a study of human existence.

PSYCHOLOGY *and* IDEALISM

If one accepted this radical shift, while claiming at the same time that religion generally or Christianity in particular remains of vital importance, then what is the essence of religion or Christianity can be found by studying the way in which the human mind works. If this is the case, much of the theorizing about religion since the Enlightenment, in what has been described as the idealist tradition, can be said to be psychological. Max Müller is a good example of this.[3] He defined religion as the 'perception of the infinite'. Müller states that what he means by 'perception' in this definition is what happens in the mind when it is stimulated by contact with the external world by means of the senses. He claims that the simple process of looking at things in the natural world, and particularly at those things that have an element of the 'tremendous' in them, is what leads humans to perceive the Infinite. This perceiving must be a type of intuitive recognition that is akin to seeing beauty in an object. This is obviously a psychological theory of the source of religion. When he first formulated this theory, he used the term 'faculty' to describe this human ability to go beyond the visible. In so doing, he was reflecting a psychological theory of the construction of the mind that was being rejected by the middle of the nineteenth century. Not surprisingly he then dropped the term, but still insists upon an ability of the mind to see beyond the

---

[2] *The Concise Oxford Dictionary* (Oxford: OUP, [9]1995).

[3] See ch. 1, 'The idealist classics', pp. 34–37.

objects of mere sense. Obviously a conviction that there is Something there to see, beyond sense, is fundamental to this theory.

Müller's full definition of religion is 'the perception of the infinite under such manifestations as are able to influence the moral character of man'.[4] The introduction of the moral aspect is out of respect for Immanuel Kant.[5] But the original religious impulse was still firmly placed in the feelings, which locates Müller in the theological tradition that traces its origin to Friedrich Schleiermacher. Müller followed Schleiermacher[6] in finding the key to the essence of religion in the emotional or intuitive way in which the human mind responds to the external world. From the point of view of theology or religion, Schleiermacher's theory was a brave attempt at a defence against the corrosive forces of rationalism and empiricism. What he did in effect was to surrender reason and logic but hang on to feelings. So scriptures and religious doctrines and traditions could be merrily torn apart, while what was really important in religion, the experience, was left untouched.

The downside of Schleiermacher's defence was that theology was really reduced to psychology or later to anthropology. In trying to find an impregnable fortress for religion, he abandoned any hope of dogmatic truth. To illustrate this point very simply, when we study the New Testament we are not studying the truth about God as revealed in Jesus Christ but an account of the experience of the truth as revealed in Jesus Christ. The Truth itself is ineffable, beyond our verbal understanding. So we can have no knowledge of God in the sense of being able to say that some statement or other about God is true. We can take as an example the beginning of the Apostles' Creed: 'I believe in God the Father Almighty, Maker of heaven and earth . . .' This is not a statement about an all-powerful being who has made everything, whose character can be appropriately described by the term 'Father', but an attempt by Christians in the first few centuries of Christian history to put their experience of God into words. In so doing, they were obviously drawing on the ancient tradition of the Jews. They were able to do this because their experience in some sense or other corresponded. So theology is not knowledge or study of God, but knowledge or study of the experience which others have had of God. It is really reduced to the study of religious states of mind. In this sense it can be argued that liberal theology, that is, theology which traces its foundational principles to Schleiermacher, is actually psychology of religion.

---

[4] *Natural Religion* (London: Longmans, [2]1892), p. 188.

[5] Müller had published a two-volume translation of Kant's *Critique of Pure Reason* in English in 1882.

[6] See ch. 1, 'The idealist classics', pp. 27–30.

Ninian Smart: idealism and psychology in Beyond Ideology

A good example of this approach to religions can be seen in the way in which Ninian Smart deals with Buddhist and Christian teaching in his *Beyond Ideology: Religion and the Future of Western Civilization.*[7] In a later article, where he expresses approval of the intuitionist view of Schleiermacher and his followers, he says that his position in *Beyond Ideology* was 'that Buddhism and Christianity are complementary traditions, giving alternative views of the transcendent X that can nourish and criticise each other'.[8] This is obviously not the case at the verbal or intellectual level. How can a tradition like Buddhism, that denies the existence of a person, complement a tradition like Christianity that is intensely personal? But he says that this 'should not stop us from seeing that in some ways the impulses towards the Transcendent both in Buddhism and classical Christianity may have a convergence in the mystical life'.[9] What he is saying is that, though there may be no convergence on the verbal level, there may be convergence on the level of experience. It may be that in both Christianity and Buddhism the real aim is a 'purified consciousness', so that they differ only in technique and verbalization.

The problem with this view, even if we accepted that the aim of either Christianity or Buddhism is a 'purified consciousness', is that the only access that we have to what either religion means by the term is by way of their verbalizations which, however, are so radically different. The Buddhist and Christian forms of 'purified consciousness' are as incompatible as are the basic dogmas of the two traditions. This is sufficient illustration that Smart's approach to religion is psychological. What he describes are psychological responses to 'the transcendent X'. It is not at all surprising that he can make statements such as the following that are very reminiscent of the pragmatism of William James: 'The paradox can be put most sharply by saying that after all it does not matter whether God does or does not exist; his powers would be just as great.'[10]

One of the stranger episodes in the history of Christian theology was the 'Death of God' movement of the 1960s. It would seem a contradiction in terms for a theologian, that is, someone devoted to the knowledge of God, to declare that 'God' has died. But the movement does at least become intelligible if theology is really only the study of people's experience of God in the

[7] London: Collins, 1981.

[8] 'Our Experience of the Ultimate', *Religious Studies* 20 (1985), p. 22.

[9] *Beyond Ideology* (London: Collins, 1981), p. 84.

[10] *Ibid.*, p. 185.

Schleiermacherian tradition. What Harvey Cox and Thomas Altizer (the leading exponents of the movement), and even John Robinson, were saying was that 'God', in the sense in which he was described in the historic creeds of Christianity, was no longer alive in people's experience. People just did not experience 'God' in that way any more. So it is just as well to declare 'God' in that sense dead, and look for more adequate verbalizations, such as the 'ground of being', to express modern people's experience of the Beyond. The merits or otherwise of their case is not in view here. It is probably true to say that what they were describing was the experience of a few intellectuals rather than the mass of ordinary Christians. The point of referring to the movement is to illustrate what can happen when psychology, in the sense of simply what happens in human experience, is made the basis of theology.

PSYCHOLOGY *and* POSITIVISM

When we turn from the idealistic to the positivist stream, we find that the theories of religion were just as psychological. But whereas in the idealistic stream the emphasis is on the feelings, in the positivist stream, initially at least, the emphasis is on cognition. E. B. Tylor's animistic theory of the origin of religion, which was adopted by James Frazer, owed much to 'Association Psychology'. Association psychologists held that everything in the mind comes by way of the senses, and that stimuli were organized according to principles such as similarity, contrast, and proximity of place or time. So primitive 'man', just emerging from animality, associated experiences such as sleep, dreaming and death in such a way as to come to the conclusion that since a part of a person is able to wander at will while the person is sleeping, what happens at death is that this part wanders off never to return. So, thinking through a series of associations, the primitive philosopher came to believe in souls. This belief was the basis of all religion which, since it was founded on a false process of reasoning, could have no foundation in reality.

In due course Association Psychology, which focused on the cognitive aspect of human experience, began to give way to other theories which took more account of the feelings and the will. A case can be made that even Emile Durkheim's theory was a psychological theory in which emotion played a key role. He definitely thought that collective emotion was the basis of religious life and ritual, though that was only a part of his theory. This psychological emphasis was also apparent in Alfred Radcliffe-Brown. He believed that there were two main categories of religious rites. The first was the rites centred on the death of members of the community. The rites and the beliefs associated with them were the result of the collective emotional response to death. The second category was the rites and beliefs associated with personified natural phenomena. The origin of these were cognitive, rather than emotional, because they arose as a result of primitive peoples' infantile psychological tendency to view things in personal terms. R. R. Marett, though a social anthropologist, went in an idealistic direction with his view of religion as that which was able to drive the will in the direction of what is good, despite what the mind may say to the contrary. This combination of emotion and will almost brings us back full circle to Müller.[11]

the PSYCHOLOGICAL ESTABLISHMENT *and* RELIGION

If much of what has been said about religion in the last hundred years can be described as psychological, in the same period Psychology is also a science which has won its right to a place in the academic world. We must now turn to what Psychology in this academic sense has contributed to the discussion about religion. What has already been said about the development of Sociology can be applied to Psychology as well. Like Sociology, it has argued for a place in academia on the basis of being 'scientific'. It is now a fully fledged profession with a clearly defined field of interest protected by professional organizations. In the United States no-one can practise as a psychologist without an approved doctorate.

Basic Psychology textbooks describe the discipline as 'the study of mental processes and behaviour in humans and animals'. The type of questions considered under this general heading include:

1. Perception/attention – conscious experience of the environment.

2. Emotion/motivation – the way in which internal states impact behaviour. This area may also include discussion of sex and sexuality, sleep and dreams.

3. Learning/thinking/memory – the way in which information is acquired and stored.

4. Personality – the way in which various aspects of mental-being hang together. This understanding can then be expanded to include mental disorder and its treatment. Dreams are considered very important by those who are involved with therapy in this area.

5. Intelligence – the development of techniques for assessing ability.

6. Social Psychology – deals with the way in which individuals interact. There is an obvious overlap with Sociology here.

---

[11] For a longer parade of psychological theories of religion, see E. E. Evans-Pritchard, *Theories of Primitive Religion* (London: OUP, 1965), ch. 2.

It is interesting to note that, while every introductory textbook in Sociology has a substantial section devoted to the Sociology of Religion, a section on the Psychology of Religion is conspicuous by its absence from Psychology textbooks. The indexes of some of the most popular introductory textbooks in Britain do not even mention religion.[12] This suggests that Psychology has nothing to say on the subject of Religion.

Ignoring something is not necessarily an indication of hostility or of a conviction that what is being ignored is of no consequence. Psychology as an academic discipline was certainly born out of an ethos that was hostile to religion, and it may be that its absence does display a residual hostility. But there may be other factors that explain the apparent disappearance of religion from the psychologist's agenda. There was a period at the turn of the nineteenth century, particularly in the United States, when the Psychology of Religion was very popular. Liberal theologians played a major part in the establishment of Psychology as a discipline and, given their psychological view of religion, it is possible that the more positivist psychologists such as J. B. Watson (1878–1958), the founder of Behaviourism, were keen to free Psychology from any institutional link with religion. The divorce does seem to have been complete. Psychology as an academic discipline does not consider religion as part of its field of study. So Psychology of Religion, if it exists, is not a sub-discipline of Psychology but of Religious Studies.

the PSYCHOLOGY of RELIGION

The contribution of William James

William James (1842–1910) is a pivotal figure in any attempt to understand the Psychology of Religion, because he straddles the two main streams that contributed to its development.[13] These two streams are the psycho-physiological and depth psychology. The psycho-physiological focuses on the conscious mind and attempts to understand the mental processes involved in religious experience by gathering information from individuals. Two topics that were discussed by James in this way in his famous *The Varieties of Religious Experience* were 'Conversion' and 'Mysticism'. 'Conversion' was a particularly

---

[12] The outline that follows on the content of Psychology is based on a number of basic textbooks and the article 'Psychology' in *Encyclopaedia Britannica*, vol. 9, Micropaedia (Chicago, [15]1994).

[13] See ch. 3, 'The ambivalent classics', pp. 57–60.

popular topic of the American psychologists of religion because it was such an important element in the revivalism of North American Protestantism. Other issues that were subjected to this type of analysis were 'Cult', in the sense of the ritual of worship, 'Revivals' and 'Prayer'.[14] Most of the material was drawn from Protestant Christianity, with the occasional reference to other Christian and non-Christian traditions. The purpose of this approach seems to have been the integration of Psychology into the stream of liberal Protestantism. There has been something of a revival of interest in this approach recently in connection with the appearance of a large number of new religious movements, often referred to as 'cults'. Interest has focused on why people join cults, the cult leaders, and how people can be released from their influence. This interest was reflected in what might be thought of as a very weak television serial drama entitled 'Signs and Wonders', broadcast by BBC2 at the beginning of 1995.

In his study of 'Conversion' and 'Mysticism', William James came to the conclusion that the key to understanding these phenomena lay in what he called the 'subliminal', or what came to be more generally called 'the subconscious mind'. James also believed that studying pathological states would help in understanding this particular facet of the human personality. He came to the conclusion that this was the part of our human make-up where contact is made with 'God'. What we have here really is an apologetic for religion in the tradition of Schleiermacher. The subconscious is a part of our being that is real but beyond rationality. This James viewed as a great advantage: 'Higher Criticism and Rationalism and Naturalism might do their worst. Only the outworks of religion were open to their attack, and the man of faith might when he chose retire to the impregnable fortress of the Unconscious Self.'[15] It belongs to that indefinable area of our being, where all sorts of emotive and primitive instinctual forces are at work. We cannot know what goes on there, we can only observe some of the effects in our conscious life. If this is the entrance for the transcendent, we can then judge whether it is genuine or not by its effects in the conscious life. So we get to James's pragmatism. We cannot know anything about 'God' because she/he/it touches human life at the subconscious level. All we can say is that, if the consequences are good, the source must have been good. So if religion works, whatever that religion may be, it must be a good thing.

---

[14] See the works of G. S. Hall, J. B. Pratt, G. A. Coe, *etc.*

[15] J. B. Pratt, *The Religious Consciousness* (New York: Macmillan, 1920), p. 49.

Freud and religion

While James was delivering his lectures on the varieties of religious experience, Sigmund Freud (1856–1939) was also shaping his theories in what became known as 'Depth Psychology', which came to very different conclusions.[16] For James the unconscious was a window looking out on to eternity, whereas for Freud it was a door into the dark cellar of our physical and moral existence. In Freud's division of the personality into the id, ego and superego, the id is unquestionably the dominant force. The id is the physical substratum of the personality and the powerhouse of all psychic energy. What goes on in the ego and superego is driven by this energy. The ego exists to relate the unconscious drives of the id to the external world, and the superego is created during childhood in order to protect from or control the imperious demands of the id.

> Instead of identifying mind with consciousness, and understanding both as distinct from the body, Freud saw consciousness as a small – and derivative – part of a mind which is largely unconscious in character, a mind whose behaviour ultimately stems from forces which are biological.[17]

The most powerful biological force is the sexual. In order to control the insatiable desire of this psychic energy for satisfaction, the ego created the divine guardians of the moral order, who are nothing more than fictional characters of the superego.

Other gods who appear in the world's mythology are products of what Freud calls the 'primary process' of the id. The instinctive drives of the id demand instant satisfaction. This is the 'pleasure principle' which drives the id. It demands that its desires are satisfied as soon as possible. The immediate satisfaction of desires is called a 'reflex action'. If someone is hungry or has a sexual desire, tension is created. A reflex action is to find something to eat or a sexual partner immediately, so that the tension can be relieved. But this is not always possible, so what happens is what Freud calls a 'primary process'. As a substitute for reflex action, tension is diffused by forming a mental image. So an image of food or of a woman or man is formed. These mental images of what the id desires he calls 'wish-fulfilment'. The best place to see this 'primary process' at work is in dreams, which are invariably motivated by wish-fulfilment according to Freud. The same process is at work in mythology, so that the gods are really nothing more than the result of the process of wish-fulfilment.

[16] See ch. 2, 'The positivist classics', pp. 47–50. *Cf.* J. N. Isbister, *Freud: An Introduction to his Life and Work* (Cambridge: Polity, 1985).

[17] C. Stephen Evans, *Preserving the Person* (Leicester: IVP, 1979), p. 37.

Carl Gustav Jung

In the Freudian system, therefore, the unconscious is certainly not the point where people come into contact with a transcendent realm. The unconscious id is the biological foundation of existence, and the superego, which is also mainly unconscious, is only a creation of the conscious self to deal with the powerful psychic demands of the id. There have been many critics of Freud from the scientific as well as the religious and theological side of the fence. One of his main critics was C. G. Jung (1815–1961), initially one of his very close collaborators in the first decade of the nineteenth century, but who then broke away from him over Freud's resort to sex as *the* key to understanding human personality and its aberrations. Jung eventually came to head an opposing psychiatric school called 'Analytical Psychology'. He put a very positive value on religion, and read widely on the world's religious traditions. He even said that among his patients

> . . . in the second half of life . . . there has not been one whose problem in the last resort was not that of finding a religious outlook on life. It is safe to say that every one of them fell ill because he had lost that which the living religions of every age have given to their followers, and none of them has been really healed who did not regain his religious outlook.[18]

As in Freud's case, Jung's views are not now favoured by many psychologists, but his shadow can still be seen, if only in terms like 'complex' and 'introvert/ extrovert'. His influence in Religious Studies is rather more than shadowy, however, because of his influence on Mircea Eliade (see chapter 9) and because his thinking is more consistent with its theoretical ethos. In New Age thinking he is still a significant influence.

Jung's life story

It helps in understanding Jung to know something of his life history. He was born into a family of clergymen. His father and eight of his uncles were clerics! The home was very religious, though his father, who was a sombre, introverted type, suffered from doubt, and used to get irritated when the young Jung asked awkward questions. His mother, on the other hand, was an open, extrovert type, whose faith was much more based on her feelings than on intellectual conviction. She was also endued with extrasensory perception. It was impossible to be insulated from the apparent controversy between religion and science at that time. Jung was pulled in both directions, but he decided very early in his

---

[18] *Modern Man in Search of a Soul* (New York: Harcourt Brace Jovanovich, 1933), p. 135.

intellectual development that it is experience that matters in religion. Though he opted for science and medicine as a career, he was fascinated by the paranormal fringe of religious experience, a fascination which most probably had its roots in his mother's ESP. His MD thesis entitled 'On the psychology and pathology of so-called occult phenomena' was a study of a medium.

From 1907 to 1913 Jung was closely associated with Freud. After their acrimonious parting, he resigned his post in Zurich and spent four years in a very unstable mental state. During this time he had very vivid dreams, visions and paranormal experiences, which he describes in his very popular volume *Memories, Dreams, Reflections*. In these dreams and visions, a figure called Philemon kept appearing. According to Jung he became a sort of spirit guide, or what the Indians call a 'spirit guru'. This is a guru that appears to his disciples in dreams rather than in the flesh.[19] Philemon taught Jung that 'there are things in the psyche which I do not produce, but which produce themselves and have their own life. Philemon represented a force which was not myself.'[20] Jung was severely tempted during this period to turn his back on science and allow himself to be absorbed into his unconscious. But he decided that 'in the final analysis the decisive factor is always consciousness, which can understand the manifestations of the unconscious and take up a position towards them'.[21] In 1916 he wrote down what Philemon, and others who appeared to him in his dreams and visions, were saying. While he was writing, odd things began happening in his family. He said that 'the whole house was filled as if there were a crowd present, crammed full of spirits'.[22] 'They' went when he finished writing.

There is one more biographical point to be made before looking at Jung's mature analysis of the personality and the place of religion in it. By 1920 he had discovered the symbolic form called a 'mandala' in the Tantric Hindu and Buddhist traditions. Linking this type of picture used in Tantric ritual and meditation with the images that he and his patients were seeing in their dreams, he says that he 'began to realise that the goal of psychic development is the self. There is no linear evolution; there is only circumambulation of the self.' 'I knew', he says, 'that in finding the mandala as an expression of the self I had attained what was for me the ultimate.'[23]

---

[19] *Cf.* the experience that the social anthropologist Katherine Ewing had with a *sufi* guru (see pp. 126–127).

[20] *Memories, Dreams and Reflections* (London: Fontana, 1973), p. 207.

[21] *Ibid.*, p. 212.   [22] *Ibid.*, p. 215.   [23] *Ibid.*, pp. 220, 222.

Jung's psychology and religion

On the surface, at least, what Jung meant by the Ultimate was the ultimate understanding of the way in which the human personality operates. The idea of the 'self' was the coping-stone which bound the rest of the structure together. Like Freud, Jung divides the personality into three main systems: the ego, the individual unconscious, and the collective unconscious. It is only the ego that is similar in the two schemes. The ego is the conscious mind. This is what gives the individual a sense of identity and continuity. Since it is the point at which everything becomes manifested, it is a kind of centre of the personality. It is something like the point in a factory at which the final product becomes visible. Behind that point are most of the processes that go on in the factory. It is like this in the personality. Most of the significant processes go on unseen and unmanifested at the unconscious level.

Having said as much, the level of the individual unconscious is closely linked to the ego. Much of what is found in the unconscious was once part of the conscious mind, but for one reason or another has been pushed into the unconscious background. It is populated by a mixture of repressed, suppressed, forgotten and ignored experiences. There is also plenty of traffic between these two systems, with some things coming into the conscious mind and others being pushed into the individual unconscious all the time. The individual unconscious is also populated by complexes. A complex is formed when a group of feelings, thoughts, perceptions and memories cluster around a particular nucleus. These complexes exist in every individual unconscious. They become a problem when they seize control of the ego and begin to use the personality for their own ends. This is what happens in mental illness and also in the case of people like Adolf Hitler, who was 'possessed' by a power complex.

The nucleus of complexes leads us to the next system in the personality, because these complexes sometimes arise from the collective unconscious. This level is the most powerful and influential system in the personality, because it contains what every individual inherits as a result of being part of the human race. There is nothing individual in the collective unconscious. It contains that which is characteristic of every human being, a sort of racial memory bank, in which a psychic residue has been stored, from generation to generation, from the pre-human animal instinctual phase up to the modern period in human history. If this collective unconscious exists, there are elements in every personality that do not belong to the individual at all. This is what Philemon revealed to Jung, when he taught him that there are some things in the psyche that were not produced by him at all but which have a life of their own.

Jung did not believe in the reality of the collective unconscious simply on the evidence of Philemon. The sources of information that he used to prove its existence were dreams, active imagination, mythology, religion and the occult sciences. The analysis of dreams is foundational. All the other sources of information are used to expand and confirm what Jung discovered in dreams. Unlike Freud, Jung analysed dreams in series rather than individually. In doing this he found that certain images were repeated over and over again. He would then encourage patients while conscious to let their imagination run free on one of the dream images – or even a conscious mental image – and then record what they 'saw'. This is what he meant by 'active imagination'. When he realized that the dream images bore some resemblance to the symbols found in mythology, religion and the occult sciences, this led him into a massive comparative study of these areas. He believed that the consistency with which certain images appear in individual dreams and in these other areas was conclusive proof of the existence of a common psychic substratum to the human personality – the collective unconscious.

The images which Jung found appearing again and again were images of the archetypes. Archetypes are 'pre-existent forms . . . which can only become conscious secondarily and which give definite form to certain psychic content'.[24] Reminding us that the background of his thinking at least was positivist, Jung goes on to say that 'the archetypes are the unconscious images of the instincts themselves . . . they are the patterns of instinctual behaviour'.[25] But even if everything is related to biological processes, he distinguishes very clearly between such processes and what he calls 'psychic life'. Psychic life cannot be reduced to biological processes even if it cannot be divorced from them. The archetypes which are completely unknowable in themselves appear in consciousness as symbols. 'The significance of symbols', Jung says, 'is not that it is a disguised indication of something that is generally known but that it is an endeavour to elucidate by analogy what is as yet completely unknown and only in the process of formation.'[26] This points to an important facet of his thinking. He believed in the purposeful development of the personality. Each individual has an aim. This is not something that is consciously adopted in the first place but something which is almost imposed from the collective unconscious. The

---

[24] *The Archetypes and the Collective Unconscious*, in *The Collected Works*, vol. 9, part 1 (London: Routledge & Kegan Paul, ²1969), p. 42.

[25] *Ibid.*, p. 44.

[26] *Collected Papers on Analytical Psychology* (New York: Moffat, Yard & Co, 1917), p. 468.

instinctual forces push the archetypal symbols into consciousness, and as symbols they present the individual with the pull of a transcendental goal. This goal is transcendent, because it is the goal of the human race springing up from the collective unconscious and not the goal of some divine being which transcends human existence altogether.

Jung describes a whole range of archetypal symbols. The 'persona' (or mask) is that which the world sees of the personality, and it witnesses to the importance of social interaction in the history of the race. The 'anima' in the case of a man and the 'animus' in the case of the woman witness to the bisexual nature of the individual. A man has a feminine aspect to his personality and a woman has a masculine aspect to hers. It is interesting to note that, during his crisis experience after splitting with Freud, Jung was tempted by his anima to give up science and rationality and opt for experience and irrationality. (Not something which could be suggested in a post-feminist age!) But the most important archetypal symbol of all is 'the self'. When he discovered this in conjunction with discovering the significance of the mandala, he believed that he had found the ultimate key to understanding the human personality. Not surprisingly, this symbol is also the key to his understanding of religion.

Remembering that the archetypal symbol represents something unknown in the process of coming to be in human consciousness, the 'self' represents wholeness, equilibrium and unity. The personality is made up of a whole series of different aspects which need to reach the fullest degree of differentiation and development. This is true of the three main aspects of the personality and also of the complexes and archetypes. For example, the persona has a specific and important goal which needs to be realized if the individual personality is to reach full maturity and the human race as a whole is to achieve its goal. But crucial to the proper development of all the various aspects is that which binds them together into a unity. That is what Jung means by 'the self'. The ultimate goal of human development is self-actualization. There is something of a contradiction in Jung's thinking at this point, because the balance of psychic energy which is the goal of selfhood would involve the cessation of that energy which is required to sustain psychic life. He denies that the goal can be reached, but if it were possible the result would be something like the Buddhist *nibbana*.

We are now in a position to look at the way Jung fits religion into his system. 'God', he says, 'is an obvious psychic and non-physical fact, that is a fact that can be established psychically but not physically.'[27] What he means by this is that the symbols of 'God' which he found in the world's religions correspond to

[27] *Answer to Job* (London: Routledge & Kegan Paul, 1954), p. 169.

psychic symbols that he discovered in treating his patients. The most satisfactory symbol is the mandala. In the first place, the mandala is a circle which represents wholeness or completeness – the fundamental characteristic of the ultimate archetype of the self. Secondly, the mandala is divided into four segments. This again represents completeness, but a completeness in which opposites are brought into harmony. The psychic harmony to which the self aspires must contain the dark and evil as well as the good and light sides of the psyche. That is why Jung believes that the Eastern images of 'God' are more adequate than the Christian or Jewish images, because evil is included in the 'godhead'.

Jung was very conscious of the reality of evil in the human personality. It was represented primarily by the archetypal symbol of the shadow. It had its roots in the dark animal past of the human race, and when it was projected outward it threw up the figure of the devil, while its inward projection gave birth to the idea of original sin. Though very real and potentially harmful, the shadow cannot be eliminated or denied, so self-actualization must mean that evil or the shadow is also somehow brought into balance with everything else in the personality. There is no question of the elimination of the shadow. So, when he comes to discuss the Christ image, even though he says that 'Christ is our nearest analogy of the self and its meaning', he goes on to say the following:

. . . although the attributes of Christ . . . undoubtedly mark him out as an embodiment of the self, looked at from the psychological angle he corresponds to only one half of the archetype. The other half appears in the Antichrist. The latter is just as much a manifestation of the self, except that he consists of its dark aspect. Both are Christian symbols, and they have the same meaning as the image of the Saviour crucified between two thieves. This great symbol tells us that the progressive development and differentiation of consciousness leads to an ever more menacing awareness of the conflict and involves nothing less than the crucifixion of the ego, its agonising suspension between irreconcilable opposites.[28]

It is important to emphasize that 'the self' is the primary concept for Jung, so that what he means by 'the Christ image' is the way in which Christ symbolizes the self. He believes that the existence of the archetype of the self is a 'proven scientific fact'. So the Christ image is interpreted in terms of the archetypal self. Since 'the self' means completeness and the Christ image focuses on perfection, the latter cannot be a fully adequate symbol of the self. He does argue that there

---

[28] *Aion: Researches into the Phenomenology of the Self* in *The Collected Works*, vol. 9, part 2, trans. R. F. C. Hull (London: Routledge & Kegan Paul, ²1968), p. 44.

are elements in the Christ image that point in the direction of wholeness, such as the existence of Antichrist or the crucifixion between two thieves, but his arguments are not at all convincing. The light/darkness or good/evil polarity in the accounts of Christ are very clear. The concept of repentance which is fundamental in Jesus' teaching means the rejection of evil in order to embrace the kingdom of God or salvation. His argument that it was the theologians of the early church who created the Christ image of perfection is not convincing, since the roots of their theology are very firmly based in the New Testament. It may be possible to argue that their idea of evil as a negation of good, and therefore non-existent in ultimate terms, owes more to Greek philosophy than to the New Testament. But that does not mean that the New Testament teaching on evil sees it as a positive quality that needs to be brought into equilibrium with other aspects of the soul. Salvation as taught by Jesus includes the command to go and sin no more. The elimination of evil and not its integration is the aim.[29]

Such arguments would not convince Jung, of course, because the evidence from historical religion is secondary. All he is interested in is evidence that confirms what he believed to be his objective scientific findings. Given his early interest in the paranormal, it may be significant that he finds the greatest confirmation of his theory in a heretical Christian movement like Gnosticism, in alchemy with its strong links with magic, and in Eastern tantric symbolism. The 'objective scientific' discovery was that the collective unconscious pushes into consciousness symbols that depict

> . . . the union of warring opposites as already accomplished, and thus eases the way to a healthier and quieter state ('salvation'). For the present, it is not possible for psychology to establish more than that the symbols of wholeness mean the wholeness of the individual. On the other hand it has to admit, most emphatically, that this symbolism uses images or schemata which have always, in all the religions, expressed the universal 'Ground', the Deity itself.[30]

He insists that this is not a statement about some reality outside the physical. He remains agnostic about the metaphysical. All he claims is that he has discovered strong parallels between what is ultimate in the human personality, the self, and what has been considered ultimate metaphysically in the world's religious traditions.

---

[29] For a fine discussion of this subject, see Henri Blocher, *Evil and the Cross: Christian Thought and the Problem of Evil* (Leicester: Apollos, 1994), pp. 85f., 105ff., 131–133.

[30] *Ibid.*, pp. 194–195.

Jung's legacy: the cult of self-actualization

What then is Jung's legacy? His psychological theories have been generally rejected or ignored. He had enthusiastic followers among psychiatrists, especially during his lifetime, and they established the Bollingen Foundation in order to propagate his ideas. Enthusiasm has now waned considerably. Because of its size, the American psychological establishment dominates psychology in the English-speaking world. With its strong roots in experimental psychology, Jung has been very generally ignored or rejected by that establishment. Because it ignores religion, it is not surprising that anyone who writes a lot about religion should be considered suspect. To be fair, it is also true to say that Jung's theories are not amenable to experimental testing, so it is understandable that they have been ignored. A scientific theory is, by definition, a theory that can be experimentally tested. It would be very difficult to design an experiment to test the existence of the collective unconscious. So the psychological establishment has viewed Jung's theories as belonging more to the world of the arts than the sciences.

It can be argued, nevertheless, that his idea of self-actualization has become a dominant concept in the world of psychiatry and psychological counselling. Whether this is a case of direct influence is not possible to gauge. It may be that he articulated one of those ideas that characterize a particular historical moment. For example, Carl Rogers (1902–87), who laid the foundations of most contemporary counselling practice, built his whole system on a particular theory of the self. His theory 'pictures the end-point of personality development as being a basic congruence between the phenomenal field of experience and the conceptual structure of the self – a situation which, if achieved, would represent freedom from internal strain and anxiety'.[31] Like Jung, Rogers sees health (salvation?) in terms of the balance of elements in the self. Another psychologist who has had a profound influence on personality theory and its application in various areas, such as management, is A. H. Maslow (1908–70). According to him, human beings have needs which can be arranged into a hierarchy. Physiological needs are found at the bottom of the ladder, but at the top is self-actualization. Self-actualization is the need to develop and realize one's individual potential to the full. One major difference between Jung and both Rogers and Maslow is that Jung did take the dark side of the self seriously.

---

[31] C. R. Rogers, *Client-centered Therapy* (Boston: Houghton-Mifflin, 1951), p. 532.

Conclusion

This brings us back to where we began this chapter and to the suggestion that psychology is taking over from religion as the West's answer to the meaning and purpose of human life. The intense preoccupation with the individual self and its well-being that is so characteristic of our Western culture is a strong evidence for this tendency. The big question now is how the individual can achieve self-fulfilment. Self-esteem is the key dogma, and not self-sacrifice. This has become such a pervasive philosophy that even Christians are being influenced by it. Becoming and being a Christian is now often presented as a means to self-actualization. People are invited to come to Jesus so that they can live happy, healthy and fulfilled lives in material comfort. Counselling is fast replacing confession and repentance as the Christian route to life.

Even more significant than Jung's emphasis on self-actualization is the way in which he married this emphasis with an intense interest in religion. He is particularly significant in this context, because his interest in religion focused primarily on its Eastern esoteric and magical manifestations. It is not surprising that he is therefore now seen as one of the prophets of the New Age movement. New Age is essentially a marriage between various twentieth-century psychological views of the human being and a whole range of esoteric religious beliefs and practices. Jung himself experimented a little with occult and paranormal experience, but his New Age followers have plunged headlong into every possible form of esoteric belief and practice. It is no surprise that he is seen as a pioneer in this movement, which is a strange mixture of the modern and the magical.

Another reason for Jung's popularity with the New Age movement is his pluralist theory of religion. He believed that he had discovered one psychological reality at the root of the diversity of religious manifestations. Such a claim is also of interest to more academic students of religion, particularly those who are pluralists. Mircea Eliade, one of the key figures in contemporary Religious Studies and the subject of the next chapter, was unquestionably influenced by Jung.

– 9 –

MIRCEA ELIADE: HISTORIAN *of* RELIGION?

BIOGRAPHY

Mircea Eliade (1907–86)[1] was born in Bucharest, Romania. He graduated in philosophy at the University of Bucharest, his early development having been heavily influenced by Ion Ionesco, the leading Romanian Greek Orthodox thinker of his day. He then spent four years studying yoga under Surendranath Dasgupta at Calcutta from 1928 to 1932. During this time he spent six months in an *ashram*, where he came into close contact with the traditional Hinduism of the ordinary people in India. This experience in India, coupled with his appreciation of the type of Orthodoxy practised by the ordinary people of Central Europe, was crucial in the formation of his view of religion in general. It is possible to see his whole output as an attempt to bridge the gap between the Western European intellectual tradition that he had come into contact with in the University and the religious experience of ordinary Romanians and Indians.

Eliade taught in the University of Bucharest from 1933 to 1940 and then spent five years in the diplomatic service between 1940 and 1945. After the Second World War, he decided to return to academic life as an exile, taking up the post of a visiting professor at the Sorbonne, Paris. He remained in Paris until 1957, when he embarked on a second exile and became professor of the History of Religions at the University of Chicago. He remained in Chicago until his death in 1986. Almost all his major works on religion were first published in French in the period 1948–65, and were also translated into English during that period. In 1976 the first volume of his three-volume *A History of Religious Ideas*

---

[1] There is a useful, brief biography of Eliade by Kitagawa in *Encyclopedia of Religion* (New York: Macmillan, 1986), vol. 4.

appeared in French. By the time he died, this large work had been almost completed and a translation made into English, the third volume of which appeared in 1985. In the preface to this work, Eliade states that it 'will probably be my last contribution to a discipline that is dear to us', but subsequently he saw through to publication, as general editor, a sixteen-volume *Encyclopedia of Religion*, which is likely to supersede Hastings' *Encyclopaedia of Religion and Ethics*. When one adds to Eliade's output the founding of the journal *History of Religions* in 1961, which has justifiably earned its place as one of the major journals in the area of Religious Studies, plus a steady stream of learned articles, it is not surprising that Eliade held an imposing position in his discipline right up to the time of his death.

ELIADE *and his* INTERPRETERS

One clear piece of evidence that someone has 'arrived' in the academic world is the appearance of interpretations of his or her work. There are plenty of interpretations of Eliade. The diverse ways in which he is understood by different authors testify not only to the wide-ranging nature of his work, but also to the manner in which he has interwoven into his thinking so many of the approaches to religion that have been developed in the twentieth century. He has been regarded not only as a historian of religion but also as a phenomenologist. Others see him as belonging to the tradition of the great anthropologists, and yet others see him as primarily a psychologist of religion in the tradition of Jung. Since he has been charged with just about all the different approaches to religion that have been examined in the second part of this volume, a brief look at his ideas and the way in which they have been interpreted will serve as a conclusion to this whole section. One thing will become very obvious, and that is that there are no clear demarcation lines between the various approaches.

A number of Eliade's interpreters are adamant that he is a phenomenologist through and through. Douglas Allen in his study of Eliade describes him as 'the foremost contemporary phenomenologist of religion'.[2] Others, such as John

---

[2] *Structure and Reality in Religion: Hermeneutics in Mircea Eliade's Phenomenology and New Directions* (Berlin: Mouton, 1978), p. xi. *Cf.* Kees Bolle, 'Myths and other religious texts', in F. Whaling (ed.), *Contemporary Approaches to the Study of Religion* (Berlin: Mouton, 1984), p. 324; W. L. Brenneman, S. O. Yarian and A. M. Olson, *The Seeing Eye: Hermeneutical Phenomenology in the Study of Religion* (Pennsylvania State University Press, 1982), pp. 57ff.; K. Rudolph (trans. G. D. Alles), 'Mircea Eliade and the "History of Religions"', *Religion* 19 (1989), p. 106.

Saliba, treat him as more of an anthropologist.[3] More rarely he is seen as belonging to the Depth Psychology school of Jung. Eric Sharpe, for example, discusses Eliade's contribution to Religious Studies in a chapter on 'Religion and the Unconscious'.[4] But, as the title of his journal shows, Eliade himself prefers to call his discipline the 'History of Religions'. In fact he is quite firm on this point.

> [The] work of deciphering the deep meaning of religious phenomena rightfully falls to the historian of religions. Certainly, the psychologist, the sociologist, the ethnologist and even the philosopher or the theologian will have their comment to make . . . But it is the historian of religions who will make the greatest number of valid statements on a religious phenomenon *as a religious phenomenon* . . . On this particular point the historian of religions also differs from the phenomenologist.[5]

We shall begin, then, by looking at what Eliade meant when he called himself 'a historian of religions'.

ELIADE'S VIEW *of* HISTORY *of* RELIGION

One of Eliade's overriding concerns in his study of religion is to avoid reductionism.[6] He began his study of religion in the late 1920s when the influence of positivists such as James Frazer, Emile Durkheim and Sigmund Freud was still felt particularly amongst the intelligentsia. Many then thought that religion belonged to a passing phase in history, a history which saw humans developing from being slaves of their circumstances to being masters of their own destiny. History is, therefore, the story of people's increasing ability to 'make themselves'.[7] It is the story of the way in which human beings came to free themselves from their limitations so that they can be truly creative. For us moderns every day is supposed to bring new possibilities for self-realization, spontaneity and creativity. The opportunities for us to express our ability to make ourselves is supposed to be endless. Unlike the many generations that have gone before, post-scientific humanity has the enviable privilege of making, rather than suffering, history.

[3] *'Homo Religiosus' in Mircea Eliade* (Leiden: Brill, 1976), pp. 104ff.

[4] *Comparative Religion: A History* (London: Duckworth, 1975), pp. 210ff.

[5] *Shamanism: Archaic Techniques of Ecstasy* (London: Routledge, 1964), p. xv.

[6] See *The Quest* (Chicago: University of Chicago Press, 1969), p. 70.

[7] *The Myth of the Eternal Return or Cosmos and History* (Princeton, NJ: Princeton University Press, 1954), pp. 155f.

In describing the modern mentality of the intelligentsia in these terms, Eliade is very conscious of the development of philosophy in the West since the Enlightenment. He sees this development as culminating in the apotheosis of 'man' as seen in the various '-isms' of the twentieth century. Here Eliade quite rightly makes no distinction between the positivist and idealist tradition. According to him, in historicism, Fascism, existentialism, Marxism, and so on, 'man' is god. All these philosophies deify humanity and its potential to create its own future. Eliade is convinced, however, that they have not given humanity the freedom that they claim to offer.

Historicism and existentialism, for example, have left humans floundering in the dark as to how they should act. Historicism may be defined as

> The belief that an adequate understanding of the nature of anything and an adequate assessment of its value are to be gained by considering it in terms of the place it occupied and the role it played within a process of development.[8]

All that it is possible to know about the past is the meaning of individual events in their context. It is not possible to discover the purpose of history, to say that history is going towards a specific end. Neither is it possible to find invariable principles for action from within the flow of history. Wilhelm Dilthey (1833–1911), one of the main representatives of historicism at the beginning of the twentieth century, reluctantly admitted that the historicist approach could only end up with relativism. 'The relativity of all human concepts is the last word in the historical vision of the world.'[9] So human beings are left by the historicist as makers of history without any real clue as to how they should go about making it.

The existentialist, in a sense, merely takes the matter one step further than the historicist, arguing that since there is no hope of knowing how we should act we must just go ahead and act anyway. This means that humans must make themselves, even though they can never know whether their actions have ultimately any point at all. Eliade also lived through a period of intense political ferment which had a profound impact on Romanian life in general and on his own life in particular. First came a period of totalitarian rule by the king of Romania, followed by the impact of Nazi Fascism, and then by the domination of a Marxist ideology. So, on the intellectual and the political level, loud claims to think and act in the interest of human freedom were not matched in Eliade's

---

[8] Maurice Mandelbaum, 'Historicism', in *Encyclopedia of Philosophy*, ed. P. Edwards, vol. 4 (New York: Macmillan, 1967).

[9] *The Quest*, p. 51; cf. *The Myth of the Eternal Return*, p. 150.

experience by an increase in freedom in reality. It is not surprising that he came to this conclusion:

> It is becoming more and more doubtful . . . if modern man can make history. On the contrary the more modern he becomes . . . the less chance he has of himself making history. For history either makes itself . . . or it tends to be made by an increasingly smaller number of men who not only prohibit the mass of their contemporaries from directly or indirectly intervening in the history they are making . . . but in addition have at their disposal means sufficient to force each individual to endure . . . the consequences of this history . . . Modern man's boasted freedom to make history is illusory for nearly the whole of the human race.[10]

It is important to realize, if one is to understand Eliade, that he approaches the whole issue of the history of religions from this very broad perspective. It can quite justifiably be described as a religious perspective because he is fundamentally concerned with the spiritual well-being of humankind, with the most basic questions that humans face as we seek to make our life in the world something meaningful. It is this perspective on things that leads to his rejection of 'historicism'. For Eliade, it is not enough to describe a series of unique and unrepeatable events without showing any concern for their meaning. For him, the meaning of the story of humankind is of paramount interest. So the historian's work has not been completed when all the historical circumstances in the historicist sense have been classified and understood. This does not mean a denial that every expression of culture is historically conditioned[11] and that the geographic, physiological, economic, sociological, *etc.*, aspects have to be taken into account if a correct assessment is to be made of a historical phenomenon. But even when all this has been done, understanding in its fullest sense has not been achieved, since understanding involves going beyond the details to the essence, to that which gives unity and continuity to the story and thus ensures that it makes sense. Eliade states:

> We must not confuse the historical circumstances which make a human existence what it actually is with the fact that there is such a thing as human existence . . . the historicity of a religious experience does not tell us what a religious experience ultimately *is*.[12]

---

[10] *The Myth of the Eternal Return*, p. 156.

[11] *The Quest*, p. 35.

[12] *Patterns in Comparative Religion* (London: Sheed & Ward, 1958), pp. 2–3.

This position does make Eliade liable to the charge of being anti-historical. The way in which he marshals evidence without any great regard for its historical location in *Patterns in Comparative Religion* also confirms this charge. Almost as if to prove that he was not anti-historical, his last major work was the massive *A History of Religious Ideas*, of which only three volumes had been completed before he died. In this work he set out to look at religious phenomena in historical or chronological sequence. But he did not forsake his anti-historicist stance in doing so, because he still emphasizes the unity of human history. 'I hold', he says, 'that any historical study implies a certain familiarity with universal history . . . It is simply a matter of not losing sight of the profound and indivisible unity of the human mind.'[13] Individuals have histories, but for Eliade there is also a history of humankind. A history of religions that is content simply to describe the beliefs, practices and development of the various religions remains on the level of the histories of individuals. If it is to have any significance, it must be raised to the level of a history of humankind. There is, therefore, as the older idealists insisted, a history of religion in the singular as well as histories of religions in the plural. Eliade's aim is to develop a methodology that will lead to an understanding of the history of religion in the singular.

It almost goes without saying, in view of this, that Eliade presupposes the reality of religious experience. There is something in religious experience that cannot be reduced to anything else. In his preface to *The Quest* and again in the preface to *A History of Religious Ideas*, he states that 'the "sacred" is an element in the structure of consciousness and not a stage in the history of consciousness'.[14] Very much in the tradition of Max Müller and Rudolph Otto, he insists upon the continuing validity of religious experience, the implication being that there is something 'there' beyond what can be analysed in physiological, psychological or sociological terms. The term which Eliade uses for this 'beyond', albeit on rare occasions, is 'the transconscious'.[15] We shall return to this concept later in this chapter when looking at Jung's influence on him.

'ARCHAIC MAN'

Having looked at some of the basic principles of Eliade's approach, we can now consider some of the consequences of their application. According to Eliade himself – up to 1958 at least – his most significant book was *The Myth of the*

---

[13] *A History of Religious Ideas*, vol. 1 (Chicago: University of Chicago Press, 1979), p. xvi.

[14] *The Quest*, p. 1; *cf. A History of Religious Ideas*, vol. 1, p. xiii.

[15] E.g. *Patterns in Comparative Religion*, p. 450.

Eternal Return or Cosmos and History.[16] The central thesis of this volume is that historicism in its various forms has obscured the 'sacred' dimension to human experience even though that dimension persists as an element in the structure of human consciousness. He argues that two basic approaches to 'history' are open to us, what he calls the 'archaic' and the 'modern'.

The archaic is in fact the religious approach. This is the approach that sees a meaning in life beyond the details of human existence. For the archaic person,

> . . . neither the objects of the external world nor human acts, properly speaking, have an autonomous intrinsic value. Objects or acts acquire a value, and in so doing become real, because they participate . . . in a reality that transcends them.[17]

Therefore a religious person is not at the mercy of events because he or she has access to a transcendent realm which can give meaning to events and which can alleviate what Eliade calls the 'terror of history'. Examples of the freedom from history which religion provides would be the strength acquired by means of religion to face suffering brought about by inhumanity through faith in some overriding purpose of a god or gods. Another example is freedom 'from the recollection of sin, *i.e.* of a succession of personal events that, taken together, constitute history'.[18] 'Archaic man', which is really Eliade's descripion of a religious person, is the one who rejects history and reaches out to the permanent beyond change, who rejects 'existence' and prefers 'being':

> It is more probable that the desire felt by the man of the traditional societies to refuse history and to confine himself to an indefinite repetition of archetypes, testifies to his thirst for the real and his terror of 'losing' himself by letting himself be overwhelmed by the meaninglessness of profane existence.[19]

Hierophanies: the sacred and the profane

'Archaic man' becomes conscious of this 'sacred' realm which is opposed to the 'profane' realm of history as a result of a large number of hierophanies. 'Hierophany' is a word made up of two Greek terms meaning 'sacred' and 'to appear' or 'become manifest'. So its meaning is 'manifestation' or 'appearance of the sacred'. The idea of hierophany is really Eliade's idea of revelation. The transconscious, or the trans-historical dimension which he calls the 'sacred', has a

---

[16] See Preface of *The Myth of the Eternal Return*, p. xv.
[17] *Ibid.*, p. 4.   [18] *Ibid.*, p. 75.   [19] *Ibid.*, p. 91.

life of its own, but throughout history it has broken in upon profane existence in various ways. All religious beliefs, myths and ritual are various responses to the breaking in upon human consciousness of this transconscious being. All religious phenomena, in their origin at least, are the result of hierophanies. From the side of the religious phenomena, what we find is that human beings have considered just about every object as a hierophany at some time or other. Stones, mountains, trees, sun, moon, stars and so on have all been venerated as sacred. The veneration itself is a historical matter which can be understood with the help of anthropology, sociology, psychology and so on. The anthropologist, for example, can describe the way in which people venerate certain stones, and the place of their veneration in their lives as a community. In doing this they will find, invariably according to Eliade, that the worship of a particular object is understood within a system of beliefs and behaviour, of myths and rituals. A comparative study of these theories or explanatory systems of hierophanies would lead, he believed, to an understanding of their essence.

This is what Eliade set out to provide in *Patterns in Comparative Religion*. The conclusion he came to was that

> . . . the paradoxical coming-together of sacred and profane, being and non-being, absolute and relative, the eternal and the becoming is what every hierophany, even the most elementary, reveals. One might even say that all hierophanies are simply prefigurations of the miracle of the Incarnation, that every hierophany is an abortive attempt to reveal the mystery of the coming together of God and man.[20]

The hint of a Christian apologetic (of the type that Christianity is a fulfilment of the other religions) contained in this quotation needs to be put into the context of Eliade's ideas about the ultimate meaning of the hierophanies developed towards the end of the volume. Here the 'most basic definition of divinity' is the meeting of opposites beyond rationality:

> . . . myth reveals more profoundly than any rational experience ever could, the actual structure of the divinity, which transcends all attributes and reconciles all contraries . . . the myths of 'quest' and of 'initiation trials'

---

[20] *Patterns in Comparative Religion*, p. 29. *Cf.* footnote on p. 30: '. . . far from thinking of pagan religious ways . . . as false and degenerate stages in the religious feeling of mankind fallen into sin, one may see them as desperate attempts to prefigure the mystery of the Incarnation. The whole religious life of mankind . . . would, from this standpoint, be simply a waiting for Christ.'

reveal, in artistic or dramatic form, the actual act by which the mind gets beyond a conditioned, piece-meal universe, swinging between opposites, to return to the fundamental oneness that existed before creation.[21]

'God' is basically rest beyond opposites, the point at which all things become united, and the Incarnation is just another symbol of this fundamental aspect of all religion.

'MODERN MAN'

So much for archaic or religious man. 'Modern man', on the other hand, according to Eliade, in the name of 'history', seeks to suppress or obscure all hierophanies and to insist that only the profane exists. Modern people believe that humans can make themselves without any help from some transconscious realm. This modern approach has made most headway in the West and, according to Eliade, it is the cause of much of the frustrations and anxieties of the modern Western world. The West has exported this 'historicism' to many parts of the world with the 'swallowing up of the ancient societies in the economic framework of colonialist and semi-industrialist societies', an export which Eliade describes as an 'absolute spiritual catastrophe'. However, the situation is not hopeless because

. . . the dialectic of hierophanies allows of the spontaneous and complete *rediscovery* of all religious value, whatever they may be and at whatever historical stage may be the society or individual who rediscovers them.[22]

The history of religions can thus, in the last analysis, be expressed in terms of the drama of the losing and rediscovery of those values, a loss and rediscovery which can never be final. Human beings may be able to obscure, but they cannot annul, the 'sacred'.

Eliade also sees great significance in the fact that we are living at a time when the Eastern peoples and those from the once colonized parts of the world are beginning to play a part in world history as active subjects rather than passive objects. His hope is that the entrance of the East, especially on the stage of world history, together with what Eliade considers its stronger hold on the sacred, will lead to the rejuvenation of religion in the West. This reflects the tremendous impact upon Eliade of the four-year period he spent in India studying yoga. He saw the History of Religions as a discipline playing a part in the development

[21] *Ibid.*, pp. 419, 428.   [22] *Ibid.*, pp. 464, 465.

towards what he calls the *'planetization* of culture',[23] that is, the creation of a culture, which includes religion, for the whole of humankind. The big question, therefore, is:

> . . . how to assimilate *culturally* the spiritual universes that Africa, Oceania, Southeast Asia open to us. All these spiritual universes have a religious origin and structure. If one does not approach them in the perspective of the history of religions, they will disappear as spiritual universes; they will be reduced to *facts* about social organizations, economic regimes, epochs of pre-colonial and colonial history *etc.* In other words, they will not be grasped as spiritual creations: they will not enrich Western and world culture – they will serve to augment the number, already terrifying, of *documents* classified in archives, awaiting electronic computers to take them in charge.[24]

The acid onslaught in this latest quotation on the reduction of people's spiritual life to the collecting of facts brings us to the heart of what Eliade understood by the 'history of religions'. History of Religions uses modern techniques to prove the value of the religious experience of 'archaic man'. It may not prescribe what people should believe, but it could play a part in the salvation of 'modern man' if it had the moral courage to withstand historicism and highlight the reality of the transconscious which is still being experienced as a reality in many parts of the non-Western world.

ELIADE *and* PHENOMENOLOGY

Having looked at what Eliade himself meant by the 'history of religions', we can now return to some of the assessments of him. Quite a few of his interpreters are adamant that he is a phenomenologist. There is some justification for this opinion. The way in which the material is divided up in *Patterns in Comparative Religion* is very reminiscent of the work of avowed phenomenologists. The table of contents is, for example, very similar to that in Friedrich Heiler's *Phenomenology of Religion*. It is even possible that Eliade influenced Heiler. Again, the way in which he seeks to go beyond the cataloguing of facts to grasp the meaning of religious phenomena, and his insistence on their irreducibility, remind us of the phenomenologists. But he still insists that he is not primarily a phenomenologist.

With his early training in philosophy, Eliade would understand the close link between philosophical phenomenology and the tradition which he sees as the great enemy, historicism. In the philosophical context, phenomenology was a

---

[23] *The Quest*, p. 69.   [24] *Ibid.*, pp. 70–71.

new method to get at what is there to be observed, freed from all subjective and presuppositional baggage. It was a way of seeing the unique event in its true historical uniqueness. In the hands of religious phenomenologists like Gerardus van der Leeuw, this exercise was preliminary to the work of comparison, and the works that they produced are similar to Eliade's in many ways, but it is not surprising that Eliade fixed on the preliminary exercise. He was not satisfied with seeing the historical phenomenon in all its purity. His interest was in the way in which patterns of meaning become manifested in history. Human religious consciousness must witness to some deep reality in human nature. He believed that an analysis of the products of this consciousness would yield an intelligible pattern or system. At the heart of his system are his ideas of the archaic view of existence and the transconscious as well as the hierophany. Eliade sees his system as an attempt to interpret the meaning of religon in general. This is why he calls it a 'creative hermeneutic'. It is not a case of meaning appearing from a study of history, because he is concerned with transcending history. The system of the religious consciousness is radically beyond history, and is the only place where humans can escape from the terrors of history. He looks for meaning beyond history, while in his estimation the phenomenologist looks for the meaning of history.

This is what makes Eliade appear anti-historical, which is strange in view of his strong preference for history of religions as a description of his discipline. But what he rejects is the development or evolutionary view of history, which he calls 'historicism', and particularly the idea of progress which was used to justify the superiority of Western European civilization. His insistence that there is something in religious experience that is classified as 'primitive' by the superior Western 'scientific' culture, which is essential to human well-being, is an attempt to break this tyranny of historicism. At this point he is obviously in sympathy with the psychology of C. G. Jung.

Eliade and Jung

Here again Eliade denies that Jung had influenced him directly, even though he had a long association with him through the annual Eranos conferences, and some of his works were published by the Bollingen Foundation that had been set up to propagate Jung's ideas. There is some justification for this denial, because by the time he became associated with the Eranos group in 1950, Eliade had already published the French edition of *Patterns in Comparative Religion*. But there is no doubt that both Jung and Eliade breathed the same intellectual air and that the latter's use of terms like 'archetype' and 'symbol', though possibly not directly derived from Jung, expresses a similar view of reality. This is also certainly true of Eliade's idea that the most fundamental religious archetype is the union of opposites (*coincidentia oppositorum*). And again, Eliade's idea of the 'transconscious' is very similar to Jung's idea of the 'collective unconscious'. He may have abandoned the use of 'archetype' in favour of 'exemplary pattern', 'model' or 'paradigm' to distance himself from Jung, but many of his statements are undeniably 'Jungian'. For instance, he says:

> Myths decay and symbols become secularised, but they never disappear, even in the most positivist civilisations . . . Symbols and myths come from such depths: they are part and parcel of the human being, and it is impossible that they should not be found again in any and every existential situation of man in the cosmos.[25]

Like Jung also, Eliade seems to see an imbalance in Christianity's representation of the religious system. Jung expresses this view in discussing the union of opposites. Eliade, who shares Jung's view of the importance of this archetype, focuses on the close link between Christianity and history. He sees the succumbing of Western thought to historicism as a fall. This is the real fall which the Genesis story metaphorically portrays. The high value which Christianity places on the unique historical events centred on the person of Jesus Christ puts it into the category of a 'fallen' religion. Eliade states:

> Christianity incontestably proves to be the religion of 'fallen man': and this to the extent to which modern man is irremediably identified with history and progress, and to which history and progress are a fall, both implying the final abandonment of the paradise of archetypes and repetition.[26]

a PROPHET of 'the SPIRIT'

Eliade is unquestionably a prophet of the spirit in our secular or desacralized West, and it is not by accident that his books are addressed to the educated generally rather than to the more limited clientele of the world of Religious Studies. The danger, however, of being a prophet of religion in general is that we are left in doubt as to which god we should worship. It is not enough for us to know that religion offers us something which is good for us. We also need to know which religion, and what the good is that we are being offered. In the last analysis, one

---

[25] *Images and Symbols*, p. 25, quoted by M. L. Ricketts in 'In Defence of Eliade', *Religion* 3 (1973), pp. 25–26.

[26] *The Myth of the Eternal Return*, p. 162.

wonders whether Eliade himself is too infected with the historicism that he castigates to bring himself to choose a god to worship and adore. It is possible to argue that what he says to Western man is that 'archaic man' has an access which is not available to us in the West because we are so infected by the historicist bug that we inevitably neutralize any hierophany by our insistence on making it an object of analysis, the plaything of 'man the maker'. But we are assured that ultimate desacralization is not possible, and that what we need to do at present is to explore the living spirituality of archaic man as found supremely in India and in those areas of the world where ancient practices such as shamanism are still alive, and hope that one day the windows will be opened for us to experience the sacred once again. Religion is a system that is beyond any particular manifestation, but it would seem that at present our only hope of approaching that essence is through an appreciation of Indian and other ancient spiritualities.

E. M. Cioran, a life-long friend of Eliade, describes his predicament very graphically, and this is a predicament in which many students of Religious Studies find themselves. Referring to Christianity, Cioran states quite correctly that perhaps Eliade 'stands, from all evidence, on the periphery of this religion'. Then he goes on:

> But perhaps he stands on the periphery of *every* religion, by profession as well as by conviction. Having refused to marshal them into a hierarchy, how can he be partial? Which belief can one sponsor? which divinity can one invoke? It is impossible to imagine a specialist in the history of religions *praying*. Or, if indeed he does pray, he thus betrays his teaching, he contradicts himself, he damages his *Treatises* in which no *true* god figures, all the gods being viewed as equivalent . . . he cannot blow life into them, having tapped them of their sap, compared them with one another, and, to complete their misery, frayed them with rubbing until they are reduced to bloodless symbols useless to the believer, assuming that at this stage of erudition, disillusion, and irony there is somebody around who still truly believes. We are all of us, and Eliade in the fore, *would-have-been* believers; we are all religious minds without religion.[27]

the WEAKNESS of a BIG THEORY

Eliade is a scholar of immense erudition who produces evidence for his theories to the point of tedium at times. Many of his volumes are mainly catalogues of

[27] J. M. Kitagawa and Charles Long (eds.), *Myths and Symbols: Studies in Honour of Mircea Eliade* (Chicago: University of Chicago Press, 1969), pp. 413–414.

examples which justify his generalizations, and the generalizations represent an attempt to penetrate beyond the diversity to the unity that underlies the religions. In this his approach is reminiscent of earlier anthropologists such as E. B. Tylor, James Frazer and Wilhelm Schmidt. The encyclopedic collection of information also leaves him exposed to criticism from historians who are more focused on a particular religious tradition or on a particular topic.

Going for breadth often leaves Eliade compromised in depth. For example, Richard Gombrich, an expert on Buddhism, severely criticizes the way in which Eliade interprets some Buddhist texts in his *Yoga: Immortality and Freedom* to justify linking the Buddha and shamanistic traditions. There seems little doubt that Eliade was mistaken in his understanding of key Buddhist texts.[28] Another example is Eliade's view of the belief in a 'high god' in pre-literate societies. He held that this belief was universal in pre-literate societies, but he maintained that the 'high god' was otiose, for it played no active part in the people's religious life. He also believed that the high god was always a sky god. John Saliba shows that the ethnographic evidence does not support Eliade on this point. According to the *Human Relations Area Files*, 'there are 156 cultures where belief in a high god has been recorded, 104 cultures where this belief is absent and 140 societies which have to be excluded because of scanty evidence.' In more than half of the 156 cases of belief in a high god, the god is not otiose. Furthermore, the evidence is not clear enough to prove the link between the high god and the sky in most cases.[29] This does not mean that Eliade is necessarily wrong. It is possible that those gathering the evidence have misunderstood the truth of the situation. Even in science, theories are often vindicated despite the apparent contradiction of the data. The extent of the discrepancy, however, does seem to weigh against him in this case. But in the last analysis, Eliade's core theory of religion cannot be invalidated by historical evidence. His theory is not the result of historical research but what makes historical research intelligible. Any substantial criticism of Eliade must therefore be made on the level of belief and not of factual evidence.

THE MYTH OF THE ETERNAL RETURN

The volume which comes nearest to a statement of the way Eliade views religion in general is *The Myth of the Eternal Return*. The two poles of religious

[28] R. Gombrich, 'Eliade on Buddhism', *Religious Studies* 10 (1974), pp. 225–231.

[29] John A. Saliba, *'Homo Religiosus' in Mircea Eliade: An Anthropological Evaluation* (Leiden: Brill, 1976), pp. 107–108.

MIRCEA ELIADE: HISTORIAN OF RELIGION?

development are archaic religion and the suppression of religious consciousness in modern Western European mentality. Archaic religion is the 'original' religion, and evidence for it is sought in prehistoric archaeology, among contemporary 'primitives', and in the folk traditions of Europe which are believed to go back to pre-Christian times. Here again, in his quest for the original religion and his belief that it will bring us to an understanding of what religion actually is, Eliade reminds us very much of earlier anthropologists. Archaic religion, then, is the religion that appeared first in the history of religion. This religion, according to Eliade, was dominated by myths of the origin of the world as an ordered reality, that is, cosmogonic myths. At this stage our ancestors were able to come to terms with everyday existence (history) by returning periodically through certain rituals to the time of the beginning of things. This return to the beginning led essentially to a transcending of all the contradictions of existence in an experience in which all opposites were united. Light and darkness, good and evil, the universal and the particular, being and existence, subject and object are all ultimately united in the One.

This coincidence of opposites is the most basic definition of divinity, and it belongs to human religious experience from the beginning as the fundamental meaning of myths and rituals. In fact, it seems to belong more to the religious experience of 'archaic man' than to anyone else. This being so, it is not surprising that Eliade exalts the 'primitive' in his study of religion. This can be seen, for example, in his large volume on shamanism,[30] which is defined as a technique to achieve an ecstatic unity with the divine and as such is a type of return to the beginning. Also, in the third volume of A History of Religious Ideas, it is significant that he concentrates on the history of magic and alchemy when discussing European religion since the Middle Ages. It might be true that the religious significance of these movements has been neglected in the study of European religion, but Eliade sees their persistence as evidence of the persistence of the original religious impulse. The occult world, according to him, witnesses to the very essence of religion. It is not surprising, therefore, that volume three of A History of Religious Ideas ends with a discussion of Tibetan religion with its strong occult emphasis. Here again he is right to emphasize the strong occult element in the Eastern religious traditions and to see that in religion people believe that they come into contact with the ultimate source of power. What is disturbing in Eliade's case, however, is that his idea of the unity of opposites stops him from taking the possibility of spiritual evil seriously, since good and evil in the spiritual realm are ultimately indistinguishable. This brings us back

[30] Shamanism: Archaic Techniques of Ecstasy (London: Routledge, 1964).

to Cioran's perceptive observations on the historian of religion that, despite all his efforts to understand religion, in the end he is not really able to treat it seriously. If Eliade thinks, as he seems to, that the evil we experience in the world can in some way be united with the ultimate good, then everything is reduced to the same plane, and it does not really matter what we believe as long as we believe something or have some dealing with the sacred. It does seem odd, however, that a scholar bred in the scientific twentieth century, and who has laid heavy emphasis on the objectivity of the History of Religions, should end up exalting the occult as the place where the true meaning of religion is still visible.

CONCLUSION

Eliade belongs unquestionably to the twentieth century, and he represents an attempt to rediscover the meaning of religion in a post-religious age. He deplores the way in which his own modern mentality rejects religion, but hopes that the application of the scientific methods to the religious worlds of the East will re-awaken that religious consciousness in modern people. What is significant is that he sees the suppression of the religious aspect of consciousness primarily in terms of the rejection of archaic mentality and not the rejection of Christianity. The return to religion is then seen as a return to archaic religion and not a return to Christianity.

It is not surprising that, like Jung, Eliade is now seen as one of the prophets of the New Age. He is seen as one of the main instigators of renewed interest in shamanism, not as an interesting historical phenomenon, but as a practical method of getting in touch with the divine. There is certainly nothing in Eliade's thinking that would discourage this step from understanding to practising. He seems to approve of any move in the direction of the revival of archaic religion. In what must have been one of the last pieces that he ever wrote, he sees a renewed interest among scientists and technologists in the United States in the more esoteric side of religion as evidence of the correctness of his theories. Religious consciousness may be suppressed, but it can assert itself again at any time.[31] For many of Eliade's colleagues in the History of Religion, the fact that his theories leave a door open for the renewal of religious practice is condemnation enough. They still cling to the idea of so-called scientific objectivity. But Eliade may be more in tune than they with the spirit of what is now called the post-modernist age, with its greater openness to a whole variety of

---

[31] '*Homo Faber* and *Homo Religiosus*', in J. Kitagawa (ed.), *The History of Religions: Retrospect and Prospect* (New York: Macmillan, 1985).

human experiences that were frowned upon in the age of scientific modernity. He has certainly encouraged many to take religion more seriously. Whether any religion will do, or whether the religion of 'archaic man' is the true religion, is another matter.

III

SOME BASIC ISSUES

– 10 –

AUTHORITY

INTRODUCTION

Authority means 'the power or right to enforce obedience'. It is that which is able to control and direct the way in which people think and live. That it is a key theme in religions is unquestionable. Religious authority is still a power that is able to control the lives of the vast majority of the world's population even today. It is even possible to argue that those who have embraced a secular ideology are still controlled by an authority which can only be described as religious.

Within the Christian tradition, authority has been a burning issue since the beginning. Authority was one of the key issues of debate between Jesus and the religious leaders of his day. Fundamental to their dispute was Jesus' rejection of the oral tradition of interpretation of the Old Testament law (*torah*) which the religious leaders considered authoritative. When the Christian church had been established, the question of authority became particularly relevant when there was a need to determine whether some new teaching or practice was consistent with the teaching of Jesus as preserved in those churches which had been founded by his immediate followers. Eventually the apostolic documents which these churches possessed were gathered together to form the collection of documents that became known as the New Testament. This together with the Old Testament became the fundamental authority for all Christian belief and practice.

Christians would agree that God is the ultimate authority over their lives. Disagreements arise about how God's will is known. Traditionally, all agreed that the Bible is God's Word, but some would say that God also speaks through the oral tradition of the church or through the structures of authority in the church that are claimed to have been established by Jesus. Others have argued that the foundation for these objective sources of authority is reason, the conscience, or the emotions. The way in which these various possibilities have been mixed together is what differentiates many of the Christian denominations from each other and, often, people within denominations as well.

The intention in this chapter is first of all to look at the various ideas of the sources of religious authority in the Christian tradition, and then to consider them in the context of some other religious traditions. In looking at what may be very familiar to those of us who belong to the Christian tradition in the unfamiliar context of other religions, what is fundamental to religious authority may come more clearly into focus. This exercise is open to the charge of Christian imperialism. However, the justification for proceeding in this way is that the whole question of authority has been generally ignored in the studies of religions other than Christianity. Books dealing with traditions such as the Hindu or Buddhist, for example, have given very little attention to the question of authority.[1]

The article on 'Authority' in the *Penguin Dictionary of Religions*, edited by J. R. Hinnells, illustrates this point very clearly. The whole article is about the question of authority in the Christian tradition. No other religion is mentioned. Added to this, every reference to authority in other articles in the same volume have to do with Christianity. *The Encyclopedia of Religion*, edited by Eliade, does have a more general article on 'authority' in the world religions, but the bibliography states that there 'are no comprehensive presentations on the theme of authority in the general history of religions based on comparative or typological studies'.[2] There can be no doubt that authority is an issue in all religions. Since discussion of it has received more scholarly attention in Christianity than any other tradition, it would seem reasonable, therefore, to use the Christian experience as a paradigm for understanding the issue in other religions.

[1] Since there is a link between authority and revelation, there is some relevant material in a recent volume by Keith Ward entitled *Religion and Revelation: A Theology of Revelation in the World's Religions* (Oxford: OUP, 1994). Part III, 'Four Scriptural Traditions', sounds promising, but it is more of a comparative study of the content of 'revelation' in the four traditions than of the way in which the authority of revelation is mediated. (This material is more relevant to the chapter on 'God' in this volume.) The material most relevant for this chapter is a section on 'Authority and Autonomy', pp. 302–310. This latter section confirms some of what is said about the significance of the religious 'expert' in this chapter.

[2] 'Authority', in *The Encyclopedia of Religion*, vol. 2 (New York: Macmillan, 1987), p. 6.

AUTHORITY *in* CHRISTIANITY

As stated above, discussion about authority in Christianity has centred on how God exercises his power or right to enforce obedience. There is a long list of possible loci of authority, such as the Bible, tradition, church, theology, dogma, reason, conscience, moral will, experience, emotion or feeling. This list can probably be reduced to five main loci.

1. The Bible

Basically, what is meant by 'the Bible' is the thirty-nine books of the Old Testament, which Christians share with the Jews, and the twenty-seven books of the New Testament. In some Christian denominations the Apocrypha, which covers the period between the two Testaments, is bound with the Bible and readings from it are included in the lectionary. In the Roman Catholic Church, there are twelve apocryphal books which were given canonical authority in 1546, and in the Greek Orthodox church there are four which were given canonical authority in 1672. Protestants do not recognize any of the apocryphal books as authoritative scripture, though some churches, such as the Anglican, have retained the practice of reading from them in their liturgy.

If the issue of the Apocrypha is set to one side, Christians have generally accepted the Bible as an authoritative book since the canon of the Old and New Testament was finally recognized by the church in the fourth century CE. It is believed that the words of this book are in one way or another the words of God himself. It follows that to obey what the Bible asks of human beings is to obey what God himself demands. God is the supreme authority, but since the Bible is a revelation of his will, to obey the Bible is to obey him. A written revelation has obvious advantages because it is very stable. There is plenty of scope for disagreement about the precise meaning of the text, but when all is said and done, the text remains as it was before any discussion.

In the Protestant tradition, the doctrine of the divine authority of the biblical text is very closely linked with the doctrine of the Holy Spirit. Human beings, who are sinners, are seen as entirely dependent on the Holy Spirit's enlightening grace before they can accept what the Bible says as God's Word. In the Roman Catholic tradition, this subjective role of the Spirit is taken by the objective teaching authority of the Church as it is concentrated, in the last analysis, in the person of the Pope.

2. Tradition

A 'tradition' is an opinion or belief or an action that has been transmitted orally or through practice. Every church, denomination or sect, to use the sociological typology of different groups in Christianity, soon develops its own traditions. But some groups, such as the Roman Catholics or Anglo-Catholics, elevate tradition to the same level of authority as the Bible. Side by side with the movement that led to the writing of the New Testament books, they believe that there was a body of oral tradition which was transmitted directly from the apostles to their successors, who in turn transmitted it to their successors and so on up to the present. This makes possible the development of beliefs and practices which are clearly not taught in the Bible, such as the immaculate conception and bodily assumption of the virgin Mary.

Protestants can accept that some claim to apostolic authority could be meaningful in a church that had been established by an apostle for the first few generations of leaders that succeeded him. The arguments of second-century CE church leaders against heretics, on the basis that the heretical teaching was not found in the churches founded by apostles, makes sense. To claim that whatever was being taught and done in those same churches, 400 years later, is authoritative because the churches were founded by apostles is another matter altogether. Protestants part company with Catholics and Orthodox on this extra-biblical oral tradition. The pronouncements of the Ecumenical Councils of the first four centuries, such as Nicea or Chalcedon, are universally recognized by Christians. But Protestants claim that their respect for the Councils is based not on oral tradition but on respect for the tradition of biblical interpretation in the church, which gave birth to the ecumenical creeds promulgated by these Councils.

3. Experience

What is in view here is the claim that certain subjective states enable the person who experiences them to claim that they know what the will of God is. There have been those throughout the history of the church who have claimed that God has spoken to them through visions, dreams or an inward voice. It is a common phenomenon even today in many Pentecostal churches and in churches that have been influenced by the charismatic movement for individuals to have 'a prophecy' or 'words of knowledge' during their services. God is believed to be speaking directly to the congregation or to certain individuals in the congregation through the 'prophecy' or 'word' that is directly revealed in this way. Charismatics and Pentecostals would deny that such messages can override the Bible, but if they are consistent with biblical teaching their authority is often accepted. Church policy, marriages and all sorts of detailed decisions that affect the life of individuals are sometimes determined in this way.

Experience is also very commonly seen as the final proof of the truth of the revelation in Jesus Christ. A popular song of some years ago started with the line, 'I serve a risen Saviour', and finished with the couplet, 'You ask me how I know he lives, He lives within my heart.' It is on the authority of a personal experience of Jesus that one is able to say that he did rise from the dead. This type of authority has an ancient pedigree in the church because the immediate followers of Jesus were described as witnesses – their authority was based on their experience of the risen Lord. Present claims are not often based on sense experience, and are derivative in the sense that they are founded on the recorded testimony of the original apostolic witness. This emphasis is particularly characteristic of the evangelical stream of Christianity with its roots in the Methodist revival of the eighteenth century, but it is also found in other Christian traditions.

The development of this emphasis in one particular direction by Friedrich Schleiermacher – who was brought up in German pietism, a movement parallel to British Methodism – has had a profound influence on Protestant thinking about authority. Despite its heavy emphasis on experience, pietism, as a Protestant movement, still looked to the Bible as the final authority in all matters of belief and behaviour. Christian experience was an experience of the truth of what is taught in the Bible. What Schleiermacher did was to reverse this order. Experience becomes the foundation of the truth in the Bible, and not the result of accepting the Bible as truth. This shift from seeing 'Scripture' to seeing the experience that is believed to underlie 'Scripture' as the final authority, not only in Christianity but in all religion, is, as we have already seen, crucial to any understanding of the modern study of religions.

The almost total neglect of the question of authority in the modern study of religions is evidence of the dominance of this idea. Beginning from the premise that experience is *the* authority, Western scholars have focused heavily on the more experiential aspects of non-Christian religions. So the impression given is that the Hindu tradition is really about the experience of Unity and the way to achieve it as taught in the various yogic traditions. It seems irrelevant that this type of experience has been true for only a very tiny minority of Hindus, for whom the authority of priests or medicine men is much more of a reality. It is true that one sees the odd *sannyasin* (wandering, scantily clad, holy man) in India, but the overwhelming impression is that they are not at all central to Indian religious life.[3] A proper understanding of religions will not be possible until

---

[3] See S. C. Dube, *Indian Village* (Bombay: Harper, 1967), p. 88: 'A text-book knowledge of the religious lore of India, and an acquaintance with her ancient classics and their modern expositions will hardly give us a true picture of the actual religious beliefs, thoughts, feelings and practices of the people now living in the countryside.'

scholars have been freed from the reductive dominance of this experiential view of religious authority. Having begun as a foundational doctrine of liberal Protestantism, this idea has become a dogma of much contemporary Religious Studies. There is no hope of really understanding religions while it dominates.

4. Persons

This term did not appear in the list of possible loci of authority near the beginning of this chapter because persons become authorities as functionaries of church or group, or as experiential specialists. These two aspects are also often united in the one person. What is in view here is the two types of religious leader which the sociologist Max Weber has called the 'prophet' and the 'priest'. The first is the one who majors on experience, while the second is the guardian of the tradition.

Bryn Jones, an 'apostle' of a Restorationist charismatic Christian group based in England, is a contemporary example of the 'prophetic' type of leader. He has tremendous authority over the church which he leads. This authority is based not on any tradition but on his experience of God and on the gifts of the Spirit which he is believed to manifest. Interestingly, being Welsh, he also fits into the Welsh Non-conformist tradition of giving great authority to the preacher in the life of the church. There have been many preachers in the history of Wales, such as Martyn Lloyd-Jones in the twentieth century, whose words have been accorded great authority. Those who respect such leaders would insist that they are respected because of their faithfulness to the biblical authority. However, the way in which an appeal to their words is believed to clinch many a discussion about certain doctrines or actions suggests that at times there is a thin line between the authority of the Bible and that of the Bible teacher.

The authority of the priest, on the other hand, is very much a traditional authority. Roman Catholics believe that certain truths that are not found in the New Testament were revealed to the original followers of Jesus. These truths were passed from one generation of leaders to another and were gradually shared with the faithful. As guardians of this secret tradition, the priests came to possess a tremendous authority over the lives of the flock. They became essential in the process of communicating the grace of God to ordinary people. The giving of God's blessing to ordinary people came to depend on the performance of priestly ritual. The priests were the guardians of the truth, the masters of the saving ritual, the mediators of God's will and blessing. This priestly class developed into a hierarchy, with the Bishop of Rome at its head. Eventually the Pope became the promulgator of doctrine and ritual, and in 1870 was declared the infallible authority when he speaks officially (*ex cathedra*) as the voice of the church. It is primarily through the ritual that the priest's authority is expressed. This is seen, for example, in the mass, where the priestly ritual is believed to convert the elements of bread and wine in some mysterious way into the body and blood of Jesus that is able to feed the souls of the communicants. Confession is another example, where the priest is able to proclaim the sinner absolved.

Informed readers of the previous two paragraphs who come from the Restorationist and Roman Catholic traditions would probably protest that their apostles or priests are secondary authorities. One would be happy to bow before the protest. Yet it is debatable that many ordinary people who belong to a Restorationist or Roman Catholic Church make such distinctions. Do many Restorationists make this distinction when Bryn Jones speaks in their convention meetings? When the Pope, the Holy Father, speaks to and celebrates mass with hundreds of thousands of enthusiastic worshippers during his foreign tours, one does wonder who is being worshipped.

5. Reason

The human ability to weigh up various possibilities and draw conclusions from them has had an important part to play in the history of Christianity. On the whole this ability has been appreciated as a servant of biblical or traditional authority. The status of reason in the history of Christianity can be summed up in Anselm's famous phrase, 'I believe that I might understand.' Reason's authority was seen as strictly derivative. Its place was to help to make clear all the ramifications of faith.

With the Enlightenment of the eighteenth century, reason declared itself independent of revelation. The dramatic discoveries of science and the development of technology boosted the confidence of some intellectuals in the ability of human beings to manage their affairs without depending on a divine revelation. There was a strong element of anti-clericalism in this movement – fired by the devastating religious wars of the seventeenth century, the identification of the religious establishment with an oppressive state, particularly in Roman Catholic France, and the unfortunate Roman Catholic opposition to Copernicanism.[4] For many, these factors were reason enough for the complete rejection of all organized religion. For others, it meant that, in order to retain any

---

[4] The sad story of Galileo, whose book of 1632 entitled *Dialogue concerning the Two Principal Systems of the World* remained on the Catholic Index of prohibited books until 1831, is a clear illustration of the unfortunate obscurantism of the Roman Catholic Church in the seventeenth and eighteenth centuries. See Colin A. Russell, *Cross-currents: Interactions between Science and Faith* (Leicester: IVP, 1985), pp. 42–46.

credibility, Christianity had to make itself consistent with the latest discoveries of independent reason. The rational religion of the Deists was the typical product of this movement in the early eighteenth century. God was seen as the great mechanic who created the world to operate according to inherent laws that needed no divine intervention. God started the machine, and he would be there at the end to assess how it had performed but, in between, humans were free to arrange things in the best possible way and were equipped with reason to do the job. Reason had become the ultimate authority in religion.

It was the acceptance of the belief that reason had destroyed the credibility of a simple belief in the Bible that drove Schleiermacher to regard feelings as the ultimate source of authority in religion. This explains the strong link between respect for reason and the denial that reason can have the last word in religion that has persisted in liberal theology ever since. Ninian Smart, for example, is insistent on the need for Religious Studies to be scientific, which is a bow in the direction of reason, but is just as insistent that the root of religion is a genuine experience of the divine. Since the formulation of Werner Heisenberg's indeterminacy principle, confidence in the ultimate rationality of the universe has also been severely dented, so that reason does not seem to figure quite so much as a religious authority as it used to. Its main significance is now, probably, as the outdated background to the intuitionists' theories.

Authority in Christianity: A conclusion

It should be apparent that a full discussion of the question of authority in the Christian tradition could have led us into a further discussion of the many theories of religion that have already been considered in this volume. This should alert us to the fact that Religious Studies is a Western phenomenon with strong roots in the discussions about the nature of religion and the possibility of revelation within Protestant Christianity since the Enlightenment. Study of religions other than Christianity was really sucked in to a discussion that was going on in the West. We should therefore expect all manner of distortions as religions have been forced into the Western framework of debate. Granted, if we want to learn about religions we have no alternative but to use the textbooks that are available, but it is just as well to be conscious that what we read may have been seen through the very heavily tinted glasses of Western European thinking since the eighteenth century.

Though it may be possible to describe various types of authority in theory, in practice it is much more difficult to isolate them from each other. What makes various Christian churches different is not the different authorities to which they appeal, but the different patterns of authority that they follow. We can take

Protestantism as an example. It is true that 'sola Scriptura' ('the Scripture alone') is one of its major mottoes. But even a superficial study of any Protestant denomination will show that tradition, particular persons, experience and even reason have a place in the overall pattern of authority. Protestants claim to represent the authentic tradition of the early church as well as the tradition of the Reformation. Martin Luther, John Calvin and others are revered, as are those contemporaries with profound experiences. Protestants who sing that Jesus lives because he lives in the heart also argue that their faith is reasonable. The same could be said of all other Christian traditions. The difference, which is not without significance, is one of pattern and priority.

In moving on to consider the question of authority in religions other than Christianity, one other important point needs to be made. This point has already been touched upon in chapter 7 on 'The Social Dimension' of religion. It has to do with the marginalization of what is perceived as religious authority in the Western nations. The story of the division of sacred and secular authority in the West is extremely complicated. It must not be represented as an unmixed evil, because it made possible a pluralist society where people of various religious persuasions can co-exist in the same state without fear of persecution. What is unfortunate in this development is the now-common conviction in Western countries that religion is a private matter which has nothing of relevance or significance to say about social life in general. God may have something to say about how we run our private lives, but human beings can order their public affairs quite well without him.

The acceptance of experience as the religious authority by liberal Protestantism has helped to accelerate this process – to lock believers in their private little world of experience, unable to say anything about God that is true for other people. How often have we heard the statement that our religion is fine for us and that we are perfectly at liberty to practise it as long as we do not try to impose it on anyone else – where 'impose' means just telling someone else that they ought to consider turning to God.

Knowledge of God, which in Kantian terms is impossible, is one side of the equation. The other side of the equation corresponds to Immanuel Kant's practical reason. Here the way in which human beings ought to behave can be known, and the origin and end of this knowledge is rooted in God. Focus on this other side of the equation has led to a strong emphasis on social behaviour in liberal Protestantism. What was called 'the social gospel', which flourished in the USA in particular in the first quarter of the twentieth century, is a good example of this. One of the major problems with this equation is that it is much more difficult to evoke an experience of an unknowable God than to proclaim a clear path of social morality. It is not at all surprising, therefore, that experience of God tends to be neglected and Christianity is reduced to morality. When this process of secularization has happened, as it did in the United Kingdom in the twentieth century, religious experience is left high and dry and perceived as an irrelevance in public life.

This division between religious authority, which is believed to be private, and the public secular authority is a Western phenomenon. Many religious people in the West are not happy with it, and there are signs here and there that it is being challenged. In the non-Western world, where religious traditions other than Christianity are often dominant, this particular dualism is not very prominent as yet. It is becoming more popular as the so-called Second and Third World nations strive to model themselves on what they perceive to be the successful pattern of the West. But generally speaking, where the major world religions remain dominant, there is no division between the secular and sacred authority.

AUTHORITY *in* JUDAISM

Chronologically, Christianity is sandwiched between Judaism and Islam. All three religions look to a book as a central authority. Christianity has absorbed the Jewish book into its Bible, as the 'Old Testament', while Islam makes extensive use of it. In Judaism, tradition is as important as the book in determining the will of God. The fundamental revelation is the Pentateuch, the five books of Moses. This is the revelation of the law (*torah*) that is so precious in Jewish eyes. But the Pentateuch and the *torah* cannot be entirely identified with each other. *Torah* is more than a book. It is the way of life of the wise man. *Torah* is the embodiment of a way of thinking and living in its fullness. It means something like the Greek idea of *logos*, the reason or order that infuses everything, the creator's pattern that is at the root of everything. It is so exalted that one rabbi has said that even God studies the *torah*.

There may be an eternal *torah* and a *torah* of the Pentateuch, but the *torah* that has guided the daily life of the Jew for centuries is the *torah* of the Talmud. A simple description of the Talmud is that it is a huge body of teaching containing the expositions and discussions of the rabbis on the Mishnah of Rabbi Judah ha-Nasi. Judah was the recognized leader of the Jews in the period after the vicious persecution of the Emperor Hadrian came to an end in 138 CE. By this time, the temple in Jerusalem with its ritual had been destroyed and the Jews who survived were scattered to the four winds. What Judah and his followers did was to re-establish the Sanhedrin in Galilee and codify in order the legal traditions which had been preserved mainly in oral form up to that time. He gathered the legal decisions and open-ended discussions of the rabbis under six headings. This is called the 'Mishnah'.

For about three hundred years after Judah had done his work, the teachers of the law (*amoraim*) in Palestine and Babylonia added further case histories and discussions to the Mishnah. The Mishnah together with the record of the deliberations of the *amoraim* forms the 'Talmud'. At first there were two Talmuds, the Babylonian and Palestinian, but gradually the Babylonian Talmud came to represent the supreme authority over every aspect of Jewish life. It is a massive literary corpus containing around two and a half million words on 5,894 folio pages! Until the eighteenth century the Talmud was practically the only subject of Jewish education. Any contact that a Jew had with the Torah was via the Talmud. This means that the other two sections of what the Christians call the 'Old Testament', the Prophets and the Writings, have been relatively neglected. Since the Talmud is basically a law book, it is not surprising that what it means to be a Jew is seen more in terms of a way of life than of adherence to a system of beliefs. What is crucial to the Jew is knowledge about how to live in such a way so as to preserve Jewish identity. It is not surprising that, apart from some of the mystical movements, experience has not figured very much in the Jewish pattern of authority. Rabbis, on the other hand, have wielded great authority, and still do, in certain Jewish sects.

Since the eighteenth century, the development of ideas about authority in Judaism runs parallel with the developments in the Christian tradition. Things changed when Jews were granted cultural, political and social freedom in various European countries in the eighteenth century. Some, such as Moses Mendelssohn (1729–86) in Germany, embraced a rationalist perspective and argued for the reform of Judaism to make it consistent with modern thought. This type of thinking led to the formation of Reform Judaism, which used the vernacular for synagogue worship, emphasized the moral at the expense of the ritual law, played down messianic hope, and in some cases abandoned any intent to re-establish the state of Israel. As we would expect, this Reform movement led to the reassertion of traditional values in some quarters. So today Jews who do not live an entirely secular life – and there are many who do – are broadly divided into Reform and Orthdox synagogues. The Reform look to the Torah, which they interpret in the light of modern thought, while the Orthodox stick closely to the Talmud.

Interestingly, when the Jews were in a position to re-establish the state of Israel in 1948, they did not establish a theocracy but a secular state in the Western style. It was not until the electoral success of Menahem Begin in the 1980s that Orthodox religious parties came to play any significant part in the government of Israel, and then only as a small minority whose support was important for the survival of Begin's government. Recently there has been a significant growth of fundamentalist groups in Judaism, which parallels the growth of fundamentalist groups in Islam and Christianity.[5] Unlike the Christian groups, the Jewish and Islamic groups' political programme is theocratic and strongly anti-democratic. It remains to be seen whether in Israel factors such as the peace process will be a strong enough incentive for them to become really significant players on the political stage. If that did happen, the political scene in Israel would be very different from what it is at present, with the Talmud being enthroned as the unified authority over the whole of life.

AUTHORITY *in* ISLAM

Islam provides the best operational example of a unified principle of authority in the modern world. The foundation of authority in Islam is Muhammad's claim to a new revelation of God (Allah) through the angel Gabriel, which supersedes all other revelations. Gabriel's messages to the illiterate Muhammad are the content of the Muslim's holy book, the Qur'an. This book is seen as a direct gift from Allah to humankind, and is so holy and authoritative that Muslims have been very reluctant to translate it from Arabic into any other language.

Although the Qur'an is such a holy book and is without question the final authority over the life of a Muslim, it does not deal with all the circumstances of everyday life where divine guidance is required. This gap is filled by the *hadith*, the body of traditions or stories about the way in which Muhammad himself acted in various circumstances. Since he is the supreme example of what it means to be a Muslim, these stories about what he said and how he acted are very authoritative. Muslim law (*shari'a*) was formulated on the basis of the Qur'an and the *hadith*. Some aspects of Muslim law, such as the sentence of death for adultery, are based exclusively on the *hadith*. It is not surprising, therefore, that some modern interpreters of Islam have appealed to the Qur'an in opposition to the *hadith* in an attempt to remove such punishments, which are obnoxious to the West, from the *shari'a*. In following the *shari'a*, the Muslim follows the standard of behaviour (*sunna*) of Muhammad. *Sunni* is the name given to the largest Islamic grouping and it means simply those who follow Muhammad's standard of behaviour. The other main Islamic grouping, the *Shi'a*, would claim that they were *sunni* in this sense too. They differ from the *Sunni* on the question

[5] G. Kepel, *The Revenge of God* (Cambridge: Polity Press, 1994) is a study of this fundamentalist revival in the three Semitic religions.

of the leadership of the Muslim community in its early years. The *shari'a* is a legal system that covers the whole life of the Muslim. There is no secular/sacred dichotomy. Political, social and private life is subject to the will of Allah.

In the modern period, Islam has come under severe pressure from the West, particularly as some of its major centres have come under the direct influence of Western imperialist power. In some areas even the idea that political authority could be distinguished from the spiritual was welcomed. The best example of this is the Turkish constitution established by Ataturk in 1923. Ataturk established a state on the Swiss model, which meant the banishment of *shari'a* from the political life of the country. This experiment has survived so far without any sign of weakening the influence of Islam over the population. The Shah in Iran and Zulfikar Ali Bhutto, Benazir Bhutto's father, in Pakistan were going along the same path as Ataturk before they were stopped in their tracks by a revival of Islamic fundamentalism. For fundamentalists like Ayatollah Khomeini, there can be no compromise with Western democracy. He stated:

> The difference between the Islamic government and the constitutional governments, both monarchic and republican, lies in the fact that the people's or the king's representatives are the ones who codify and legislate, whereas the power of legislation is confined to God . . . and nobody else has the right to legislate and nobody may rule by that which has not been given power by God . . . The Islamic government is the government of the law and God alone is the ruler and legislator.[6]

What this means practically in a country like Pakistan, where there has been increasing pressure to apply *shari'a*, is the persecution of minority groups. The conflict betwen Islamic fundamentalism and a more Western view of state authority was graphically illustrated by the case of a thirteen-year-old boy, who was sentenced to death in 1994 for showing disrespect to the Prophet but who was released by the High Court in 1995. The imposition of *shari'a* has led to Christians being barred from certain professions. They are also placed on separate electoral rolls so that they can be politically marginalized, and their testimony in court is worth only half the testimony of a Muslim. In the Sudan, the attempt of the Muslim North to impose *shari'a* on the Christian South has led to a thirty-year civil war, which remains unresolved. Algeria is now locked in a brutal conflict between the forces of democracy and Islamization. In many other Muslim

---

[6] Ayatollah Khomeini, 'Islamic Government', in J. J. Donohue and J. L. Esposito, *Islam in Transition* (Oxford: OUP, 1982), p. 317. *Cf.* 'The Universal Islamic Declaration', in Salem Azzam (ed.), *Islam and Contemporary Society* (London: Longman, 1982), pp. 253ff.

countries, the forces of fundamentalism backed primarily by Iran are very active.

A full analysis of authority in Islam would yield a range of possibilities similar to that seen in Christianity, but with the growth of fundamentalism the focus must be on *shari'a*. From the beginning Islamic authority is something that can be imposed on people, by force if necessary. Muhammad was a prophet who was also a conquering king. His religion spread by military conquest. It may have been influenced in the direction of moral persuasion by the West in modern times, but with the rise of fundamentalism the survival of such an emphasis has been put in doubt. Scholars may argue about which approach is true to the essence of Islam. History seems to be on the side of the fundamentalists. What would happen if they succeeded in their aim of mobilizing the world-wide Islamic community in the service of *shari'a* is a horrifying prospect. The question of authority in religion is not just an interesting topic for academics!

AUTHORITY *in* HINDUISM

In moving from Islam to the Hindu tradition, we move into a very different world. To begin with, Hinduism, if there is such a thing, is extremely complex, and to add to our problems the study of Hinduism is in a state of flux at present. When 'Hinduism' was discovered by Western scholars in the nineteenth century they focused on the sacred literature. This is understandable, because sacred books were crucial in seeking to understand the three main religions that were already known to them – Judaism, Christianity and Islam. So they set about mastering the sacred books of the East with the conviction that a system of beliefs and practices would emerge from their study. A system did emerge, but it is questionable whether it represents what actually happens in Indian religion. This brief account of authority in Hinduism will attempt to get behind the Western picture to what actually happens.

We begin by noting that Hinduism is basically an ethnic religion. Traditionally, the only way to become a Hindu is to be born into one of the four classes into which Indian society has been divided. The four classes are priests (*brahmin*), rulers (*kshatriya*), workers (*vaisya*) and servants (*sudra*). Each class is further subdivided into castes. While there are thousands of castes, they each belong to one of the four classes. The members of these different classes are different types of human beings graded on a scale of purity–impurity, with the priests being the purest and the servants the least pure. There is a major difference between the first three classes, who are 'twice-born', and the fourth class. To be 'twice-born' refers to a particular ritual which boys from the first three classes went through to make them full members of the Hindu fold. This ritual is now observed only among the *brahmins*, but the term 'twice-born' is still used to distinguish the spiritual status of the first three classes from the fourth.

Communities are still generally organized with respect to class, particularly at village level, which is where most Indians live. This has definite repercussions on people's lives. For example, if there is only one well in a village, the upper classes will have first claim on the water and can take it without any regard for the needs of others. People from a lower class will not be allowed to go to the well at the same time as those from a higher class, and so on. Some people thus have an authority simply because of their class. Others exist to respect and serve. The hierarchy of class, which is still the context of the lives of most Hindus, is a spiritual authority structure which defines the place and behavioural parameters for everyone in society. All other religious authorities operate within or with reference to this system.

At the most basic level of mere survival, the Hindu villager relates to a whole range of spirits, demons and localized deities. The authorities who can deal with these spiritual beings are the priests of local temples and local seers or healers. Astrologers are also very important, because of the need to do a whole range of things at the right or propitious time.

On another level, the Hindu needs to be in touch with the law that controls his class. It is very important to keep the class law or *dharma*. *Dharma* is the correct way to live within the context of class in order to make sure of a good rebirth in a future existence. Members of the priestly class are the guardians of *dharma*. They know the rules, and particularly the rules of worship, called *puja*. Not everyone from the priestly class acts as a priest, but priests normally come from that class. As guardians of the *dharma*, they are also responsible for teaching the scriptures. Ordinary Hindus do not read their scriptures. A father may pay a priest to teach some scripture to his sons, but studying them is not part of normal living. The authority of tradition is much more important than scripture.

Added to this there are two traditions that transcend the class system: the ascetic tradition of the *sannyasa*, and the ecstatic tradition of *bhakti*. In the first case, having lived to middle age and so fulfilling one's *dharma*, there is the option of forsaking everything to seek final release from the wheel of becoming. Normally this is not done by means of individual study of scriptures, such as the Upanishads, in order to learn the theory and practice of *yoga*, but by attaching oneself to a *guru*. It is part of Indian ascetic discipline that the disciple subjects himself completely to the authority of the *guru*. Different gurus claim to have discovered a unique way to release persons from the round of rebirth, so India is full of sects. *Bhakti*, which is a way of devotion to a personal god, also has its many gurus and a host of different sects. Many of the gurus have left an account of their particular path to the Truth, which has the authoritative status of scripture in the sect. Tulsi Das was a famous guru of the sixteenth century in the *bhakti* tradition of devotion to Ram. He wrote the *Ram Carit Manas*, which has been called the Bible of North India in the twentieth century. This is the source of the *Ram Lila*, the dramatic presentation of the life of Ram that is so important in the lives of millions of Hindus.

The standard introductions to Hinduism would normally begin not with the actual religious experience of Hindus but with the history of the development of a scriptural tradition, beginning with the Vedas and reaching its full development in the Upanishads. Then would come the books of the various philosophical schools, the law books, the epics and the books of various *bhakti* sects. But Hinduism is not a book religion like Judaism, Christianity and Islam. It may be a whole collection of religions that have a book but, if it is a religion at all, it is ruled by tradition and a tradition that is dominated by the most rigid class system in the world. So far this authority has survived the establishment of a secular state that officially outlaws it. This is probably because the vast majority of Indians still live in villages. The drift to the big cities is accelerating, however, and it is more difficult to hang on to the class system in the factory than in the fields. Hinduism is still very much alive in the great cities of India, but its character may be changing under the pressure of Western industrial and political ideologies.

AUTHORITY *in* BUDDHISM

As with Hinduism, the study of Buddhism is in a state of flux. It is becoming more and more apparent that the picture of Buddhism created by Western scholars since the nineteenth century is woefully inadequate. The studies of contemporary scholars like S. J. Tambiah, Richard Gombrich and Martin Southwold show this very clearly. In the case of Buddhism, the situation is also made more complicated because it is a missionary religion which has firmly established itself in many Eastern countries. Since it has no central authority to guide its development, such as one manageable book or an institution like the Papacy or the Patriarchate, its development has been far from uniform. The influence of various Indian centres was crucial as Buddhism spread over much of the Far East, but Buddhism practically died out in India in the Middle Ages, so the religion had to go its own way in the various countries where it found root, without reference to the land of its origin.

We shall look briefly at Southwold's study of village Buddhism in Sri Lanka.[7]

[7] M. Southwold, *Buddhism in Life* (Manchester: Manchester University Press, 1983).

Sri Lankan Buddhism belongs to the tradition of Theravada, which looks to the Pali Canon as its authoritative source of information about the Buddha's teaching. According to Western scholars, this is the body of authoritative teaching in Buddhism that approximates most closely to the original teaching of the Buddha himself. In the hands of the translators of the Pali Text Society under the leadership of Rhys Davids, 'a rather favourable picture of Ancient Buddhism emerged, strongly influenced by rationalist and Protestant ideas. Miraculous, ritual and devotional elements in the literature were viewed as later innovations.'[8] The austere and intellectualist picture of early Buddhism created by Western scholars was gladly embraced by Buddhist modernists, who were very happy to give back to the West a religion that had been first created by Western scholars and which could be fitted into the modern Western mind-set. But it is a far cry from the Buddhism of actual Buddhists.

To the Theravada Buddhists with whom Southwold lived in a village in Sri Lanka, what Western scholars had represented as the heart of the Pali Canon is hardly relevant at all. They do respect the scripture, but they do not study it and they know very little of its content. This is true even of their priests. Southwold got the impression that the *dhamma* (Pali word for *dharma*) was more of an authority than the Pali Canon. *Dhamma* is a notoriously difficult term to translate. M. Nyanatiloka lists the following definitions: the constitution (or nature of something), norm, law, doctrine, righteousness, quality, a thing, object of thought, phenomenon, the law leading to freedom discovered by the Buddha.[9] Buddhists who have been influenced by Western thought emphasize the doctrinal aspect. For them, Buddhism is a dogmatic system that explains the nature of existence and the way to real freedom. Therefore the first step in the direction of the light is to accept the authority of the Buddha's teaching.

A first impression of the Noble Eightfold Path, which is a popular way of presenting the *dhamma*, would seem to support this view. The first two aspects of the Path are Right View and Right Thought. The possession of these two qualities is Wisdom. Then come the three aspects of *sila* (precepts, moral instructions): Right Speech, Action and Livelihood. The last three aspects are Right Effort, Mindfulness and Concentration, which have to do with mental discipline. Scholars disagree about the precise nature of this Path, whether it is a series of steps up towards enlightenment or whether it is one path that is made up of various aspects like colours in the rainbow. Southwold is of the opinion that

---

[8] L. S. Cousins, 'Buddhism', in J. R. Hinnells (ed.), *A Handbook of Living Religions* (Harmondsworth: Penguin, 1984), p. 299.

[9] M. Nyanatiloka, *Buddhist Dictionary* (Colombo: Frewin, ²1956).

it is more like a set of stairs but that, practically, what would appear to be the first two steps have been moved from the bottom to the top of the stairs. Wisdom is way beyond the reach of ordinary Buddhists, but they can relate to the demands of *sila*. So the ordinary Buddhists of Sri Lanka see their faith as a matter of behaviour. Mental discipline and wisdom are left for the monks in their monasteries in the jungle.

L. S. Cousins points out that there is one aspect of Buddhist life that comes even before *sila*. This is *dana*, which means giving alms to the monks. This is seen as a particularly meritorious act which can prepare one for higher states in future lives. It also underlines the authority of the monastic order, the *Sangha*, in the Buddhist system as a whole.[10]

When Southwold asked what it meant to be a Buddhist, the answer he was given more often than not was 'not to harm any animals'. He believes that this reflects the Five Precepts, which is a very popular way of representing Buddhist morality. The first of the Five Precepts is the law of *ahimsa*, which means refraining from harming living things. Southwold believes that in referring to the first of the Five Precepts, the villagers were taking it as representative of them all. What they were saying really was that Buddhism was a matter of keeping certain precepts.

What, then, about the authority of the Buddha himself? Southwold found that some brought offerings to him not because they believed that he was a living reality able to help them, but because bringing offerings is good for their mental condition and contributes merit toward a better rebirth. This has been the Western scholarly understanding of offerings to the Buddha in the Theravada tradition. But in Southwold's study, many did believe that the Buddha is a living reality who is actually able to help them.

For the ordinary Buddhists of Sri Lanka, therefore, their religious authority is fundamentally the moral teaching of the Buddha. This teaching has become so ingrained that it is really equivalent to a traditional way of life. The Sangha, the Pali Canon and the Buddha himself have their place, but they are very much in the background. As in Indian villages, however, Sri Lankan villagers also believe in a whole range of supernatural beings and seek the help of a similar range of experts to deal with them.

CONCLUSION

This brief look at authority in the world's major religious traditions has shown how thinking about religious authority in the West has influenced the study of

[10] Cousins, *op. cit.*, p. 301.

AUTHORITY

religions generally. It led to the creation of pictures of religions such as Hinduism and Buddhism in the image of Western liberal Protestantism in particular. These pictures are now in the process of being dismantled and a more realistic picture is coming into view. One result of this move is that the more supernaturalistic aspects of the major Eastern traditions are being recognized. There are also signs that the 'modern' idea of the authority of experience, which has been dominant in Religious Studies, may give way to a more supernaturalistic view. This is certainly the emphasis of the New Age movement, the thinking of which is appearing in more and more unexpected places.

The time has come to look more closely at the way in which the authority possessed by the one who is studying religions relates to the ideas of authority of religious adherents. There is much need of a critical assessment of the view common in Religious Studies that either the person who is studying religions does not have a religious authority or that, as a student of religion, one must be free from the constraints of any religious authority. This dogma of objectivity has led to very distorted views of religion. Without such a critique, what confidence can we have that new views, which may be still operating on the same principles, are not just as distorted? There is a pressing need for a critique of the authoritative foundations of the modern study of religions. In the next chapter, we shall look in more detail at the experiential view of religious authority that from the beginning has been so central in the dominant idealistic stream of the modern study of religion.

— 11 —

MYSTICISM: *the PHILOSOPHIA PERENNIS?*

MYSTICISM *and* RELIGIOUS EXPERIENCE

'Religious experience' is one of the 'in phrases' of Religious Studies which has been repeated many times already in this volume. Ninian Smart's very popular book on the world's religious traditions is called *The Religious Experience of Mankind*. We have also looked at the theological tradition with its roots in Friedrich Schleiermacher that makes religious experience normative in understanding religion. Smart is one of the foremost representatives of that tradition. Wilfred Cantwell Smith is another, with his theory that religion can be divided into 'faith', which is the one ineffable experience at the root of all religions, and 'belief', the diversity of historically conditioned doctrines that have been formulated to express the essential experience of faith. In that tradition mysticism has been seen as the religious experience *par excellence* and a possible point at which different religions can be seen to coalesce. In discussing the need to formulate a theology of faith — as opposed to the various theologies of beliefs — Smith looks to the mystics as a model. 'As a matter of sober fact,' he said, 'in the past it is primarily the mystics who have produced religious statements that can at all legitimately or even approximately be called a theology of religions.'[1] This chapter will look at what is meant by 'religious experience' and examine the claim that all mystical experiences are the same and, therefore, prove the unity of religions.

Aldous Huxley and the philosophia perennis

The view that mysticism witnesses to the one religious experience at the root of

---

[1] W. Cantwell Smith, *Towards a World Theology: Faith and the Comparative History of Religion* (London: Westminster Press, 1981), p. 126.

all religions received a tremendous impetus from Aldous Huxley's account of his experiments with the hallucinogenic drug, mescaline. On a bright May morning in California in 1953, he took a dose of mescaline. The account of what happened as a result was given in *The Doors of Perception* (1954), with further analysis in *Heaven and Hell* (1956).[2] Before experimenting with mescaline, Huxley was already committed to what was called the *philosophia perennis*. R. C. Zaehner defines the *philosophia perennis* as

> . . . that philosophy which maintains that the ultimate truths about God and the universe cannot be directly expressed in words, that these truths are necessarily everywhere and always the same, and that, therefore, the revealed religions which so obviously differ on so many major points from one another, can only be relatively true, each revelation being accommodated to the needs of the time and place in which it was made and adapted to the degree of spiritual enlightenment of its recipients . . . All are rather facets of the same truth . . . The truth itself is that experienced by the mystics whose unity of thought and language is said to speak for itself.[3]

Huxley came to the conclusion that, under the influence of mescaline, he had mystical experiences. He states that, as he looked on a small glass vase containing three flowers:

> Words like Grace and transfiguration came into my mind . . . The Beatific Vision, *Sat Chit Ananda*, Being-Awareness-Bliss — for the first time I understood, not on the verbal level, not by inchoate hints or at a distance, but precisely and completely what those prodigious syllables referred to. And then I remembered a passage I had read in one of Suzuki's essays. 'What is the Dharma-body of the Buddha?' . . . Now it was all as clear as day . . . Of course the Dharma-body of the Buddha was the hedge at the bottom of the garden. At the same time, and no less obviously, it was these flowers, it was anything that I — or rather the blessed Not-I released for a moment from my throttling embrace — cared to look at.[4]

Central to Huxley's idea of mysticism was the experience of ego-lessness — the experience of losing a sense of individual identity in being merged into the one reality of the All. Looking at it from the physiological and chemical angle, he argued that there is something in normal consciousness that inhibits the

---

[2] Published together as a single volume by Penguin Books in 1959.

[3] R. C. Zaehner, *Mysticism Sacred and Profane* (London: OUP, 1957), p. 27.

[4] *The Doors of Perception & Heaven and Hell* (Harmondsworth: Penguin, 1959), p. 18.

realization of this All or what he calls Mind at Large. Normal consciousness is utilitarian and needs only that which is important for survival. But in religion and the arts there is a need for something more, for a wider and deeper experience of what is. Some have a natural ability to get round 'the reducing valve' of normal consciousness; others get round it by means of spiritual or religious exercises, or hypnosis or by using drugs. What happens when Mind at Large seeps past the reducing valve varies from person to person. Huxley says:

> [Some] discover a world of visionary beauty. To others again is revealed the glory, the infinite value and meaningfulness of naked existence . . . In the final stage of ego-lessness there is an 'obscure knowledge' that All is in all — that All is actually each.[5]

Experiencing the All left Huxley with a dilemma:

> This participation in the manifest glory of things left no room . . . for the ordinary, the necessary concerns of human existence, above all for concerns involving persons. For persons are selves and, in one respect at least, I was not a Not-self, simultaneously perceiving and being the Not-self of things around me. To the new-born Not-self, the behaviour, the appearance . . . of other selves . . . seemed . . . enormously irrelevant. Compelled by the investigator to analyse and report on what I was doing (and how I longed to be left alone with the Eternity in the flower, Infinity in four chair legs, and the Absolute in the folds of a pair of flannel trousers!), I realized that I was deliberately avoiding the eyes of those who were with me in the room . . . [They] belonged to the world from which . . . mescaline had delivered me — the world of selves, of time, . . . of over-valued words, and idolatrously worshipped notions.[6]

He resolves this dilemma by reminding himself that mystics have been good and kind people in 'this world' of limited consciousness, while witnessing to that other world of heightened consciousness which is far better. But note again that 'this world' is a world of 'over-valued *words*, and idolatrously worshipped *notions*'.

Huxley represents the more popular end of the appeal to mysticism as the route to grasping the essence of religion. He himself had moved from atheism to an intellectual acceptance of the theory associated with Vedantist mysticism in India. Vedanta is a monistic philosophy that denies the ultimate existence of everything except Brahman. It asserts that the essence of every individual — the Atman — is identical with Brahman. The aim of the philosophy is the experience

[5] *Ibid.*, p. 24.   [6] *Ibid.*, p. 31.

of this unity by means of various meditative techniques (yoga). However, Huxley had not had a mystical experience before he took mescaline. It is interesting that he explains his experience after taking mescaline in terms of the philosophy that he had espoused. His experience with mescaline also convinced him that the use of drugs in order to bring about 'mystical' states of consciousness should be advocated. In this he was able to point to the extensive use of drugs in ancient religious traditions and in the contemporary traditions of Native America and the indigenous peoples of Latin America. It is not surprising that he also became something of a prophet for the hippy movement of the 1960s, particularly for those, like Timothy Leary and Alan Watts, who saw the use of drugs like LSD as the route to a generally higher level of consciousness, with its attendant peace and well-being among humankind. It is not surprising, either, that his *philosophia perennis* remains as a potent concept in the contemporary New Age movement. Such an influential idea in the academic study of religion and in the popular arena deserves close scrutiny.

MYSTICAL EXPERIENCES DESCRIBED

There can be no doubt that when Huxley's experience under the influence of mescaline is put side by side with accounts of similar experiences, we are faced with something that needs explanation. One interesting point that needs to be made before quoting some accounts of mystical experiences is that there seems to be a sort of scholarly folklore of these accounts. Many of the accounts of such experiences outside the main religious traditions come from scholars such as William James or C. G. Jung. It would be interesting to find out whether people still have this type of experience now.

1. The *experience of Karl Joel*, which was first used by Jung:

> I lay on the seashore, the shining waters glittering in my dreamy eyes; at a great distance fluttered the soft breeze; throbbing, shimmering, stirring, lulling to sleep comes the wave beat to the shore — or to the ear? I know not. Distance and nearness become blurred into one; without and within glide into each other. Nearer and nearer, dearer and more homelike sounds the beating of the waves; now like the thundering pulse in my head it strikes, and now it beats over my soul, devours it, embraces it, while it itself at the same time floats out like the blue waste of waters. Yes, without and within are one. Glistening and foaming, flowing and fanning and roaring, the entire symphony of the stimuli experienced sounds in one tone, all thought

becomes one thought, which becomes one with feeling; the world exhales in the soul and the soul dissolves in the world.[7]

2. The *experience of Lord Tennyson*, first used by William James:

> I have never had any revelations through anaesthetics, but a kind of waking trance – this for lack of a better word – I have frequently had, quite up from boyhood, when I have been all alone. This has come upon me through repeating my name to myself silently, till all at once, as it were out of the intensity of the consciousness of individuality, individuality itself seems to dissolve and fade away into boundless being, and this not a confused state but the clearest, the surest of the surest, utterly beyond words – where death was an almost laughable impossibility – the loss of personality (if so it were) seeming no extinction, but the only true life. I am ashamed of my feeble description. Have I not said the state is utterly beyond words.[8]

3. The *experience of Dr Bucke*, which was also first used by William James:

> I was in a state of quiet, almost passive enjoyment, not actually thinking, but letting ideas, images, and emotions flow of themselves as it were, through my mind. All at once, without warning of any kind, I found myself wrapped in a flame-colored cloud. For an instant I thought of fire, an immense conflagration somewhere close by in that great city; the next, I knew that the fire was within myself. Directly afterward there came upon me an immense exultation, of immense joyousness accompanied or immediately followed by an intellectual illumination impossible to describe. Among other things, I did not merely come to believe, but I saw that the universe is not composed of dead matter, but is, on the contrary, a living Presence; I become conscious in myself of eternal life.[9]

4. The *initiation of Ramakrishna* into the way of Advaita (non-dualism), as described by himself:

> After initiating me, the Naked One[10] taught me many sayings expressing the philosophy of non-dualism. He told me to withdraw my mind from all

---

[7] From P. C. Almond, *Mystical Experience and Religious Doctrine* (Berlin: Mouton, 1982), p. 27.

[8] William James, *The Varieties of Religious Experience* (London: Longmans, 1907), p. 384 (also used by Zaehner and Almond).

[9] James, *ibid.*, p. 399 (loosely quoted by Wainwright).

[10] Referring to Tota Puri, Ramakrishna's vedantin guru who went naked.

creatures and objects, and plunge into contemplation of the Atman. But when I sat down to meditate in this way, I found that I couldn't make my mind go quite beyond name and form. I couldn't stop it working and make it still. My mind could stop being conscious of creatures and objects – that wasn't difficult; but whenever it did this, the Divine Mother [Kali] appeared before me in that form I knew so well – that form which is made of pure consciousness . . . I almost despaired. I opened my eyes and told the Naked One. 'No – it can't be done. I can't stop my mind from working. I can't plunge into the Atman'. The Naked One got excited. He scolded me severely . . . Then he looked around the hut till he found a bit of broken glass. And he stuck the point of it into my forehead, between the eyebrows. It was sharp as a needle! 'Fix the mind here,' he told me. So I sat down to meditate again, firmly determined. And as soon as Mother's form appeared, I took my knowledge of non-duality as if it was a sword in my hand, and I cut Mother in two with that sword of knowledge. As soon as I had done that, there was nothing relative left in the mind. I entered the place where there is no second – only the One.[11]

5. A *description of the aim of Zen Buddhism*, by D. T. Suzuki. It is interesting but not surprising that he refers to the Christian non-dualist mystic, Eckhart, in explaining Zen to a Western audience:

The time comes when traditional logic holds true no more, for we begin to feel contradictions and splits and consequently spiritual anguish . . . Evidently the repose we seemed to enjoy before we were awakened to the contradictions involved in our logic was not the real one . . . Where then is the ground of non-dualism on which the soul can be really and truthfully tranquil and blessed? To quote Eckhart again, 'Simple people conceive that we are to see God as if He stood on that side and we on this. It is not so; God and I are one in the act of my perceiving Him.' In his absolute oneness of things Zen establishes the foundation of its philosophy.[12]

6. An account of *the experience of Julian of Norwich*, the female Christian mystic:

Also in this He showed me a little thing, the quantity of an hazel-nut, in

---

[11] C. Isherwood, *Ramakrishna and his Disciples* (London: Shepheard-Walwyn, 1986), p. 118. Tota Puri left Ramakrishna in this deep state of meditation and had to go in to rouse him three days later!

[12] D. T. Suzuki, *Essays in Zen Buddhism*, vol. 1 (London: Rider & Co, 1949), pp. 269–270.

the palm of my hand; and it was as round as a ball. I looked thereupon with eye of my understanding, and thought: *What may this be?* And it was answered generally thus: *It is all that is made.* I marvelled how it might last, for me-thought it might suddenly have fallen to naught for little[ness]. And I was answered in my understanding: *It lasteth, and ever shall {last} for that God loveth it.* And so All-thing hath the Being by the love of God.

In this Little Thing I saw three properties. The first is that God made it, the second is that God loveth it, the third, that God keepeth it. But what is to me verily the Maker, the Keeper, and the Lover, – I cannot tell; for till I am Substantially oned to Him, I may never have full rest nor very bliss: that is to say, till I be so fastened to Him, that there is right nought that is made betwixt my God and me.[13]

7. *A description of Islamic mysticism* (sufism) by the great Muslim scholar and mystic al-Ghazali:

The mystics, after their ascent to the heavens of Reality, agree that they saw nothing in existence except God the One . . . Nothing was left to them but God. They became drunk with a drunkenness in which their reason collapsed . . . However, when their drunkenness abates and the sovereignty of their reason is restored . . . they know that this was not actual identity, but that it resembled identity as when lovers say at the height of their passion: 'I am he whom I desire and he whom I desire is I; We are two souls inhabiting one body.'

. . . There is a difference between saying, 'The wine *is* the wineglass', and saying, 'It is as if it were the wineglass'! Now, when this state prevails it is called 'naughting' (*fana*) with reference to the person who experiences it . . . This condition is metaphorically called identity with reference to the man who is immersed in it, but in the language of truth (it is called) union.[14]

These accounts of mystical experiences from sources which were not particularly religious, from Hinduism, Buddhism, Christianity and Islam, confirm at least that mystics use similar language when trying to describe their experiences. The extracts have also been carefully selected to show that the idea of 'unity' is very common in the language of the mystics. It is understandable that those who have been looking for some place where the diversity of religious

---

[13] Julian of Norwich, *Revelations of Divine Love*, in *Treasures from the Spiritual Classics* 3, compiled by Roger L. Roberts (Oxford: Mowbray, 1981), pp. 14–15.

[14] Almond, *op. cit.*, pp. 39–40 (used also by Zaehner).

traditions can be unified should claim to find it in mysticism. But for those who advocate this position, the existence of non-religious 'mystical' experiences, and in particular mystical experiences that are caused by taking drugs, is problematic. For those who see mysticism as the pinnacle of religious achievement to claim that such experiences can be had, simply by taking a dose of mescaline[15] or some other hallucinogenic drug, is outrageous. It is like someone buying all the right equipment and then making the effort to get to the top of Snowdon on foot, only to find a whole host of people completely unequipped for mountaineering having arrived there effortlessly by train! It was the sense of outrage at such a suggestion in Huxley's *Doors of Perception* that drove Zaehner to pen his *Mysticism, Sacred and Profane*.

R. C. Zaehner's view of mysticism

Zaehner defined mystical experiences as those 'in which sense perception and discursive thought are transcended in an immediate apperception of a unity or union which is apprehended as lying beyond and transcending the multiplicity of the world as we know it'. So he accepted that mystical experience is a category of experience that is amenable of a general definition. But just as there are many different breeds of the general category 'dog', there are different types of the general category 'mystical experience'. Zaehner argues that there are three main types: panenhenic, monistic and theistic.

The sort of experience described by Karl Joel, Dr Bucke, Tennyson and Suzuki would fit into the panenhenic category. They are experiences where time and space are transcended by heightening sensory experience. This can happen as a result of contemplating the natural world or by purposefully using some technique or other, such as repeating one's name as in Tennyson's case, to bring about a consciousness of timelessness. Huxley's experience would also belong to this type, which is not necessarily religious at all and is the lowest type of mysticism in Zaehner's estimation.

The experience described by Ramakrishna fits into the monistic category. Whereas Suzuki speaks of the oneness *of* all things, Ramakrishna speaks of the One *as opposed to* all things. When he achieved enlightenment, Ramakrishna had his eyes closed in order to block out the flow of sensory experience so that he could deal with the problem of diversity in the mind. Once the mind had also been emptied of all impressions the end was achieved – which was a very deep formless trance out of which he would never have emerged without someone else's intervention.

[15] Cited in Almond, *op. cit.*, p. 25.

Finally there is the theistic type, which is described in the quotations from Julian of Norwich and al-Ghazali. Here, despite the emphasis on unity, the distinction between the devotee and God/Allah is retained. Zaehner sees a huge gulf between those who believe that 'God' and what is essential to the individual are ultimately the same thing, and those who believe that, though he is so much greater and the root and cause of their existence, the ultimate experience is to stand in the presence of God. According to Zaehner, the theistic type, and the Christian in particular, is the highest type of mysticism.

Criticism of Zaehner

Zaehner's theories have been subjected to much criticism since they were first published. The distinction which he makes between panenhenic and monistic mysticism seems to be particularly problematic. As one would expect, in an area in which loud claims to scientific objectivity have been made, his grading of mystical experiences so that Christian mysticism appears at the top of the pile has also been severely criticized. What many of his critics did was try to refine or redefine his types of mysticism. W. T. Stace, for example, argued that there were only two main types, the extrovertive and the introvertive. Both types share five main characteristics: a sense of objectivity or reality; blessedness and peace; a feeling of the holy, sacred, or divine; paradoxicality; and ineffability. They differ in two areas. The extrovertive experience is a Unifying Vision, whereas the introvertive is an experience of Unitary Consciousness. The extrovertive is a more 'concrete apprehension of the One as an inner subjectivity, or life, in all things', while the introvertive experience is non-spatial and non-temporal.[16] Stace's extrovertive type corresponds to Zaehner's theistic, and his introvertive to the monistic-panenhenic type. Contrary to Zaehner, Stace argues that the introvertive (monistic) is the highest type of mystical experience.

Ninan Smart criticizes Zaehner because of his failure to give full weight to the interpretation of mystical or religious experiences by those who experience them and those who observe those who experience them. In the tradition of Schleiermacher, Smart gives precedence to the religious experience. On the basis of this assumption, he then attempts to understand the way in which religious experience has been expressed. He believes that there are two basic types of religious experience, the numinous and the mystical. The numinous experience, which he describes in Rudolph Otto's terms, is basically the same as Zaehner's theistic type. Smart limits mystical experience to Zaehner's monistic

---

[16] See Steven T. Katz, *Mysticism and Philosophical Analysis* (London: Sheldon Press, 1978), pp. 49–50.

type. Even though they are apparently opposites, the numinous and the mystical do sometimes mix, as in the Hindu *bhakti* or Christian and Muslim mysticism. This, according to Smart, is the best or highest form of religious experience. But, in the last analysis, everything depends on the way in which the core experience is interpreted. The extract which was quoted from al-Ghazali was an interpretation of monistic experience by an external observer, who favoured mysticism but who was also an orthodox Muslim theologian. (It should also be noted that al-Ghazali had himself followed the mystic way for ten years or so.) What we have is a description of a monistic experience which is interpreted in the context of Muslim theology. So the description of identity between Allah and his devotee could not possibly be literal but metaphorical. This type of interpretation leads Smart to conclude:

> If the monistic category includes heterogeneous high auto-interpretations, there is no guarantee that we should not place all mystics, including theists, in the same category; and explain their differences not in terms of radically different experiences, but in terms of varied auto-interpretations.[17]

A rejection of the dualism of the essence and form of mysticism

Fundamental to scholars like Zaehner, Stace and Smart, and to a more popular view such as Huxley's, is the conviction that the mystical experience itself and its interpretation are two different entities. The experience itself is one, but there is a diversity of descriptions or interpretations. These differ in the way they classify and grade the descriptions/interpretations, but they are all dualist in their analysis of the phenomenon of mysticism. However, this dualism is not without its critics. Even in the 1950s, G. G. Scholem, an expert on Jewish mysticism, was saying that there is no such thing as mysticism in general – there is only Hindu mysticism, Christian mysticism, Jewish mysticism, and so on. The foremost contemporary exponent of his view is Steven T. Katz. In his introduction to a volume entitled *Mysticism and Religious Tradition*, which he edited and which was published in 1983, he says that the dualist view of mysticism was still the 'regnant scholarly orthodoxy'. He says of this orthodoxy:

> At the exalted level of the mystic experience, the specificity of given religious systems is transcended in a sense of oneness which is common to all true mystics . . . Tragically, the mystic must descend from his height and then, caught up again in the fetters of tradition and history, space and

---

[17] 'Interpretation and Mystical Experience', *Religious Studies* 1 (1965), p. 83.

time, he must express what is truly inexpressible in the inadequate symbols and syntax of his particular faith community.[18]

Katz argues that, as far as our knowledge of mysticism is concerned, it is impossible to get beyond the symbols and syntax of the mystic's faith community. This stands, even though the mystics themselves claim that their experience is ineffable and ultimately inexpressible, so that when they talk about it they don't really mean what they say or say what they mean. This would seem to support the dualist position. But, says Katz:

> If the mystic does not mean what he says and his words have *no* literal meaning whatsoever, then not only is it impossible to establish my pluralistic view, but it is also impossible to establish any view whatsoever. If none of the mystics' utterances carry any literal meaning then they cannot serve as the *data* for any position . . . and certainly not the view that all mystical experiences are the same, or reducible to a small class of phenomenological categories.[19]

So, if we take what the mystics say about their experiences, the only conclusion we can come to is that there are different mysticisms, not different types of mysticism.

In trying to describe the essence of mystical experience, 'dualists' like Stace have used general terms like 'the sense of objectivity or reality', 'feeling of the holy, sacred or divine', and so on. But to say, for example, that all mystics have an experience of ultimate Reality says nothing about the essence of mysticism. When we look at what the mystics themselves say about the ultimate Reality, we come up against phrases like Henry Suso's 'intoxication with the immeasurable abundance of the Divine House . . . entirely lost in God [that is, the God of Christianity]'; the Hindu Upanishad's '*sat* [what is] . . . is expressed in the word *satyam*, the Real. It comprises this whole universe: You are this whole universe'; and the Buddhist's 'dimension of nothingness'. An indefinite term like 'reality' can be used to describe something that is common to mysticism but it says so little that it is hardly worth the bother. What is meant by 'Reality' in mysticism obviously differs from one religious tradition to another. The Christian 'abundance of the Divine House', the Hindu 'You are

---

[18] Steven T. Katz (ed.), *Mysticism and Religious Traditions* (New York: OUP, 1983), Editor's Introduction.

[19] 'Language, Epistemology, and Mysticism', in *Mysticism and Philosophical Analysis*, p. 40.

SOME BASIC ISSUES

this whole universe', and the Buddhist 'dimension of nothingness' are obviously not talking about the same reality.

Those who have looked to the mystics for a key to the unity of religions see them as the athletes of the spirit, as those who are at the cutting-edge, pushing religion beyond the boundaries of mere 'belief' to the ineffable reality of 'faith'. Katz examines this claim with particular reference to Christianity in his chapter on 'The "Conservative" Character of Mysticism'. Interestingly, if they were supposed to be so radical, hardly any of the great Christian mystics have been branded as heretics, let alone suffered martyrdom at the hands of church authorities.

> Augustine, Francis of Assisi, Bernard, Suso, Tauler, Thomas à Kempis, Teresa, John of the Cross, all, though not free of tension, were in holy orders, lived out their lives in regularised Christian ways, continued all their life to participate in Christian ritual and sacramental activity, were not permanently excommunicated, did not die outside the church.[20]

It is true that Eckhart came into conflict with the church authorities and was excommunicated after his death. But even his posthumous excommunication was only temporary.

The reason why these mystics were not rejected was that their view of the nature of existence, their ontology, was fundamentally Christian. They believed that the world is the creation or emanation of a personal God; that humans, who are also his creations, are alienated from him because of their original sin; that God has provided a means for overcoming this alienation through the mediation of his incarnate Son, the Christ, the second person of the Trinity. The soul can respond to God's mediation because

> . . . it is created by the Divine being, incorporates the Divine, or is (depending on the technicalities of the different thinkers) Divine in itself. However, even the soul's divine origin is no guarantee of salvation unless God in his grace awakens the soul from its sensual, this-worldly, imprisonment and turns it towards its maker and master.[21]

This is not to deny that the 'image' type of Christian mysticism associated with the likes of Eckhart was not heavily influenced by the neo-Platonist mysticism of Plotinus (205–270 CE).[22] What Katz emphasizes is that even these influences were christianized and absorbed into a Christian ontological framework. Those who

---

[20] *Mysticism and Religious Traditions*, p. 33.

[21] *Ibid.*

[22] Plotinus was the founder of the neo-Platonist school of philosophy. He was a

view their Christianity in the light of the Reformation may question whether or not the medieval mystics were true representatives of the Christian tradition, but Katz is able to prove that, within their own context, they did not step outside their Christian parameters. They were *Christian* mystics. So what they experienced was not the same as what was or is experienced by Buddhist mystics, Muslim mystics or any other mystics. There is no such thing as the *philosophia perennis*.

the MYSTICAL ILLUSION

It has been a commonplace of the Western understanding of the Hindu tradition that it is essentially a mystical tradition, and Indian scholars like Radhakrishnan have been more than happy to encourage this belief. The story begins in the Vedic era, and reaches its apex in the enigmatic and 'mystical' verses of the tenth book of the Rig Veda. This theme is developed in the Upanishads, where the Brahman-Atman doctrine appears, and further developed by great mystics like Samkara. *Bhakti* then comes along to put a more personal and theistic gloss on Samkara's tradition of Advaita (non-dualism). Hinduism can then be sold to the West as a mystical tradition, which can include theistic devotion but which goes beyond it to the fulfilment of all religion in the experience of non-dualism. However, the reality of Indian religion is encapsulated in the word 'caste', not 'mysticism', but our Western understanding is so conditioned by the 'mystic illusion' that students from very respectable institutions that teach Hinduism can visit India and not see the significance of caste at all.

H. H. Penner shows how significant caste is to the right understanding of the Hindu mystical tradition in the chapter entitled 'The Mystical Illusion' in *Mysticism and Religious Traditions*. Following Katz, Penner emphasizes the fact that a right understanding of mysticism is dependent on its context. In the case of Indian mysticism, he claims that it is the 'distorted understanding of yoga and Buddhism as semantically independent of the world of caste which perceives yoga or Buddhism as the paradigm of the religious life in India'.[23] Penner agrees with L. Dumont[24] that caste is a religious system based on a 'complementary ritual relation between the pure and the impure'.[25] So within the caste system

---

contemporary of Origen at Alexandria but later moved to Rome. For a brief and helpful outline of his ideas and influence, see article on 'Platonism', in *New Dictionary of Theology*, ed. S. B. Ferguson and D. F. Wright (Leicester: IVP, 1988), pp. 517–519.

[23] Penner, in Katz (ed.), *Mysticism and Religious Traditions*, p. 102.

[24] See L. Dumont, *Homo Hierarchicus* (London: Paladin, 1972).

[25] Penner, in Katz (ed.), *op. cit.*, p. 105.

SOME BASIC ISSUES

there is a hierarchy dependent on the relative purity or impurity of its members. The most pure are the brahmins, and the most impure the unclean Sudras. The outcastes are neither pure nor impure because they are outside the system altogether. Within the system everyone is subject to *karma*. *Karma* means 'works', so to be subject to *karma* is to be subject to action and its consequences. How everyone should act is determined by *dharma*, which is the law or principle conditioning the life of every stratum in the system. The central responsibility of the higher castes, the twice-born, is threefold. They are obliged, firstly, to pay their debt to the sages by learning the sacred texts, the Vedas; secondly, they must pay their debt to the gods by performing *puja* (worship); and, thirdly, they must pay their debts to the ancestors by establishing a household. In this, marriage is central in that it is through marriage that sons are born to learn the Vedas and perform *puja*. Living within this system has been, and still is, the lot of the overwhelming majority of Hindus.

Since adopting the mystic path means stepping outside the caste system, Penner is right to emphasize that the significance of Indian mysticism can be understood only in relation to caste. Just a glance at the Yoga Sutra of Patanjali, or the Noble Eightfold Path of the Buddha, clearly illustrates this point. The first branch or limb of Patanjali's ascetic way is abstention. This means non-violence, speaking the truth, not stealing, chastity and eschewing all possessions. To do this necessarily involves the renunciation of caste. How could a member of the *kshatriya*, which is the warrior/ruler caste, accept non-violence without breaking caste? Most significant is the adoption of chastity or celibacy. This cuts across the fundamental caste duty of marrying in order to establish a household, which is fundamental to the whole system. It is not surprising that in the Law of Manu the path of the renouncer is seen as something that should be considered in later life when all three debts have been paid. So, ideally, it is after observing the *dharma* of one's caste in the jurisdiction of *karma* that one can contemplate rejecting *karma* and become an outcast of the system in the pursuit of the non-karmic aim of liberation (*moksha*). The difference between Buddhism and Hinduism at this point is that the Buddha invited anyone at any time to renounce caste in the search for enlightenment. In the light of his analysis, Penner is justified in coming to the conclusion that 'the meaning of India's ascetic tradition must be discovered in the totality of the system. The significance of Indian mysticism is its relation to caste.'[26] The paradigm of religious life in India is devoted observation of caste duty. Asceticism, yoga, or the pursuit of mystical realization, is a path that is trodden by only a few. Those

[26] *Ibid.*, p. 113.

MYSTICISM: THE PHILOSOPHIA PERENNIS?

who tread it are highly respected and, as mendicants, depend on the system that they have forsaken, but it is the system itself that gives them their significance.

It may be a surprise for some to learn that India is not full of mystics and that mysticism is not at the heart of the Indian way. But this helps to place mysticism in its right place in the world's religious traditions. Buddhism is probably mystical at heart, but 'Buddhist' countries are as unmystical as any other. In all the other major religious traditions, mysticism is very much a peripheral activity. If the way of the mystics is *the* unifying way of religion, then precious few have ever walked it. It seems strange, therefore, that modern scholars should have looked to mysticism as evidence that all religions are ultimately concerned with the same divine reality. If that is the case, the overwhelming majority of the adherents of all the world's religious traditions have had nothing to do with divine reality because they have had nothing to do with mysticism. It is possible that modern scholars think that since mysticism can be found in all the major religious traditions, this somehow sanctifies the tradition as a whole. If the tradition can be expressed in a mystical way, the whole tradition must be in touch with the divine reality and therefore all its adherents are saved. Yet we have seen that this is not what actually happens. Mysticism does not exist independently of the tradition in which it occurs. There may be some similarity in the language used by mystics, but that does not point to the reality of an experience of divine reality that can be separated from a Christian, Buddhist, *etc.*, experience. The existence of mysticism does not take us, in the last analysis, beyond the existence of a series of religious traditions which make different truth claims. The mystics, like every other adherent of a religious tradition, belong to a specific tradition which marks them out as not belonging to other religious traditions.

It has been argued that what is called the constructivist view of mysticism, held by Katz, Penner and others, does not do justice to the similarities between the mystics.[27] But historical diffusion can explain similarities more adequately than the theory that mystical experiences are similar because they are experiences of the same reality. In the case of the Semitic traditions of Judaism, Christianity and Islam, mysticism can be traced primarily to the influence of neo-Platonist philosophy, and in the case of Islam to some direct Indian influences as well. It is not impossible, either, that Platonism was influenced by Indian thought. The mysticisms of the Semitic traditions are similar in some ways because they have the same intellectual roots. The mysticisms of these traditions are really a case of

[27] *E.g.* Michael Stoeber, 'Constructivist Epistemologies of Mysticism: A Critique and a Revision', *Religious Studies* 28 (1992), p. 108.

incorporating external influences into the life of the religions. The similarities between Eastern mysticisms are understandable, because of the central influence of Indian thought particularly through the Buddha.

John Hick and the Real

John Hick, though he accepts Katz's argument, still believes that mystical experiences in the various religious traditions are experiences of the same 'Real', which is his term for the one ultimate reality that he believes is at the root of all religions.[28] For Hick, the result of various encounters with the one Real, which look like a series of competing truth claims, is actually a series of different phenomenal descriptions shaped by the character and context of those who did the encountering. Hick uses Kantian terms in order to explain his thinking on this point. He postulates 'a divine noumenon which becomes the object of human phenomenal experience in a variety of forms, the difference between these different divine phenomena being due to the varying human contributions to these different awarenesses of the divine'.[29] Again, he claims that 'even in the profoundest unitive mysticism the mind operates with culturally specific concepts and that what is experienced is accordingly a manifestation of the Real rather than the postulated real *an sich*'.[30] If Hick is right, it is fair to ask what this tells us about the Real.

Like Cantwell Smith, Hick drives a very deep wedge between God/the Real and any experience of it. But if all we can know are historically conditioned descriptions of the Real, what are we to do with the contradictions in the descriptions? It seems difficult to relate to a Real, which by definition is superior to us but which leaves us in such confusion as to what it is or wants of us. The confusion is our responsibility as human beings in Hick's scheme, because contradictions arise when experience of the Real is filtered through our minds and historical context. But that still leaves us with an Ultimate Reality that is helpless in the face of human history. In the last analysis, there seems to be little difference between Hick and Ludwig Feuerbach, who argued that all 'gods' are merely the creation of the human mind, since any claim to knowledge of the Real is a human creation.

[28] See John Hick, *An Interpretation of Religion* (London: Macmillan, 1989), pp. 170–171 n. 17, and pp. 294–295.

[29] H. Coward and T. Penelhum (eds.), *Mystics and Scholars* (Calgary Conference on Mysticism, 1976), p. 61.

[30] *An Interpretation of Religion*, p. 295.

DRUG-INDUCED *and* OTHER 'MYSTICAL' EXPERIENCES

We shall return to Huxley and his experiment with mescaline before we take our leave of mysticism. Huxley believed that genuine mystical experiences could result from taking hallucinogenic drugs. His ideas led to the formation of religious movements that used drugs to bring about mystical states. This type of experimentation soon fell foul of the law in Western countries. But before this happened, a number of careful studies were made to look into the correlation between taking hallucinogenic drugs and mystical experiences. According to William Wainwright, the most significant studies were 'conducted by Walter N. Pahnke, Walter H. Clark, and Jean Houston and R. E. L. Masters'.[31]

Pahnke experimented with twenty students in a Christian theological college. He gave psilocybin to ten of them, and a placebo to the other ten, who were used as a control group. Nine of the ten who had the drug claimed to have received a mystical experience. In their descriptions of it there was a heavy bias in the direction of the type of introvertive experience as defined by Stace. In religious terms, their experience was much more monistic than theistic.

Clark administered LSD daily to eight normal subjects over a period of sixteen days. Ten months later, they filled in a questionnaire to test whether or not what they experienced under the influence of the drug could be classed as mystical experiences. Three out of the eight scored very highly on the scale that indicated a mystical type of experience.

Houston and Masters experimented with 206 subjects. They distinguished between a mystical experience and an authentic religious experience. Using Stace's typology, almost half of their subjects had extrovertive experience, but

> . . . these were not regarded as authentically religious because they involved no perception of God or Being or Ultimate Reality . . . Only eleven were judged to have had authentically religious experiences . . . It was concluded that six had had introvertive experiences. It is significant that all six were persons who 'have in the course of their lives either actively sought the mystical experience in meditation and other spiritual disciplines or have for many years demonstrated considerable interest in integral levels of consciousness'.[32]

Wainwright's conclusion on these studies is that drugs can sometimes induce

---

[31] William Wainwright, *Mysticism* (Madison, WI: University of Wisconsin Press, 1982), p. 55. A full analysis of the various studies follows on pp. 55–69.
[32] *Ibid.*, p. 61.

introvertive mystical experiences, particularly if those who take them are inclined in that direction in the first place. Since he was well into the theory of Eastern religion and the *philosophia perennis* before he took mescaline, it is not surprising that Huxley had experiences which he interpreted by means of his prior philosophy. It is particularly interesting that drugs do not seem to produce extrovertive or theistic experiences. They do not seem to lead those who take them to an experience of the sort of God that one finds in the Christian Bible. This may point to what actually happens when drugs are taken. There can be no question that as human beings we are part of the material world, whatever religious belief we espouse. Even the Bible teaches quite clearly that we have been made from the earth, from the same material as everything else. It may be that under certain conditions we can have an experience of this fact. What is experienced in introvertive unitive mysticism may be simply the fact that we are physiologically made from the same matter as everything else. This would certainly explain why theistic experiences do not seem to occur under the influence of drugs.

The extreme asceticism of the mystics also explains to a great extent why they have their strange experiences. Food deprivation and painful practices like flagellation can bring about physiological changes that make the mind more susceptible to visions and so on. The same is true of ecstatic practice such as the dance of the whirling dervishes. The fact that drugs can lead to mystical experience is proof that modifying the physiological processes of the brain does create strange and unusual experiences. Even the experiences of those who are mentally ill are sometimes similar to mystical experiences. This does not mean that we have to attribute all mystical experiences to physiological tampering of some form or other. But it does suggest that the mystical experience that cannot be explained in physiological terms may be the experience of a personal God which does not come as the result of ascetic or ecstatic practice.

– 12 –

GOD *and* BRAHMAN: *the* REAL?

INTRODUCTION

The question of authority presupposes the existence of Something or Someone that transcends the limits of our mundane existence and is able to command respect and obedience. 'Mysticism' is concerned with the possibility of being united in some way or other with this Someone or Something. In this chapter we shall focus on this Something or Someone. What will be examined is the view already touched upon in the previous chapter that there is ultimately only one Something or Someone that is experienced in the various religions of the world. This will be done by concentrating on how Christians and Hindus talk about their Ultimate.

For those who live in countries whose history has been very much shaped by Christianity, what is meant by the word 'God' is determined by the Christian tradition. Everything that we need to know about God can be found within the Christian tradition, and many theologians have spent their whole lives thinking about the implications of this knowledge without any reference to any other religious traditions. But from its earliest days there have been those in the Christian tradition who have been conscious of the wealth of other religious traditions. This was particularly true of the Greek philosophical tradition which has contributed so much to the shaping of Christian doctrine. Over the last two centuries the wealth of the great religious traditions of the East has been discovered. Theologians and those who are concerned with understanding religion are now in the process of coming to terms with this relatively new material. Questions are being asked about the relationship between the image of the Ultimate in Christianity and that in other major traditions. The two views of this relationship that have been dominant in Religious Studies are 'inclusivism' and 'pluralism'.

INCLUSIVISM

Inclusivism is the belief that it is the same 'God' that is worshipped in all the religions, but that the fullest knowledge of him is to be found in the Christian tradition. Christianity fulfils the vague longings that are expressed in other religions. This idea has an ancient pedigree in the Christian tradition. For example, Justin Martyr, a second-century CE apologist of the Christian faith, argued that Jesus, who is described as the eternal Word (*logos*) in John's Gospel, fulfils the Greek philosophical idea of the logos.[1] Justin's idea was then developed by the Alexandrians Clement (*c.* 150–*c.* 215) and Origen (*c.* 185–*c.* 254). Max Müller enthusiastically grasped this Alexandrian approach in developing his inclusivist theory in the nineteenth century.[2] E. O. James and R. C. Zaehner carried the inclusivist banner in Religious Studies well into the twentieth century.

On the whole, the advocates of this position have been theologians, churchmen and the occasional missionary such as J. N. Farquhar, who ended his days as Professor of Comparative Religion (1923–29) at Manchester. Farquhar believed that the theory of fulfilment 'satisfied the science of religion to the uttermost, while conserving the supremacy of Christ'.[3] Some of the most prominent advocates of this view in the second half of the twentieth century have been Roman Catholic theologians. Karl Rahner (1904–84) is a good example. His starting-point was despair at the lack of success of Christian missionary activity in the East. He found it difficult to accept that millions of people in the East have lived and died without knowledge of Christ or his church and therefore without salvation. Since he was concerned to remain faithful to the dogma that there is no salvation outside the church, he invented the idea of 'anonymous Christians'.[4] He argued that there are different levels of explicitness among those who belong to the church. This is true even among those who have been baptized: some take their baptism very seriously, while others do not. Rahner held that this lack of explicitness can be taken beyond baptism, and that there are some people who really belong to the church even though they have never heard of it. These are the 'anonymous Christians', who belong to the church without knowing it.

---

[1] *A New Eusebius*, ed. J. Stevenson (London: SPCK, 1974), pp. 63f.

[2] See Max Müller, *Theosophy or Psychological Religion* (London: Longmans, 1893).

[3] Quoted in E. J. Sharpe, *Comparative Religion: A History* (London: Duckworth, 1975), p. 153.

[4] See Karl Rahner, *Theological Investigations*, vol. 16 (London: Darton, Longman & Todd, 1974), pp. 390–398.

If this is the case, then the 'anonymous Christian' must have come into contact with the essence of what it means to be Christian even though he or she has never heard of Christ. The way in which Rahner describes this type of Christian experience of God is necessarily abstract, but the sum of it seems to be a view of the meaning of the incarnation that is 'worked out in moral action, a view that is very reminiscent of the nineteenth-century idealists.[5]

Hans Küng (1928–), another Catholic theologian who, unlike Rahner, has had his official recognition as a church lecturer withdrawn, goes a step further. He says that we must accept that salvation is possible outside of the church. The world religions are the ordinary way of salvation for most people, while Christianity is an extraordinary way. But 'if Christian theology today asserts that all men – even in the world religions – can be saved, this certainly does not mean that all religions are equally true'.[6] If salvation is not really an issue, it is possible to have a relatively friendly dialogue about what is true or not, particularly since truth means the right principles of behaviour as much as anything else. So cannibalism or the Hindu caste system can be condemned from the vantage-point of the higher truth that has been manifested in the Christian tradition. Obviously there is no need for anyone to convert from one religion to another. The role of Christians from their higher vantage-point is to help the adherents of other religions to be the best adherents they can possibly be within the context of their own religion. Küng does not seem to have realized that to reject caste in the Hindu context is really to put an axe to the very root of the religion.

Inclusivism is not confined to Christian thinkers. Radhakrishnan is an example of a Hindu inclusivist. 'All religions', he states, 'spring from the sacred soil of the human mind and are quickened by the same spirit. The different systems are tentative adjustments, more or less satisfactory to spiritual reality.'[7] Of course, as a Hindu inclusivist, Radhakrishnan believed that religion reached its fulfilment in the Advaita Vedanta of the Hindu tradition. He argued that,

---

[5] 'If one takes it seriously that God has become man, then . . . man is that which happens when God expresses and divests himself. Man is accordingly in the most basic definition that which God becomes if he sets out to show himself in the region of the extra-divine.' 'Prior to the explicitness of ecclesiastical faith this acceptance can be present in an implicit form whereby a person undertakes and lives the duty of each day in the quiet sincerity of patience, in devotion to his material duties and the demands made upon him by persons in his care' (Rahner, *op. cit.*, pp. 393, 394).

[6] Hans Küng, *On Being a Christian* (London: Collins, 1977), p. 104.

[7] Quoted in P. C. Almond, *Mystical Experience and Religious Doctrine* (Berlin: Mouton, 1982), p. 12.

since this type of monism can incorporate all other types of belief as steps up to the final experience of impersonal Unity, it must be the crown of all religions. What Christians worship as 'God' is only one stage in the realization of the true nature of the Ultimate. The Hindus who follow the way of *bhakti*, with its devotion to a whole range of personal gods, operate on the same level as Christianity. But this knowledge and understanding of 'god' is seen to be provisional when one experiences the impersonal Ultimate.

PLURALISM

Pluralism takes matters a step further than inclusivism and states that all religions are equally valid ways to 'God'. Religions are like board games. There is a great variety of games. They look different and the activities that the players have to perform differ, but the aim is the same – that one person complete the task demanded by the game before anyone else. So it is with religions, according to the pluralist. Religions differ, have different rules and an amazing range of different activities, but their goal is the same. There is only one transcendent reference point.

John Hick (1922–) is probably the most famous contemporary advocate of this view. He calls for a Copernican revolution in theology. Just as everyone eventually had to accept that the earth moves around the sun, Hick believes that it is time for Christians to accept that God and not Christianity is the centre of the universe of religions.[8] What this means is that every religious person of whatever religion is really reaching out to the same 'God'. As the title of one of Hick's books proclaims, 'God has many names'. He bases his belief on the similarity between the ideas about 'God' expressed in the worship of different religious groups in Birmingham – Christians, Jews, Muslims, Sikhs and Hindus. He can see only three possible explanations of their worship: that they are all worshipping different 'gods' that really exist; that one group is worshipping the true God while the others worship a creation of their own imagination; or that they are all worshipping the same God under different names. He thinks that there is enough similarity in the language used by the various groups to justify accepting the third alternative, and he states:

> There is but one God, who is maker and lord of all; that in his fullness and richness of being he exceeds all our human attempts to grasp him in thought; and that the devout in the various great world religions are in fact

---

[8] John Hick, *God Has Many Names* (London: Macmillan, 1980), p. 52.

worshipping that one God, but through different, overlapping concepts or mental icons of him.[9]

In later works Hick has abandoned the use of the term 'God' in favour of 'the Real' to describe the one transcendent reference of all religions.

Hick's thesis has been strongly supported and opposed, but it may help to clarify the issues by focusing on the Christian and Vedantist views of Ultimate reality.

the GOD *of* CHRISTIANITY

What is the Christian concept or mental icon of God? Since we have to start somewhere, we can say that God is infinite and personal. To say that God is personal leads us immediately to the persons of the Trinity, whereas the idea of infinity may fit more happily with the concept of unity. Christians believe that there is one God in three persons: Father, Son and Holy Spirit. Traditional theology usually begins with the divine unity in attempting to describe God before going on to describe the three persons. This is reasonable, because all the essential attributes of divinity belong to the three persons individually. In his essence, God is completely independent and self-sufficient, unchangeable, eternal and present everywhere. There can be only one divine being in this sense, so everything else derives its existence from him.

In saying this, Christians do not assert that God and everything that is are of the same essence. God did not emanate[10] the physical world out of his own being but created it out of nothing. God differs from his world or universe because he is incorporeal. God is spirit. But he is not the only spiritual being. Angels and humans are also spiritual beings, created with the very special ability of spiritual communication with their Maker. As creator, God is the sovereign Lord of all that he has made. He knows everything about it and is a good and just ruler. These are just a few terms that Christian thinkers have used to describe the God they believe is revealed in the Bible. There is one other term which is central to the biblical picture of God and that is the term 'holy'. Though he was not specifically concerned with explaining the biblical idea of holiness, Rudolph

---

[9] *Ibid.*, p. 48.

[10] It is traditional or orthodox theology that is being reviewed here. As stated above (see p. 206), some Christian mystics leaned in the direction of emanationism. This was one of the reasons why they were suspected of heresy. Other elements of their theology made it possible for them to remain in the Christian fold.

SOME BASIC ISSUES

Otto's *The Idea of the Holy*[11] is a classical study of the subject. As Otto explains, to say that God is holy means that God is a transcendent mystery that is experienced as both awesome and attractive. For the impure, purity is frightening but also desirable.

In the Christian tradition, all the terms used to describe God so far cannot be divorced from the idea of the Trinity. The statement that there is one God subsisting in three persons does not occur in the Bible, but the fact that it ascribes divine attributes to the Father, the Son and the Spirit makes it inevitable that any attempt to describe what the Bible says about God will have to come to this sort of conclusion. So what was said about the essence of God is true of God as Father, Son and Holy Spirit. The Father is the source, the Son is the mediator and the Spirit is the executor of everything. This is the pattern of all God's dealings with his creation. We see this when God reveals himself to humankind. We can come to the Father, the source of everything, through the Son as a result of the Spirit's work in awakening us to the truth of the Son's mediatorial death on our behalf.

When he visited Athens, the apostle Paul, who was the most significant figure in the early expansion of Christianity, was taken before the Council of the Areopagus to explain his Christian message.[12] Though not as powerful as it had been, this Council still had the right to adjudicate on matters of morals and religion in Athens. During his address Paul declared that humans live and move and have their being in God. In saying this he did not mean that humans are made of the same substance as God, but that our existence is dependent on the will and power of God. It is God who sustains our existence from moment to moment. Then Paul went on to talk about a relationship with God, not only on the basis of our creation by him but also on the basis of grace and forgiveness that are possible through the death and resurrection of Jesus Christ. The way Paul expresses this is by saying that God is giving human beings an opportunity to be reconciled to him before he comes to judge the world through his Son Jesus Christ. A personal-moral relationship between God and his human creatures is the climax of God's dealings with creation.

The New Testament also speaks, particularly in John's writings, of God indwelling those who respond to the call of Jesus Christ. This does not mean that what is essentially human is absorbed into the infinite being of God. The heart of Christian experience is getting to know the person of Jesus. It is more than knowing about Jesus, though it must include that type of knowledge. It is a

[11] Oxford: OUP, 1923.

[12] The account of Paul's visit is found in Acts chapter 17 in the New Testament.

spiritual understanding, created by the Holy Spirit, which enables Christians to experience Jesus as a real and living person. It is an experience of the holy in that Jesus is a revelation transcending understanding, who causes a profound sense of unworthiness but who at the same time is the source of forgiveness. Christian experience is not about the undermining of the essential difference between the human and the divine nature. Even most of the Christian mystics have claimed that their climactic experiences have been filled with the person of Jesus. As Charles Hodge put it, 'We should remember that we lose God when we lose our confidence in saying You! to Him, with the assurance of being heard and helped.'[13]

This very brief outline of the Christian concept of God is traditional and/or conservative. In some respects it is shaped by one particular stream in the history of Christianity. However, it does represent substantially what Christians say that they believe about God even today. This traditional, theological and conceptual framework has been under severe pressure from the forces of modernity in the West since the eighteenth century. Remarkably it has survived and is very vibrant still, particularly in the Third World. Even in the West there has been a significant swing back to traditional and conservative thinking in the last twenty-five years.

The point that is being made here is simply a matter of fact. Liberal theologians, and many conservative theologians as well, would be very unhappy with an argument that a particular doctrine must be true because it has been traditionally held by the majority of Christians. But the historian of religions, in attempting to describe to an outsider what Christians believe, is justified in saying that most Christians have traditionally held to a particular belief. Liberal theologians may have questioned or rejected that belief, and their questioning or rejection must be taken very seriously in a theological context. But, in the historical context, liberal theology is a movement that emerged in Western European Protestantism in the nineteenth century, which eventually had some influence on the Roman Catholic and Orthodox traditions as well. The Protestant theological establishment in the West is still dominated by 'liberalism', and its influence has spread to many Protestant establishments in other parts of the world as well. But the fact that 'liberalism' sets the agenda in Western theology does not mean that liberal views of God are generally held even by Protestant church leaders and their congregations. What is being highlighted here is the tension between the theory and the actuality of religion. This is clearly illustrated again as we turn to the Hindu tradition.

[13] Charles Hodge, *Systematic Theology*, vol. 1 (London: James Clarke, 1960), p. 374.

GOD *in* HINDUISM

In turning to look at a Hindu view of 'God', we are immediately caught in a dilemma which we have already encountered more than once. What Hindu view of 'God' do we opt for? If we take the religion of most Indians seriously, we will have to accept that most Hindus are frankly polytheistic. They really do believe in a multiplicity of gods. Some more educated people would argue that this multiplicity is ultimately only apparent, and that in the last analysis there is only one God. Some would go even further than that and say that ultimately there is only one Reality — which is the idea that we want to examine in due course in this chapter. But this is very remote from the experience of the overwhelming majority of Hindus. They offer prayers to Ganesh when they go on a journey or embark on a new business venture, because they really believe that there is such a being as Ganesh who is interested in what they want to do. One has met educated middle-class Indians worshipping the huge statue — it would probably be quite legitimate to use the term 'idol' in this context — of Nandi the bull in the ancient Bull Temple of Bangalore, in the hope of having children. They really believe that Nandi is a supernatural being who is able to influence their fertility. Then there was the highly educated builder-engineer who secured an important contract worth millions of rupees and who attributed his success to his pilgrimage to the temple of a little-known deity in the forests of south India. He really believed that his handsome gift to the temple of this deity had caused the god to influence the situation in his favour. Polytheism is unquestionably a pervasive religious reality in India.

The Brahman of the Upanishads

As we have already seen, this polytheism exists within a class system that is fundamentally religious. But Hindus also recognize a way of renunciation. This way not only renounces the social system but also the way of polytheism. It takes the few who tread it beyond belief in the gods and on to monism or a type of monotheism. Indian monism was first taught in that part of the sacred literature called the 'Upanishads'. Even though there is no textual evidence whatever, scholars believe that the Upanishads had been composed by 500 BCE. It is the religious ideas and practices that have their roots in this literature which Western scholars have looked to as representing half the essence of Hinduism. The other half is found in the *bhakti* tradition, which will be considered later in this chapter.

One very obvious characteristic of the Upanishads, which are often difficult and obscure, is the tendency to merge gods into each other. The religious context of the literature is a polytheism which is expressed in a complex sacrificial ritual. So the gods, sacrifices and the priests who perform the sacrifices are very much in evidence. Many gods are worshipped by means of sacrifice, but they are not self-subsisting beings. In the last analysis they are different manifestations of something greater, the 'god' behind the gods, the One or the All. The name which is given to this One or All in the Upanishads is Brahman. Its original meaning was the sound of the sacred chant which the priests used in the sacrifice, so there is a powerful ritual link in the concept as well as a strong justification for the superiority of the priestly class in the Indian hierarchy. This Brahman is the ultimate reality which is beyond description. A favourite term for it in the Upanishads is *tyat*, which means 'that', 'just that'.

The following quotation from the *Brihadaranyaka Upanishad* is a good illustration of the tendency to merge the gods. In Book 3 chapter 9, Vidagdha Sakalya is questioning Yajnavalkya about the number of the gods. Yajnavalkya's first answer is 3,306. So Vidagdha Sakalya asks again, 'How many gods are there really?' The second answer is thirty-three. And so the questioning goes on, with the number getting increasingly smaller — six, three, two, one and a half — until it finally gets to one. Vidagdha Sakalya then asks for more information about the thirty-three gods in particular. Yajnavalkya tells him who they are:

'The eight Vasus, the eleven Rudras, the twelve Adityas. That makes thirty-one. [Add] Indra and Prajapati, [and that] makes thirty-three.'
   'Which are the Vasus?' [asks Vidagdha Sakalya].
   'Fire [Agni], earth [Prithivi], wind [Vayu], atmosphere [Antariksha], sun [Aditya], sky [Dyu], moon [Chandramas] and stars [Nakshatras] . . .'
   'Which are the Rudras?'
   'The ten breaths in man [Purusha], and the eleventh is the self [Atman].'
   'Which are the Adityas?'
   'The twelve months of the year are the Adityas, for they carry off everything, though going on [themselves] . . .'
   'Which is Indra? Which is Prajapati?'
   'Indra is thunder, Prajapati is the sacrifice.'
   'Which is thunder?'
   'The thunderbolt.'
   'Which is sacrifice?'
   'Cattle.'
   'Which are the six?'
   'Fire, earth, wind, atmosphere, sun and sky . . . These six are everything [or "this whole universe"]'.

'Which are the three gods?'

'These three worlds, for all these gods are in them.'

'Which are the two gods?'

'Food and the breath of life.'

'Which is the one and a half?'

'The purifying [wind] . . .'

'Which is the one god?'

'The breath of life, and that is Brahman, the beyond [tya].'[14]

Having just noted that the 3,306 deities can be reduced to 303, and then to thirty-three, the thirty-three are then described. Yajnavalkya begins with the Vasus that represent the whole of the visible world divided into four sections: the earth, the atmosphere, the heavens and the stars. The first three are ruled by three types of fire: the ordinary hearth fire, the thunderbolt (wind?) and the sun. The world of the stars is ruled by the moon, which is identified with the drug god Soma in other passages. Everything visible subsists in these eight gods, or they are the substance of everything visible. They are the Indian gods of the elements out of which everything, including human beings, are made. The second type of gods are the Rudras. They are the subtle elements which do not belong to the visible world. They represent the invisible elements of the life force that are found in every living being (*purusha*). There are eleven of these that are active in a human being, including the five senses. The eleventh, Rudra, is the self (*atman*). The next group is the twelve Adityas that are identified with the twelve months of the year. The reason for this is that, as sovereign lords, they represent different aspects of the order of things. They express themselves in the law that rules the universe, which includes human society. They are the gods of knowledge and the different aspects of consciousness. Mitra (Friendship), who rules men's relationships, is one of them. Vishnu (the Pervader), who is responsible for the cosmic order that pervades everything, is another.

Two other gods are then added to the thirty-one, Indra and Prajapati. Something of the background of both these gods can be found in the Rig Veda, a collection of songs which is the earliest source of information about the ancient Aryan religion of India. Indra is the god of war, the lord of the three spheres and the wielder of the thunderbolt. He is the major god of the Rig Veda. Prajapati, on the other hand, is only mentioned in one hymn in the tenth book, where he appears as a sort of creator. He creates by sacrificing himself. This is the theme

[14] *Brihadaranyaka Upanishad* III.ix.1–9, from *Hindu Scriptures*, trans. R. C. Zaehner (London: Everyman's Library, 1966), pp. 57–58.

GOD AND BRAHMAN: THE REAL?

that is taken up in the Brihadaranyaka, which is also one of the most popular images of the origin and nature of physical things in the Upanishads as a whole. Indra is the thunderbolt, the fire, and the eater that continually consumes everything. Prajapati, on the other hand, is the sacrifice, the animals that are sacrificed, and that which is consumed. There is a description of this process in the *Brihadaranyaka*, Book 1 chapter 2.

> In the beginning nothing at all existed here. This [whole world] was enveloped by Death, – by Hunger. For what is death but hunger? And [Death] bethought himself: 'Would that I had a self!' He roamed around, offering praise; and from him, as he offered praise, water was born. And he said [to himself]: 'Yes, it was a joy [*ka*] to me to offer praise [*arc*-].' And this is what makes fire [*arka*] fire . . .
>
> Water too is arka. And the froth of the water was churned together and became the earth. And on this [earth] he wore himself out. And the heat and sap [generated] by him, worn out and consumed by fierce penances as he was, turned into fire.
>
> He divided [him]self [*atman*] into three parts: [one third was fire], one third the sun, one third the wind. He too is the breath of life [*rana*] threefold divided.
>
> The east is his head. The north-east and south-east are his two arms. The west is his tail . . . The sky is his back, the atmosphere his belly, this [earth] his chest . . .
>
> [Then] he longed that a second self might be born to him; [and so he who is] Hunger and Death copulated with Speech by means of mind. What was the seed became the year; for there was no year before that. For so long did he beat him [within himself] – for a whole year; and after so long a time did he bring him forth. When he was born, [Death] opened his mouth [as if to swallow him]. 'Bhan,' said he, and that became speech.
>
> He considered [within himself]: 'If I should try to take his life, I should make less food for myself.' By this word, by this self, he brought forth this whole universe, – everything that exists, – Rig-Veda, Yajur-Veda, Sama-Veda, metres, sacrifices, men and beasts.
>
> And whatever he brought forth he began to eat: for he eats up everything.[15]

What exists at the beginning is the primeval stuff of the universe. This raw material is covered by death or hunger, and from this combination everything

---

[15] *Ibid.*, II.ii.1–5, pp. 33–34.

that is arises. The story begins with the unmanifested; then comes mind, intention or will-power. The characteristic expression of this 'mind' is praise or worship. Praise or worship here is not to be understood in the Christian sense but in the Indian sense of generating heat by means of devotion. This was literally true in the case of the burnt offering of the sacrifice. Fire or heat was the means by which praise or worship was offered. By the time the Upanishads were being composed, the physical act of sacrifice was being internalized into meditative exercises that were able to generate spiritual heat or power that could lift the meditator above the limits of time and space. It is this type of heat that Death or Hunger generates in the process of producing everything out of itself by emanation. It is three of the four spheres represented by the Vasus in the passage considered above. This Original Being called Death or Hunger is identified with Prajapati by comentators on this passage. In the latter part of the passage, the birth of knowledge and action is explained. This is the word and its expression. It is when the word is spoken that consciousness of visible things comes into being from Death (Prajapati). The truth of this world is that everything is food for Death, that everything is being continually consumed. The picture of everything in the universe rushing into the jaws of Death/Hunger/Prajapati and so on is an abiding image in Indian religion.

Everything is involved in the endless cycle of appearing merely to be consumed. Returning in order to be consumed is the lot of everything and everyone. This is the doctrine of reincarnation (samsara) which appears in the Indian sacred literature for the first time in the Upanishads. The big question in the Upanishads is whether there is something which is not involved in this endless process of becoming in order to be consumed. They give no single answer to this problem. One of the most popular answers is that there is a still ground of all being called Brahman – the One in the passage quoted above. Looked at from one angle, this Brahman is the sum of everything there is. The thirty-three gods really represent the whole universe, so if Brahman is the thirty-three gods, he/it is the whole universe. But how does saying that everything is ultimately the One mean escape from the process of consumption? Where there is only One, there cannot be process; process demands a consumer and the consumed. A problem here is that the way in which the appearance of everything is represented means that Prajapati consumes himself, so to say that there is only One does not really mean escape from the process. The process goes on in the One.

Brahman is also viewed as some sort of spiritual entity that is different from everything that appears, even though everything that appears has come from it. This is true on the macrocosmic and microcosmic level. So, at the heart of the universe, there is Brahman, from which everything emanated but which is more

GOD AND BRAHMAN: THE REAL?

than the sum of everything. Its/his essence is beyond process. On this pattern there is something at the heart of every human being which is more than the sum of *samsara*. This human essence is called *atman*. The Upanishads teach that the Brahman in the universe and the atman in the human being are the same reality. Coming into an experience of the unity of Brahman and Atman means freedom from *samsara*. This involves a very negative attitude towards the physical world. The human problem is ignorance of the true nature of the human being that is obscured by living in an unfortunate world of diversity.

What happens in the Upanishads is that the Ultimate is identified with the essence of a human being. Brahman-Atman is a case of bringing 'god' from heaven to earth or raising the human to the status of divinity. This is what happens to the polytheistic religion of India in the Upanishads. There is still as much talk about the gods now as there is about Brahman into which/whom the gods merge, but the focus is 'man' – and the masculine is used deliberately here, because woman has a very inferior place in the Hindu tradition. The big question is how can man free himself from the shackles of reincarnation. The answer is by turning in on himself and, through a process of self-analysis, discovering in himself the still Ground of his being.

The seventh section of the *Chandogya Upanishad* is a good example of this. Radhakrishnan gives it the heading 'Progressive worship of Brahman'.[16] What is meant by 'worship' is not contemplating the transcendent worth of the Divine Being but generating spiritual 'heat' by meditative exercises. The content of the chapter is a series of instructions on how to meditate on various aspects of the human mind and on different concepts that will help the meditator to gain freedom from *samsara*. The aim is an experience of going beyond opposites where there is no consciousness of the difference between subject and object. This is what it means to be one with Brahman. The nearest analogy of this in ordinary human experience is deep, dreamless sleep.[17] Such a self-induced, non-conscious state is believed to represent real freedom.

Now next, the instruction with regard to the soul [or Self, *atmadesa*]. – The

[16] S. Radhakrishnan, *The Principal Upanishads* (London: Allen & Unwin, 1953), p. 468.

[17] This raises the question of whether unity with Brahman is an experience at all. There is no conscious experience in deep, dreamless sleep. It only becomes a significant experience when one wakes up! One is reminded of Ramakrishna's Vedantist experience. He went into such a deep trance that he would have died if someone else had not revived him. From outside, nothing can be said about this unitive experience other than that it means the cessation of consciousness of physical processes that is suicidal unless interrupted.

Soul [*Atman*], indeed is below. The Soul is above. The Soul is to the west. The Soul is to the east. The Soul is to the south. The Soul is to the north. The Soul is, indeed, this whole world.

Verily, he who sees this, who thinks this, who understands this, who has pleasure in the Soul, who has delight in the Soul, who has intercourse with the Soul, who has bliss in the Soul — he is autonomous; he has unlimited freedom in all worlds.

> The seer sees not death,
> Nor sickness, nor any distress.
> The seer sees only the All,
> Obtains the All entirely.[18]

The sum of this teaching is that a man can discover his salvation in himself. He lifts himself by means of meditation to an experience of the Immortal. The last word of the Upanishads is not 'Glory to God' but '*Tat tvam asi*' ('That you are').[19]

Krishna of the Bhagavad-gita

'That you are' is not the last word in the Hindu tradition on the Ultimate. There is also a strong tradition of devotion to a number of personal gods. *Bhakti* is the Hindu word to describe this type of religion. The two central deities in this movement are Shiva and Vishnu, with their wives and children and other beings that are closely associated with them. We have already referred to Vishnu's son Ganesh. Lakshmi, the Indian goddess of good fortune, is one of his wives. Vishnu has many names, one of the most popular being Hari. The core meaning of 'Hari' is to remove or take away. As applied to Vishnu it means something like 'Saviour', because he removes the ignorance from the human mind, particularly the false idea that anything can exist independently of him.

It is believed that Vishnu occasionally appears in a visible form to remove ignorance and unrighteousness from among human beings. Two of his human appearances (*avatara*), in the forms of Krishna and Ram, are very significant in the devotional life of India. The cults of Krishna and Ram, remain very popular today, particularly in North and central India. It is not surprising that the Bhagavad-gita, in which Krishna appears as the central character, has become one of the most popular Hindu scriptures. Interestingly, it is not part of the Vedas, the most ancient and sacred Hindu literature, but part of the great epic

---

[18] *Chandogya Upanishad*, 7.25.2 and 7.26.2, from R. E. Hume, *The Thirteen Principal Upanishads* (India: OUP, ²1931), pp. 261–262.

[19] *Chandogya Upanishad*, 6.12 and 13.3.14, *cf. Brihadaranyaka Upanishad*, III.vii.1–23.

poem the Mahabharata. Some Western scholars have called the Gita 'the New Testament of Hinduism'. They also argue that it proves that Indians have come to believe in a god that is very much like the Christian God, independent of the Christian revelation. The Gita teaches, they claim, that there is one god who is the source of everything and who will forgive the sin of those who worship and serve him. This claim deserves close examination.

The setting of the Gita is a battlefield. The battle that is about to commence is part of a bloody civil war. Thinking about the prospect of killing some of his relatives and former friends, the young prince Arjuna turns in despair for advice to his charioteer Krishna. Their resulting discussion about the meaning of life reaches its climax when Arjuna, who has by now realized that Krishna is an avatar of Vishnu, asks Krishna to show him his real nature. Krishna agrees to this, and in chapter 11 of the Gita there is the account of the vision that Arjuna has of what Vishnu really is. If those are right who have argued that the god of the Gita is like the God of the New Testament, we would expect to find real parallels at this point.

This is the description of what Arjuna, the son of Pandu, saw: 'Then did the son of Pandu see the whole [wide] universe in One converged, there in the body of the God of gods, yet divided out in multiplicity.'[20] This is the Ultimate as the One or All that we have met in the Upanishads. Then Arjuna sees Krishna/Vishnu as Time, the destroyer or consumer. 'Time am I,' says Krishna, 'the wreaker of the world's destruction, matured, – [grimly] resolved here to swallow up the worlds.'[21] The Ultimate as the consumer is another fundamental concept of the Upanishads. So far there seems to be no difference between Brahman and Krishna/Vishnu. In verse 37 they are clearly distinguished from each other in Arjuna's hymn of praise. 'And why should they ["the hosts of men perfected" of the previous verse], not revere You, great [as is your] Self, more to be prized even than Brahman?'[22] Accepting that Zaehner and others are correct in translating 'Brahman' here as opposed to the 'Brahma' of Shankara and Radhakrishnan, Arjuna continues immediately to describe Krishna/Vishnu in the same way as Brahman is described: 'All hail [to You],' he says, 'when I stand before You . . . [all hail to you] the All! . . . All things you bring to their consummation: hence You are All.'[23]

If Brahman and Krishna are described in the same way, there arises the

---

[20] *The Bhagvad-gita*, trans. and ed. R. C. Zaehner (New York: OUP, 1973), p. 306.

[21] *Ibid.*, vs. 32, p. 311; *cf.* vss. 25–29.

[22] *Ibid.*, vs. 37, p. 313. Shankara and Radhakrishnan translate 'Brahma' and not 'Brahman' here, so that Vishnu is seen as greater than the creator god Brahma and not the ultimate principle Brahman of the Upanishads.

[23] *Ibid.*, vs. 40, p. 316.

question of the difference between them. The answer is found in chapter 12 of the Gita, where Krishna compares the way to freedom through realizing unity with the impersonal Self, Brahman, and through love and devotion to a personal Lord. '[But] greater,' Krishna says, 'is the toil of those whose thinking clings to the Unmanifest; for difficult [indeed] it is for embodied men to reach-and-tread the unmanifested way.' There is no essential difference between Brahman and Krishna/Vishnu; the difference is in the way to freedom that they represent. The Gita is of the opinion that the way of devotion to a personal Lord is superior to the way of abstract meditation that culminates in the experience of Brahman. There seems to be no difference in the nature of the freedom that is achieved by either way. The central purpose in the Gita, as in the Upanishads, is to break free from the cruel cycle of becoming. The Gita may extol a personal Lord but the freedom that is craved through him is described in terms of identification with the All. The goal is more fundamental than the way to it. The contrast between this and the statement of Jesus, 'I am the way', is striking.

INCLUSIVISM, GOD *and* BRAHMAN

Having taken a brief look at the ideas of the ultimate in Christianity and some aspects of the Hindu tradition, we can now return to the inclusivist and pluralist theories. What, to begin with, can the kind of claim made by Farquhar, that Christ fulfils the longings of the Hindu, mean in the light of what has been said about the Christian and Hindu concepts of the Ultimate? For this claim to be meaningful in any sense, Christ would have to appear at the head of a single set of stairs that included the Hindu way of seeing things. But it seems very difficult to see how Jesus Christ and Brahman, or even Krishna, can appear on the same continuum. In what sense can the profound trance experience of Brahman that comes as the climax of a long and arduous course of meditation be a preparation for a personal experience of forgiveness through the living Christ?

Things may be a little more hopeful in the case of *bhakti*. At least Christianity and *bhakti* are ways of devotion to a personal God. But, if we compare the objects of devotion in both traditions, there is very little similarity. A very superficial comparison of the transfiguration of Jesus in the Gospels and of Krishna in the Gita shatters any hope of compatibility. Jesus is very much there as an individual when he displays his glory, whereas Krishna loses all trace of personhood or individuality.[24] It may be possible to argue that there is a longing in the heart of

---

[24] *Cf.* the accounts of the transfiguration of Jesus in the New Testament (Matthew 17:1–13; Mark 9:2–13; Luke 9:28–36), and of Krishna in the Bhagavad-gita 11.

GOD AND BRAHMAN: THE REAL?

everyone for the true God who comes in Jesus, but that there is no evidence of such a longing in the religion which has developed in India. In the experience of missionaries the opposite is true – Hindu religion is the greatest hindrance to the acceptance of Jesus as the true and final revelation of God.

In fact, from one angle it may make more sense to argue that the teaching of the Upanishads, and the system of Vedanta that was built on it, fulfils Christianity and all other religions. As Radhakrishnan argued, it is possible to see devotion to Jesus, or Krishna, or any other personal deity, as steps on a continuum that reaches its climax in the experience of non-duality. The impersonal is certainly a more unifying concept than the personal.

This becomes clear when we look again at John Hick's idea of the Real. Hick says that the Real may be either personal, or impersonal, or some mix that transcends all such distinctions. But no-one is allowed to say dogmatically that God is personal as theists have understood him. God cannot communicate his personal reality to anyone, because if he had it would be possible to claim to know that God is personal. So the Real is either unwilling or unable to communicate itself as personal, and therefore can hardly be personal as theists have claimed. In view of this lack of personal communication, it is much more likely either that the Real is impersonal or that it transcends personal being. If this is the case, Hinduism fits the bill much better than Christianity as a 'fulfilling' religion.[25]

If the most important thing is to find a unifying factor among the competing claims of the world's religions, the Vedanta view of Brahman must be one of the best candidates. The Zen Buddhist concept of the Buddha nature is another. These Ultimates fit the bill because they have no attributes. Nothing can be said about them. On a lower level of spiritual understanding it is fine to believe that the Ultimate is a personal deity with attributes, but with growing spiritual maturity the realization will come that the Ultimate has no attributes. That about which nothing can be said has to be One.

The system of Advaita Vedanta that Shankara developed was a specific attempt to unite the various streams of Indian religion. It has not, however, proved very successful in uniting the various streams of Hinduism since it was first formulated in the ninth century CE. Most Indians have been content with gods that have attributes. Of course, if finding a unifying factor in the world's religions is not the most important thing, there is no more reason to think that Advaita Vedanta fulfils all other religions than that Christ fulfils them. And it is

[25] I am indebted to Professor Stephen Williams of the Union Theological College, Belfast, for the argument in this paragraph.

at least just as valid a possibility that the Ultimate principle in the universe is personal as it is to think that it is impersonal.

Rahner approaches the issue from a different angle. He is a theologian committed to the dogma of the Roman Catholic Church who wants to make that church as inclusive as possible. His idea of the 'anonymous Christian' is a way of including good people in the Catholic Church even though they belong to non-Christian faith communities. In the context of the discussion of the concept of the Ultimate in Christianity and some aspects of Hinduism, it can be argued that Rahner's view of that which identifies someone as an 'anonymous Christian' excludes Vedantin monists. What Rahner says about the experience of the 'anonymous Christians' does seem to imply that they must experience the personal God, who is fully revealed as Father, Son and Holy Spirit. Rahner is not really interested in a unifying principle of religion but in widening the boundaries of the church so that more people will be saved in the end. There is still plenty of scope for exclusion, and Vedantins would seem to come into the category of those who will be excluded.

PLURALISM, GOD *and* BRAHMAN

In arguing for one Ultimate reference point for all religions, Hick has moved from using 'God' to using 'the Real' to describe it. In the light of the discussion of the Christian and Hindu ideas of the Ultimate, we can now explore the claim that it is the same Real that is being experienced in both traditions. What evidence is there for this position?

We can begin with the verbal descriptions. This is not very hopeful for Hick because, particularly in the case of Vedanta, there seems to be precious little that is common between the description of God and of Brahman. Ninian Smart came up against the same problem when he set out to explore the idea that Christianity and Buddhism have to do with the one divine reality. Smart's answer was to argue for complementarity. What Christianity teaches is made complete by what Buddhism teaches, and vice versa.[26] But it is difficult to see

---

[26] See *Beyond Ideology* (London: Collins, 1981). In this volume, Smart looks to the idea of self-denial as the point where Christianity and Buddhism could complement each other. In his *Christian Systematic Theology in World Contexts* (with S. Konstantine; London: Marshall Pickering, 1991), he argues that it is morally required that God should suffer like us, and that it is only Christianity that teaches that he did (p. 110). Self-denial is central here again, but there is a strong indication that its full revelation is only found in Jesus Christ. If this is so, Smart must also be numbered among the inclusivists.

how the Hindu idea of the One, or the Buddhist idea of *nirvana*, completes the Christian idea of a personal creator. In his *God Has Many Names*, Hick had been able to argue that the language used in the liturgy of the various religious groups that he had observed in Birmingham did contain a number of similarities which needed explaining. Even in that situation, he did not take the context of the words or the issue of historical diffusion seriously enough. But when the religious horizon is broadened to include movements such as Vedanta or Buddhism, it becomes much more difficult to find any common language. In this case, it seems much more reasonable to accept that there are different and contradictory ideas of the Ultimate. This allows for the possibility that some ideas may be wrong, which the existence of different doctrinal schemes requires. If the Brahman of the Upanishads is the Ultimate, the Christian is excluded from knowledge of it.

The second possibility is experience. This question was examined in chapter 11, 'Mysticism', where it was shown that it is impossible to dissociate religious experience from the overall religious framework in which it is expressed. A favourite illustration of the pluralist position – which is a Hindu illustration originally – is that of the blind men encountering an elephant. One bumps into its leg and says that they have come up against something that is like a pillar. Another gets hold of the tail and says that it is like a rope. A third comes up against the trunk and claims that it is like a pipe. So, in religion, various groups and individuals have experienced the Real as this, that or the other. But the illustration makes sense only if there is someone around who has actually seen the elephant. If this were not so, it would be impossible to say that one person has experienced it as this, and that another person has experienced it as something else, and so on. Hick accepts that it is futile to look for religious unity on the level of experience. So his claim that all religions have to do with the one Real must be a claim to the privileged position of knowing that religious people from various traditions are like blind men coming up against a creature which they have never experienced before. The pluralists' claim is a claim to knowledge that is superior to that of adherents of the world's great religious traditions.

The third possibility is behaviour. There is only one Real because the behaviour that flows from the experience of it is universally the same. It has to be admitted that what people have considered good is very similar all over the world. But we have to distinguish between religious behaviour and the way in which people treat each other in everyday life. Religious behaviour is often the opposite of what is considered to be common decency. Human sacrifice, which still persists to a certain extent, is a good case in point. The ascetic way that is associated with the teaching of the Upanishads is also a clear illustration of this point. In the description of the ideal life of a member of the Hindu priestly class, the last of the four stages is renunciation. At this stage, the twice-born has the choice of opting out of social life altogether in the search of liberation from the wheel of *samsara*. He can expect to receive the minimum support needed to sustain physical life from those that have been left behind, but as far as their well-being is concerned he becomes utterly indifferent. What we would consider as love in the Christian context is left behind as he concentrates entirely on his own salvation, which is seen in terms of absorption into the One. The contrast with the highest Christian ideal of giving up one's life for others is striking. So behaviour is not an area in which we can discern some evidence of there being one reality at the heart of religion, either.

We are forced to the conclusion that there is no evidence for the pluralist view, as typically expressed by Hick, that all the religions are equally legitimate ways of experiencing the one ultimate reality. That this position has been advocated by such as Hick and Smart, who claim to be Christians, witnesses yet again to the tremendous shift in Protestant theology which gave birth to liberal Protestantism at the beginning of the nineteenth century. Liberalism moved the focus of theology from the objective to the subjective. Giving up any claim to objective knowledge of God in response to the challenge of scientific rationalism, it looked for a firm foundation in human experience. Sadly, in their attempt to preserve religion from the attacks of rationalists, what liberals did was to put human beings and their needs, and not God, at the heart of religion. The inevitable result of this is the re-creation of God in the image of the human.

In one sense, this process also happens in Hinduism. In Vedanta, the focus is very much on the human. The central concern is not the glory of God but the release of the human from *samsara*. The Ultimate is not that important, it is the experience of the Ultimate that is centre stage. In religious and theological terms, pluralism is probably closer to certain types of Hinduism (and Buddhism) than it is to Christianity. Pluralism is certainly not an adequate theoretical framework for understanding the true nature of the world's religions.

CONCLUSION

The dominant way of thinking in Religious Studies has been, and probably still is, essentialist. Essentialism has been driven by a desire to find an essence of religion behind or underneath its multifarious forms. In many cases the attempt to find the elusive essence has been made in the name of objective science. The number of different and contradictory theories of religion that have been presented in the name of scientific objectivity in itself makes a mockery of the whole idea. If 'facts' are supposed to be transparent, they have failed to be so in the case of religion. This myth of 'scientific objectivity' therefore needs to be laid to rest.

To give up any pretence to scientific objectivity would open the door to a much more tolerant attitude, particularly towards Christians who prefer to cling to a more traditional understanding of their faith. It would then be possible for the kind of pluralism that is a reality in Western society at large to be reflected in institutions of higher education. A pluralistic society recognizes that people have the freedom to practise and propagate the religion of their choice within certain legal limits. There has been a very real resistance against allowing the same tolerance in many colleges. Because of adherence to the myth of scientific objectivity, academics who advocate a more traditional form of Christianity have been treated with some suspicion. But, as we have seen, any essentialist position is as dogmatic as that of a traditionalist Catholic or evangelical.

In their critique of John Hick's pluralist position, Peter B. Clarke and Peter Byrne conclude that 'the pluralist hypothesis itself becomes an exclusivist religious truth to which all other religions are a preparation'.[1] Anyone who teaches religions from the pluralist perspective is dogmatizing and proselytizing

---

[1] *Religion Defined and Explained* (London: Macmillan, 1993), p. 95.

CONCLUSION

as much as anyone else. In this context, a good case could be made that a conservative Jew or Muslim teaching in a college is likely to be much more tolerant in that his assumptions are 'up front' and not hidden as is often the case with 'pluralists'. What is being advocated here is openness and honesty in the area of presuppositions. What is being objected to is the impression that the so-called modern scientific approach to religion is fair, tolerant and objective, while viewing religion as a whole from the perspective of a faith commitment is bigotry. Everyone is capable of displaying this reprehensible characteristic.

It is also very clear that pluralists are not averse to making judgments on religions, particularly in the area of morality. Ninian Smart, for example, calls for pressure to be brought on Muslim states so that they become more tolerant towards other faiths and eschew a very deeply ingrained tradition that it is legitimate to keep Muslims in the faith by the threat of violence.[2] John Hick is of the opinion that the religions that really matter are the religions of the post-Axial age. Following Karl Jaspers, he believes that something special happened in religion around the sixth century BCE, which is when the Buddha, Mahavira (the founder of Jainism), Confucius, Lao-tsu (the founder of Taoism) and a few others flourished. Hick holds that significant religion from this time was really concerned with salvation which was conceived in terms of a move from self- to reality-centredness. We have seen that to describe Vedantic monism, which also belongs to the Axial period, as a move from self- to reality-centredness is questionable, but the point here is that Hick passes very definite judgments on religions. His test of religious validity in the last analysis seems little different from William James's pragmatic test. If this is the case, one assumes that Hick has no objection to the strong advocacy of a particular faith – as long as it produces the fruit of self-denial in the service of a greater reality. Though Christianity has much that is shameful in its history, it also has much that is noble, even in Hick's terms. What objection can Hick have then to the strong and devoted propagation of the religion of Jesus?

It is interesting that pluralists like Hick find Jesus a real stumbling-block. Jesus scandalizes them in his intense particularity. So they throw their weight behind those interpretations of the New Testament that diminish its historical content almost to nothing. If all we have is a record of what unscientific and primitive thinking people thought about Jesus, he can be safely turned into an idea. Once he has become only an idea, he is under human control and he can be

---

[2] See chapter entitled 'Towards a Higher-Order Agreement in Worldviews: The Coming Victory of Pluralism', in N. Smart, *Buddhism and Christianity: Rivals and Allies* (London: Macmillan, 1993).

CONCLUSION

made into just about anything we want to make of him. That is why modern thinking is so scandalized by the resurrection. A risen Jesus is out of human control. He really *is* God.

There are signs that a number of disciplines, including Religious Studies, are at present entering a period of self-criticism and analysis. In a recent volume, Tomoko Masuzawa has taken a critical look at the unspoken dictum in contemporary Religious Studies that 'Thou shalt not quest for the origin of religion'.[3] She finds this prohibition very odd, because all the founding fathers of Religious Studies took a very keen interest in the origins of religion, and religions themselves are also very interested in origins. There seems to be a real tension at this point between what Religious Studies and religion itself are all about. Masuzawa believes that this situation calls for 'a critical inquiry about the practice of knowledge and power, about the politics of writing, as it pertains to the study of religion'.[4] She believes that denying the validity of the search for origins reflects the desire of modern people to control their own lives. The quest for origins takes us beyond history, which is something that has been created by human beings, to an area where we become products rather than producers.

It is not surprising that Masuzawa finds Mircea Eliade, who was until recently the illustrious star of the department where she now teaches, a good illustration of the point she is trying to make. With Eliade's strong juxtaposition of the archaic and modern way of thinking about reality, he is seen as giving a vivid illustration of the repression of the reality of religion in the modern study of religions in the interest of control and domination. Masuzawa says, in her comments on Eliade:

> The archaic, the other of the modern, is at once the other of us, the contemporary scholars of religion. But the other of oneself is always a double of oneself . . . This other — the archaic — is presented as peculiarly marked by a single obsession with the moment of origin. What does this reflect vis-à-vis the modern scholarship on myth and ritual . . . that rather emphatically denied itself the quest for the origin of religion some time ago? . . . Does this not signal a certain displacement . . . which is a telltale sign of repression?[5]

'Western man' has got used to the idea of power and control which have been acquired particularly through science and technology. Anything, including

---

[3] *In Search of Dreamtime: The Quest for the Origin of Religion* (Chicago: University of Chicago Press, 1993), p. 2.

[4] *Ibid.*, p. 6.   [5] *Ibid.*, p. 29.

religion, which would seem to question the superior position, is unconsciously pushed to one side.

Masuzawa's theory is not presented here because it is particularly convincing. There may be better explanations of the rejection of the quest for origins. The founding fathers of Religious Studies were very enamoured of the evolutionary theory, although they divided into idealist and positivist camps as far as the meaning of evolution was concerned. At this stage, the quest for origins was clearly included in the scientific enterprise and was part of the process of subduing everything to the control of 'modern Western man'. There is no evidence that scholars like Max Müller and James Frazer felt that they had failed in their attempt to trace the origins of religion. Masuzawa is correct, however, in seeing a very profound tension in the thinking of classical authors like Emile Durkheim, Müller and Sigmund Freud between the deterministic model of scientific understanding (time, that which is beyond human control), and human self-determination (history, that which humans produce). It is not accidental that the age which sees more and more things being explained in terms of physical reactions is the age that puts a very high value on the word 'freedom'.

At this point, Masuzawa has put her finger on a fundamental characteristic of European thought since the Enlightenment that is an important factor in the theoretical structure which underlies this whole volume. Traditional Christian and biblical teaching viewed human beings as belonging to two worlds, the spiritual and physical. Both these worlds belong to God, who is their author and sustainer. The intention of the Creator was that humans would, in submission to him, find fulfilment and joy in their physical existence. Because of their rejection of God's wisdom and veracity, confusion and alienation were introduced into the spiritual dimension of human experience, which is reflected in confusion and alienation in their physical experience as well. God then takes the initiative to restore human beings both spiritually and physically. This initiative reaches its culmination when Jesus Christ, God's Son, died on the cross and rose from the grave. In this model all human life is viewed in the light of God. God is the Creator and Sustainer of human life, who has revealed his will and purpose for human life on earth. The climax of his self-revelation is the person of Jesus Christ who, as the risen Saviour who is alive for evermore, makes absolute claims on his followers. True human freedom, which can be defined as living in the way God intends, can be found only through faith in and obedience to Jesus Christ.

From the beginning, Christians have recognized that people find it difficult to accept that they need a Saviour and that salvation comes through a death on a cross. Through the ages some who have claimed to be Christian theologians have looked for ways to avoid the full weight of Christ's teaching and actions. In the eighteenth century, a coming-together of various factors opened the way to a very serious challenge to the traditional view of Christianity, particularly among the intellectuals of 'Christian' Europe. The shift in thinking that followed was not from theism to atheism, but from Christianity as defined above to deism. 'God' was not abandoned, but what God is and how humans are to live their lives in this world became a matter of human, not divine, decision.

One of the key factors which contributed to the growth of confidence in human ability, and led to the rejection of biblical and ecclesiastical authority, was an explosion of scientific discovery. This was seen as paving the way for unlimited technological advance which would hasten progress towards a utopian earthly existence. What has become apparent again and again since the eighteenth century is the fact that the ideal of freedom, embodied in the rejection of the Christian view of God, and the idea of nature, embodied in the ability of science to explain nature in terms of 'laws', are in a dialectical relationship. Freedom has to be proclaimed over and over again in the face of a nature that is continually threatening to squeeze it out of the picture.

Many of the significant figures in the story of Religious Studies illustrate this fundamental dialectic of modern thought. The idealists approached religion from the perspective of freedom, while the positivist approached it from the perspective of nature. Both started from the premise that knowledge of 'God' is of human construction. The idealists began from the presupposition that religion has been too pervasive a fact of human experience to be empty of any reality. There must be some realm other than nature where a person can find freedom from its inexorable laws. The positivist began from those inexorable laws and attempted to explain religion from within nature, so that it became an expression of a universal neurosis of society, and so on.

The pervasive tradition in Religious Studies has been the idealist. This tradition is *for* nature in that it rejects the supernatural in the biblical sense of the miraculous, but it also wants to assert something that is *other than* nature. The method which has been called 'the objective scientific method', which empties religion of its surface meaning and reduces it to something else, is accepted as essential to any right understanding of religion or religions. On the other hand, many of those who use this method in Religious Studies still want to assert that it is a good thing for people to pray! This fundamental tension is continually driving Religious Studies either in the direction of experience of the supernatural (as Jung or Eliade), or in the direction of seeing it as a purely natural phenomenon (as Durkheim or Levi-Strauss). Between these two extremes are those like Smart and Hick who are struggling to find some middle ground between nature and freedom.

CONCLUSION

It is my deep conviction that such ground cannot be found, because as humans we are created and dependent beings who are not the measure of all things. There is no ground on which we can stand where we are independent of God and able to decide what God is. It is he, as Creator, who is able to tell us who he is and what we are. It is through his revelation to us humans that we understand who God is and what we are, and not through our understanding that we decide what is or is not revelation from God. To quote again the ancient wisdom of Anselm, 'I believe that I might understand.'[6]

Anselm was explaining the link between his Christian faith and his rational understanding of the world. But recent discussion among theologians, philosophers and scientists suggests that Anselm's principle can be applied much more widely. Scientists now accept that their enterprise is sustained and motivated by faith in the rationality of the universe. This is not something that they can prove, but something that they believe and that often sustains them in their quest when what they observe does not seem to make sense.[7] While many scientists are recognizing the impossibility of objective science, it is strange that experts in Religious Studies should still cling to the ideal. This is particularly strange when the sophisticated scientific theories of so many experts in Religious Studies strongly reflect what is known of their faith commitment. When this happens, Religious Studies has degenerated into an apologetic exercise on behalf of the expert's own 'faith'. This is one of the most unsatisfactory aspects of the search for the essence of religion that is so central in the history of Religious Studies. More often than not, the 'essence' turns out to be the expert's own religious belief or belief about religion.

To reject the quest for the essence of religion is not to deny that human beings are incurably religious. Religion is still important to the vast majority of the world's population. Even in the West, and in many of the former communist countries where there was severe oppression for many years, there is a strong revival of religion. There may not be one God or Real that is worshipped in many religions, but the religious nature of human beings seems to be universal. So, while rejecting the thesis that the objects of religious devotion are only reflections of human needs and desires, the study of religions can help us to understand some of the deepest longings of the human heart — remembering that understanding follows faith!

---

[6] In trying to grapple with the dominant 'scientific' culture of our times, I have benefited greatly from the work of Lesslie Newbigin among others. See his *Foolishness to the Greeks: The Gospel and Western Culture* (London: SPCK, 1986).

[7] Newbigin, *ibid.*, pp. 70–71.

CONCLUSION

Where the objects of religion are concerned, there seems to be only one possible conclusion — they are neither different names for, nor different aspects of, the same reality. To quote the apostle Paul, 'there are many "gods" and many "lords" '.[8] Until this fact is recognized, Religious Studies will not be in a position to make a really meaningful contribution to human life in the global village.

[8] 1 Corinthians 8:5 (NIV).

BIBLIOGRAPHY

Allen, D., *Structure and Reality in Religion: Hermeneutics in Mircea Eliade's Phenomenology and New Directions* (Berlin: Mouton, 1978)

Almond, P. C., *Mystical Experience and Religious Doctrine* (Berlin: Mouton, 1982)

Azzam, S. (ed.), *Islam and Contemporary Society* (London: Longman, 1982)

Barth, K., *Protestant Theology in the Nineteenth Century* (London: SCM, 1972)

Beattie, J., *Other Cultures: Aims, Methods and Achievements in Social Anthropology* (London: Routledge, 1989)

Berger, P. L., *The Heretical Imperative* (London: Collins, 1979)

——*A Rumour of Angels* (Harmondsworth: Penguin, 1970)

Biller, P., 'Words and the Medieval Notion of Religion', *Journal of Ecclesiastical History* 36 (1985), pp. 351ff.

Blocher, H., *Evil and the Cross: Christian Thought and the Problem of Evil* (Leicester: Apollos, 1994)

Brenneman, W. L., S. O. Yarian and A. M. Olson, *The Seeing Eye: Hermeneutical Phenomenology in the Study of Religion* (Pennsylvania State University Press, 1982)

Bruce, S. (ed.), *Religion and Modernization* (Oxford: OUP, 1992)

Clarke, P. B. and P. Byrne, *Religion Defined and Explained* (London: Macmillan, 1993)

Clements, K., *Friedrich Schleiermacher: Pioneer of Modern Theology* (London: Collins, 1987)

Comte, A., *Positive Philosophy*, trans. Harriet Martineau, 3 vols. (London, 1896)

Cousins, L. S., 'Buddhism', in J. R. Hinnells (ed.), *A Handbook of Living Religions* (Harmondsworth: Penguin Books, 1984)

Coward, H., and T. Penelhum (eds.), *Mystics and Scholars* (Calgary Conference on Mysticism, 1976)

BIBLIOGRAPHY

Crosby, D. A., *Interpretive Theories of Religion* (The Hague: Mouton, 1981)

Darwin, C., *The Descent of Man* (London: John Murray, 1871)

Donohue, J. J. and J. L. Esposito, *Islam in Transition* (Oxford: OUP, 1982)

Downie, R. A., *Frazer and the Golden Bough* (London: Gollancz, 1970)

——*James George Frazer: The Portrait of a Scholar* (London: Watts, 1940)

Dube, S. C., *Indian Village* (Bombay: Harper, 1967)

Dumont, L., *Homo Hierarchicus* (London: Paladin, 1972)

Durkheim, E., *Elementary Forms of the Religious Life*, trans. J. W. Swain (London: Allen & Unwin, 1915)

Edwards, P. (ed.), *Encyclopedia of Philosophy* (New York: Macmillan, 1967)

Eliade, M. (ed.), *Encyclopedia of Religion* (New York: Macmillan, 1986)

——*A History of Religious Ideas*, vol. 1 (Chicago: University of Chicago Press, 1979)

——'Homo Faber and Homo Religiosus,' in J. Kitagawa (ed.), *The History of Religions: Retrospect and Prospect* (New York: Macmillan, 1985)

——*The Myth of the Eternal Return or Cosmos and History* (Princeton, NJ: Princeton University Press, 1954)

——*Patterns in Comparative Religion* (London: Sheed & Ward, 1958)

——*The Quest* (Chicago: University of Chicago Press, 1969)

——*Shamanism: Archaic Techniques of Ecstasy* (London: Routledge, 1964)

Evans, S., *Preserving the Person* (Leicester: IVP, 1979)

Evans-Pritchard, E. E., *Theories of Primitive Religion* (London: OUP, 1965)

Ewing, K., 'Dreams from a Saint: Anthropological Atheism and the Temptation to Believe', *American Anthropologist* 96.3 (1994), pp. 571–583

Ferguson, S. B. and D. F. Wright (eds.), *New Dictionary of Theology* (Leicester: IVP, 1988)

Fraser, D. A. and A. Campolo, *Sociology Through the Eyes of Faith* (Leicester: Apollos, 1992)

Frazer, J. G., *The Belief in Immortality*, vol. 1 (London: Macmillan, 1913)

——*The Golden Bough*, vol. 1 (London: Macmillan, ^{2}1900)

——*Psyche's Task* (London: Macmillan, ^{2}1913)

——*The Worship of Nature*, vol. 1 (London: Macmillan, 1926)

Freud, E. L. (ed.), *Letters of Sigmund Freud*, trans. T. and J. Stern (New York: Basic Books, 1960)

Glock, C. Y., B. B. Ringer and E. R. Babbie, *To Confront and to Challenge* (Berkeley, CA: University of California Press, 1967)

Gombrich, R., 'Eliade on Buddhism', *Religious Studies* 10 (1974), pp. 225–231

Grahame, K., *The Wind in the Willows* (London: Methuen, 1978)

Hegel, G. W. F., *Lectures on the Philosophy of Religion*, trans. E. B. Spiers and J. Burdon Sanderson, 3 vols. (London, 1895)

BIBLIOGRAPHY

Hick, J., *God Has Many Names* (London: Macmillan, 1980)

——*An Interpretation of Religion* (London: Macmillan, 1989)

Hinnells, J. R. (ed.), *A Handbook of Living Religions* (Harmondsworth: Penguin, 1984)

Hodge, C., *Systematic Theology,* vol. 1 (London: James Clarke, 1960)

Hume, R. E., *The Thirteen Principal Upanishads* (Oxford: OUP, ²1931)

Huxley, A., *The Doors of Perception & Heaven and Hell* (Harmondsworth: Penguin, 1959)

Isbister, J. N., *Freud: An Introduction to his Life and Work* (Cambridge: Polity, 1985)

Isherwood, C., *Ramakrishna and his Disciples* (London: Shepheard-Walwyn, 1986)

James, E. O., 'The History, Science and Comparative Study of Religion', *Numen* 1 (1954)

——*The Origins of Religion* (London: John Heritage, 1937)

——*The Origins of Sacrifice* (London: John Murray, 1937)

——*The Social Function of Religion* (London: Hodder & Stoughton, 1940)

James, W., *The Varieties of Religious Experience*, rev. ed. (London: Longmans, Green & Co., 1907)

Johnstone, R. L., *Religion in Society: A Sociology of Religion* (Englewood Cliffs, NJ: Prentice Hall, ³1988)

Jones, E., *The Life and Works of Sigmund Freud*, vol. 3 (London: Hogarth Press, 1957)

Julian of Norwich, *Revelations of Divine Love*, in *Treasures from the Spiritual Classics* 3, compiled by Roger L. Roberts (Oxford: Mowbray, 1981)

Jung, C. G., *Aion,* in *The Collected Works*, vol. 9, part 2, trans. R. F. C. Hull (London: Routledge & Kegan Paul, ²1968)

——*Answer to Job* (London: Routledge & Kegan Paul, 1954)

——*The Archetypes and the Collective Unconscious* in *The Collected Works*, vol. 9, part 1 (London: Routledge & Kegan Paul, ²1969)

——*Collected Papers on Analytical Psychology* (New York: Moffat, Yard & Co., 1917)

——*Memories, Dreams and Reflections* (London: Fontana, 1973)

——*Modern Man in Search of a Soul* (New York: Harcourt Brace, 1933)

Kant, I., *Religion within the Limits of Reason Alone*, trans. T. M. Greene & H. H. Hudson (New York: Harper, 1960)

Katz, S. T., *Mysticism and Philosophical Analysis* (London: Sheldon Press, 1978)

——(ed.), *Mysticism and Religious Traditions* (New York: OUP, 1983)

Kepel, G., *The Revenge of God* (Cambridge: Polity Press, 1994)

Khomeini, Ayatollah, 'Islamic Government', in J. J. Donohue and J. L. Esposito, *Islam in Transition* (Oxford: OUP, 1982)

King, U., 'Historical and Phenomenological Approaches,' in F. Whaling (ed.), *Contemporary Approaches to the Study of Religion*, vol. 1 (Berlin: Mouton, 1983)

——*Turning Points in Religious Studies: Essays in Honour of Geoffrey Parrinder* (Edinburgh: T. & T. Clark, 1990)

Kitagawa, J., 'Eliade, Mircea', in *The Encyclopedia of Religion*, vol. 4 (New York: Macmillan, 1986)

——(ed.), *The History of Religions: Retrospect and Prospect* (New York: Macmillan 1985)

——and C. Long (eds.), *Myths and Symbols: Studies in Honour of Mircea Eliade* (Chicago: University of Chicago Press, 1969)

Kristensen, W. B., *The Meaning of Religion* (The Hague: Martinus Nijhoff, 1960)

Küng, H., *On Being a Christian* (London: Collins, 1977)

Lang, A., *The Making of Religion* (London: Longmans, 1898)

——*Modern Mythology* (London: Longmans, 1897)

——'Mythology', in *Encyclopaedia Britannica* (^{9}1890)

Leach, E., *Levi-Strauss* (London: Fontana, 1970)

——*Social Anthropology* (Oxford: OUP, 1982)

Leeuw, G. van der, *Religion in Essence and Manifestation*, Eng. trans. (London: Allen & Unwin, 1938)

Levi-Strauss, C., *The Savage Mind* (London: Weidenfeld, 1966)

——*Totemism*, trans. R. Needham (Harmondsworth: Penguin, 1969)

Ling, T., *A History of Religion East and West* (London: Macmillan 1962)

Lovett, R., *James Chalmers* (Oxford: Religious Tract Society, 1902)

Mackintosh, H. R., *Types of Modern Theology* (London: Nisbet, 1937)

Mandelbaum, M., 'Historicism', in *The Encyclopedia of Philosophy*, ed. P. Edwards, vol. 4 (New York: Macmillan, 1967)

——*History, Man and Reason* (Baltimore: Johns Hopkins, 1971)

Marett, R. R., *Anthropology* (London, 1911)

——*Head, Heart and Hands in Human Evolution* (London: Hutchinson, 1935)

——*Psychology and Folklore* (London: Methuen, 1920)

——'A Sociological View of Comparative Religion', *The Sociological Review* 1 (1908)

——*The Threshold of Religion* (London: Methuen, ^{2}1914)

Masuzawa, T., *In Search of Dreamtime: The Quest for the Origin of Religion* (Chicago: University of Chicago Press, 1993)

McKenzie, P., *The Christians* (London: SPCK, 1988)

Menzies, A., *History of Religion* (London: University Extension Manuals, 1895)

Müller, F. Max, *Anthropological Religion* (London: Longmans, 1892)

——*Introduction to the Science of Religion* (London: Longmans, ^{2}1893)

BIBLIOGRAPHY

——*Lectures on the Origin and Growth of Religion* (London: Longmans, 1978)

——*Natural Religion* (London: Longmans, ²1892)

——*Physical Religion* (London: Longmans, 1891)

——*Theosophy or Psychological Religion* (London: Longmans, 1893)

Newbigin, L., *Foolishness to the Greeks: The Gospel and Western Culture* (London: SPCK, 1986)

Nyanatiloka, M., *Buddhist Dictionary* (Colombo: Frewin, ²1956)

O'Flaherty, W. D., *The Rig Veda* (Harmondsworth: Penguin Classics, 1981)

Otto, R., *The Idea of the Holy* (London: OUP, 1923)

——*The Philosophy of Religion*, trans. E. B. Dicker (London: Williams & Norgate, 1931)

——*Religious Essays* (London: OUP, 1931)

Perry, R. B., *The Thought and Character of William James*, vol. 2 (London: OUP, 1936)

Pratt, J. B., *The Religious Consciousness* (New York: Macmillan, 1920)

Radcliffe-Brown, A. R., *The Andaman Islanders* (Glencoe, IL: Free Press, 1964)

——*Structure and Function in Primitive Society* (London: Cohen & West, 1952)

Radhakrishnan, S., *Eastern Religions and Western Thought* (London: OUP, ²1940)

——*The Principal Upanishads* (London: Allen & Unwin, 1953)

Rahner, K., *Theological Investigations*, vol. 16 (London: Darton, Longman & Todd, 1974)

Reardon, B. M. G., *Religion in the Age of Romanticism* (Cambridge: CUP, 1985)

Ricketts, M. L., 'In Defence of Eliade', *Religion* 3 (1973), pp. 25ff.

Rieff, P., *The Triumph of the Therapeutic* (New York: Harper & Row, 1966)

Rogers, C. R., *Client-centered Therapy* (Boston: Houghton-Mifflin, 1951)

Rudolph, K. (trans. G. D. Alles), 'Mircea Eliade and the "History of Religions"', in *Religion* 19 (1989), pp. 106ff.

Rushdoony, R. J., *Freud* (Philadelphia: Presbyterian & Reformed Publishing Co., 1965)

Russell, B., *A History of Western Philosophy* (London: Routledge, 1991)

Russell, C. A., *Cross-currents: Interactions between Science and Faith* (Leicester: IVP, 1985)

Saliba, J. A., *'Homo Religiosus' in Mircea Eliade: An Anthropological Evaluation* (Leiden: Brill 1976)

Schleiermacher, F., *The Christian Faith*, ed. and trans. H. R. Mackintosh and J. S. Stewart (Edinburgh: T. & T. Clark, 1928)

——*On Religion: Speeches to its Cultured Despisers* (New York: Harper, 1959)

Sharpe, Eric J., *Comparative Religion: A History* (London: Duckworth, 1975)

Smart, N., *Beyond Ideology* (London: Collins, 1981)

BIBLIOGRAPHY

——*Buddhism and Christianity: Rivals and Allies* (London: Macmillan, 1993)

——'Interpretation and Mystical Experience', *Religious Studies* 1 (1965)

——'Our Experience of the Ultimate', *Religious Studies* 20 (1985), pp. 19–26

——*The Phenomenon of Religion* (London: Macmillan, 1973)

——, J. Clayton, P. Sherry and S. T. Katz (eds.), *Nineteenth Century Religious Thought in the West*, vol. 1 (Cambridge: CUP, 1985)

——and S. Konstantine, *Christian Systematic Theology in World Contexts* (London: Marshall Pickering, 1991)

Smith, W. Cantwell, *Faith and Belief* (Princeton, NJ: Princeton University Press, 1970)

——*The Meaning and End of Religion* (London: SPCK, 1978)

——*Towards a World Theology: Faith and the Comparative History of Religion* (London: Westminster Press, 1981)

Smith, W. R., *The Religion of the Semites* (Edinburgh: A. & C. Black, 1927)

Southwold, M., *Buddhism in Life* (Manchester: Manchester University Press 1983)

Stevenson, J. (ed.), *A New Eusebius* (London: SPCK 1974)

Stoeber, M., 'Constructivist Epistemologies of Mysticism: A Critique and a Revision', *Religious Studies* 28 (1992)

Suzuki, D. T., *Essays in Zen Buddhism*, vol. 1 (London: Rider & Co., 1949)

Tylor, E. B., 'On Language and Mythology as Departments of Biological Science', *Report of the Meetings of the British Association for the Advancement of Science* (1868)

Waardenberg, J., *Classical Approaches to the Study of Religion*, vol. 1 (Berlin: Mouton, 1973)

Waida, Manabu, 'Authority', in *The Encyclopedia of Religion*, vol. 2 (New York: Macmillan, 1987)

Wainwright, W., *Mysticism* (Madison, WI: University of Wisconsin Press, 1982)

——'Wilfred Cantwell Smith on Faith and Belief', *Religious Studies* 20 (1985), pp. 353–366

Ward, K., *Religion and Revelation: A Theology of Revelation in the World's Religions* (Oxford: OUP, 1994)

Weber, M., *The Protestant Ethic and the Spirit of Capitalism*, trans. Talcott Parsons (1930; London: Allen & Unwin, 1976)

——*The Religion of China* (Glencoe, IL: Free Press, 1951)

——*The Religion of India* (New York: Free Press, 1958)

——*The Sociology of Religion*, trans. E. Fischoff (London: Methuen, 1965)

Welch, C., *Protestant Thought in the Nineteenth Century*, vol. 1 (Yale: Yale University Press, 1972)

BIBLIOGRAPHY

Whaling, F. (ed.), *Contemporary Approaches to the Study of Religion* (Berlin: Mouton 1984)

Wilson, B., *Religion in Social Perspective* (Oxford: OUP, 1982)

Wolff, K. H. (ed.), *Emile Durkheim 1858–1917* (Colombus, OH: Ohio State University Press, 1960)

Wood, A. W., 'Rational Theology, Moral Faith and Religion', in *The Cambridge Companion to Kant*, ed. P. Guyer (Cambridge: CUP, 1992)

Zaehner, R. C. (trans. and ed.), *The Bhagvad-gita* (Oxford: OUP, 1969)

——(trans.), *Hindu Scriptures* (London: Everyman's Library, 1966)

——*Mysticism Sacred and Profane* (London: OUP, 1957)

INDEX